distributed
data warehousing
using
web technology

distributed
data warehousing
using
web technology

How to Build a
More Cost-Effective and
Flexible Warehouse

R. A. Moeller

AMACOM
American Management Association
New York • Atlanta • Boston • Chicago • Kansas City • San Francisco • Washington, D.C.
Brussels • Mexico City • Tokyo • Toronto

Special discounts on bulk quantities of AMACOM books are available
to corporations, professional associations, and other organizations.
For details, contact Special Sales Department,
AMACOM, a division of American Management Association,
1601 Broadway, New York, NY 10019.
Tel.: 212-903-8316. Fax: 212-903-8083.
Web site: www.amacombooks.org

This publication is designed to provide accurate and authoritative information
in regard to the subject matter covered. It is sold with the understanding that
the publisher is not engaged in rendering legal, accounting, or other professional
service. If legal advice or other expert assistance is required, the services of a
competent professional person should be sought.

Library of Congress Cataloging-in-Publication Data

Moeller, R. A.
    Distributed data warehousing using Web technology : how to build a more
cost-effective and flexible warehouse / R.A. Moeller.
        p. cm.
    ISBN 0-8144-0588-6
    1. Data warehousing. 2. Electronic data processing—Distributed processing 3. World
Wide Web. I. Title.

QA76.9.D37 M64 2000
658.4'038'0285574—dc21

                                                                    00–038984

Printing number

10 9 8 7 6 5 4 3 2 1

To
Louis and Mary Anna,
for a thousand reasons

Contents

Preface

Imagine a world without news magazines, cable companies, telephone service providers, daily newspapers, or television networks. Replace them with entertainment and information providers, high-speed data carriers, and knowledge stores all catering to us, the information consumers. Not much of a stretch—rather, a realistic snapshot of the near future. Today's businesses must forge ahead into this electronic future, responding the best they can to the evolutionary pressures of a fast-changing environment. And the greatest prize of all, survival, will go to the few businesses with a rapid response capability based on the best information.

A big part of this paradigm shift is fueled by distributed computing systems, which are rapidly gaining importance in our economy. In their most notorious form, the World Wide Web, they link hundreds of thousands of people across five continents into a global community. In their less conspicuous incarnation, distributed systems function daily to process millions of tasks for medium-size and large businesses worldwide. As these distributed systems grow, acquiring more computing power, better connectivity, and faster access tools, they will inevitably evolve to interactive and web-enabled data warehouses.

This marriage of communication facilities with database systems takes them from centralized, monolithic storage facilities to decentralized, almost organic entities in which shared data is the glue that binds together the dissimilar parts.

Designing a distributed data warehouse system so that the data required by its individual components, applications, and processes will be available when needed is a daunting engineering task. Both networking and data storage issues are of great importance, and the classical tenets of communications engineering and centralized database design no longer work in a distributed environment. However, new tenets must be established to provide the rapid response businesses will need in the near future.

Data warehousing has already proven it gives the best decision support for many companies. Sooner or later, every business will implement a data warehouse. The question in a business's mind cannot be if, but rather *when* and *how,* if it hopes to remain competitive. The overwhelming challenge for the developer is to design a framework that will allow the diverse parts of a distributed data warehouse to work together. Web technology is the answer.

Data warehouses come in all shapes and sizes. Some are simplistic, others complex. Some encompass a single database while others span the entire mix of the enterprise's computing systems. Whatever they may look like and whatever their complexity, data warehouses transform raw data into knowledge, empowering businesses with a competitive edge. This book, too, is about sharing knowledge, from beginning concepts in data warehousing to building and implementing a distributed data warehouse supported by an Internet/intranet environment. It analyzes technical issues, such as the placement of functions and data in a distributed environment, web-enabled computing technologies, object technologies, and more. It also discusses such business-oriented concepts as when and where to build a data warehouse, what to expect from a data warehouse, and how to get the most for your data warehousing dollars.

Acknowledgments

Writing a book is one of the most time-consuming, stressful, and ultimately rewarding tasks I have ever undertaken. It would not have been possible without the support of my family, friends, and fellow consultants. Many people helped to make this book possible, and the following deserve special mention:

Ted Codd and Chris Date, for laying the foundation for data warehousing and, on a personal note, for their generous encouragement of the author.

Patricia Ferdinandi, for both her technical expertise and her constant support and enthusiasm.

Michael Rothstein, for that "kick in the pants" needed to get the project on target and moving.

Jacquie Flynn, for her guidance throughout the daunting publishing process.

Mike Sivilli, for shepherding this book and its author through the editing and production process.

Joanne O'Neill, for her valuable input concerning data models.

Tony Vlamis, for his guidance, experience, and understanding of book-making.

Special thanks to Robert Moore, valued business partner and associate, for his many contributions to this project including reviews, proofreading, and, more important, his patience.

distributed
data warehousing
using
web technology

Introduction

At no time in the history of data processing have there been so many challenging innovations vying for the attention of computing professionals as there are right now. And at no other time in history has it been so important to the business community that their technologists make the right choices. The very survival of a corporation may depend on the architecture, computing systems, networks, and software chosen today. Computers are no longer just the "back-office operation," useful only for printing statements and addressing envelopes; corporations now depend on them for marketing and sales functions and, most important, as sources of mission-critical information.

But how are data processing professionals to chose what is right for their companies? Technological advances are continually being made in hardware, software, and methodologies. The announcement of new software products, the publication of ingenious ideas, and the introduction of faster, more powerful hardware—all bring demands from the user community for inclusion in the users' systems, whether or not there is a match between innovation and the computing environment. There is a perpetual cry for more functionality, flexibility, and performance, even if users are unaware of any particular development likely to improve matters. So the technologist designing a new application or prolonging the life of an old one must always be looking for ways of linking recent developments and ideas to the needs of the users.

One area in which new ideas and concepts are becoming increasingly viable and useful from a corporate point of view is distributed data warehousing. These systems manage data stores attached to several computers linked by communications networks and allow users to rapidly retrieve the information stored there. The basic concepts of distributed databases were first discussed in the mid-1970s. Schemes for architectures started to appear in the 1980s. Advances in hardware, software, and networking capabilities have finally reached the point that now, at the start of the twenty-first century, distributed data warehouses are a reality.

A Brief History of Data Warehousing

The original conception of a data warehouse was elegant and simple—it would be an enterprisewide information repository (Figure 1-1). All the organization's data would be homogenized and fed into a unified structure under the control of a single database product and reside at one location. From this, all users could gather a view of the organization's activities and various departments could share information. Marketing could "borrow" the customer records from all the salespeople, and a bond trader might use the securities desk's call list to prospect for new clients.

To populate this early data warehouse, all the organization's production systems would feed it their pieces of the puzzle as well as having departments and even individuals contribute important data. All extractions and transformations came under the control of a single process, usually the services of the relational database management system (RDBMS) used for data storage. Reports were printed and some extracted data was transferred to users' personal computers for use in early analytic programs.

Many businesses chose to try pilot warehouse projects, with initial deployment limited to a small subset of users in a functional department such as sales. But demand for data access always grows in direct proportion to the success of the warehouse. As the value of the warehouse came to be realized first by sales and later by other areas, demand increased dramatically, spreading from sales to marketing, marketing to research and development, and on throughout the organization. What began as an experiment grew from a few users to a corporatewide necessity. As the warehouse expanded to encompass more departments, the quantity and quality of information compounded, providing better decision support to the entire corporation.

While traditional data warehouses successfully organized and directed the information of many companies in the 1980s and 1990s,

Figure 1-1. Enterprisewide information repository.

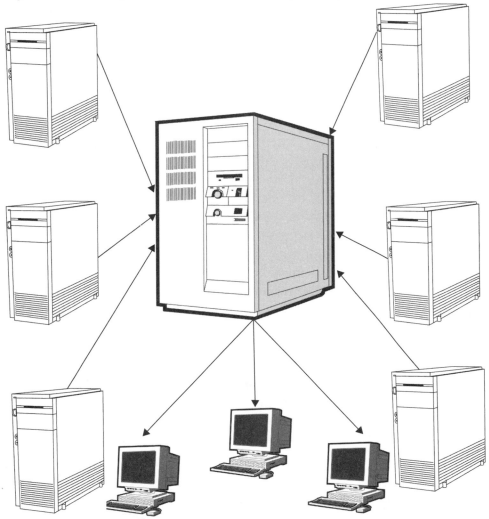

the quantity of information organizations must manage is snowballing. Organized and readily accessed data seems to breed even more data, sometimes beyond the bounds of the regular data warehouse. Rather than employ an enormous central system, some organizations are moving toward workgroup servers. The workgroup server provides the basic data processing services for a department (e.g., transaction processing or intradepartment e-mail). These workgroup servers are then attached to enterprise servers, which in turn are linked together with communications facilities, yielding a truly distributed data processing environment. This networking together of computing equipment from different "levels" within an organization is often referred to as the creation of an *n*-tiered environment.

The key component in this interconnected architecture is the distributed database that allows the warehouse's data to reside in multiple locations joined by a network. A distributed database environment creates a number of challenges:

1. Making the distributed database transparent to the users while simultaneously delivering the highest levels of performance, reliability, and availability.
2. Accommodating the heterogeneity of the supporting environment. Mix-and-match hardware, differing network protocols, and diverse operating systems are all part of the problem.
3. Locating (or building) systems management tools that will accommodate all the diverse software products and function over the network infrastructure.
4. Managing the communications network to ensure security, reliability, availability, and consistent high levels of performance.

These and other problems will be addressed later in this book.

As data warehouses continue to grow beyond the bounds of a single computing system, a way must be found to successfully connect all the participating hardware and all the users. A corporate intranet is the ideal vehicle for widespread connectivity within an organization. This access method takes advantage of Internet technologies to deliver data throughout the corporation from any connected internal source, regardless of platform or location. By leveraging Java and other web-enabled application-building tools, businesses can deploy their own custom data access applications easily, making them instantly available to everyone within the company. Many excellent, third-party data access tools are already web-enabled and waiting to be employed in an intranet environment.

Since web-enabled applications reside on a server, neither the user's physical location (provided it has access to the corporate intranet) nor the configuration of the individual personal computer are obstacles to accessing and using the product. As a result, the barriers to application deployment disappear. This thin-client approach means that mobile users (i.e., laptop users with limited storage or telecommuters with home machines) have easy access to applications and data as well.

Moving from a desktop-centric to a network-centric model is revolutionary for any organization. Installing and maintaining easy-to-use access tools on the desktop of a few users, who are all in one location, is certainly possible for a pilot project—this is a fat-client approach. However, installing software on every desktop in an organization quickly becomes overwhelming, and maintenance is a nightmare. Widespread installs and upkeep result in huge costs to a business.

By making browsers standard equipment for all enterprise desktops and installing only web-enabled software, the organization can move toward a thin-client model with a fraction of the systems management cost of the fat-client approach. The network-centric approach eliminates the need for service on every desktop computer. It saves the company time and money as well as simplifying application rollout and maintenance.

What Is a Data Warehouse?

A data warehouse is a tool used by many businesses to gain and maintain a competitive advantage. Gathered from both in-house and external data sources, the modern warehouse is a collection of information stored in a way that improves access to data. Once the information is assembled, some type of assisted query software is used on the desktop to retrieve data from the warehouse, where it is analyzed, manipulated, and reported.

In short, owning a data warehouse means faster and better access to widespread information at all levels of the corporation. The idea behind a traditional, centralized data warehouse is to put a wide range of operational data from internal and external sources into one place so it can be better utilized by executives, line managers, and analysts. Keep in mind that while a data warehouse contains data gathered from many different sources and satisfies a diverse range of analytical needs, its smaller version, the data mart, can be equally useful. A data mart focuses on a subset of data, such as sales and marketing or financials only, and produces a select view for a particular purpose—the right tool for the right job.

Large businesses often suffer from a common problem: Data is stored everywhere—some in locations known only to a few selected users—and it is associated with many different types of applications and kept in a variety of formats. In some cases, information is locked away in legacy systems to be accessed only when the data processing department is willing to write special programs to extract it. Data may also be stored for use with transactional systems (e.g., billing, inventory, and order entry) and is not organized in a manner that is useful to the user. As a result, it is impossible to consolidate data across applications or to compare data between systems; no one has a reliable picture of the business as a whole. A data warehouse resolves these issues by delivering improved information access and higher-quality decision support.

A data warehouse must be viewed as an environment, not a single product or even a convenient package. It cannot be purchased off-the-shelf, ready to go. To acquire a data warehouse, a business must build its own, from the ground up. The component parts need to be chosen carefully for compatibility and usability and to provide the appropriate information. The data warehouse environment consists of:

- Source systems from which data is extracted
- Middleware used to extract data for loading into the data warehouse
- Data warehouse structure where the data is stored
- Desktop tools used for querying and reporting, to facilitate decision support

The source systems for the data warehouse can include:

- Mainframe and minicomputer systems
- Workgroup and client/server data files and databases
- Spreadsheet data
- Data from external sources
- Data from personal computers

Middleware, the suite of tools used to populate the data warehouse, is responsible for the cleansing and transformation of the data from the source systems. These tools can be designed and coded in-house or purchased from one or more third-party vendors. The cleaning process alone can be very time-consuming and costly if the data in the source systems has not been well maintained. The data transformation process will vary in complexity from one system to the next and can include:

- Field translations (i.e., PC to mainframe formats)
- Data formatting changes (i.e., Julian date to Gregorian date)
- Field reformatting (i.e., truncate or pad fields to accommodate the field characteristics specified in the warehouse)
- Reformatting data structures (i.e., reordering table columns)
- Substitution through table lookups (i.e., replacing transaction codes with reporting codes)
- Logical data transformations (based on user-defined business rules)
- Aggregation of low-level data into summary information

Some third-party data transformation tools are also able to schedule extractions from source systems and loads of the data into the warehouse. Unlike the cleaning operations, which are generally only done once for the initial warehouse load, data transformation is an ongoing process. It is often the most difficult and expensive continuing task required to maintain a data warehouse.

The heart of any data warehouse is its database, where all the information is stored. Most traditional data warehouses use one of the relational products for this purpose. Because they can manage extremely large amounts of data (hundreds of terabytes) mainframe relational databases, such as DB2, are used for some of the world's largest data warehouses. Universal data servers such as those from Oracle or Informix may be a good choice for medium-size warehouses because they manage a variety of data types extremely well. Multidimensional databases are also becoming more popular, but limit the size of the warehouse to less than 5 gigabytes for now. These multidimensional databases typically run on single- and multiprocessor hardware using either the Microsoft Windows NT or the UNIX operating system.

Users have employed a variety of tools to query the data warehouse. With the development of online analytical processing (OLAP) and relational online analytical processing (ROLAP) tools, this task has become easier. OLAP tools work against data stored in multidimensional databases, whereas ROLAP tools work against data stored in relational databases. Some of these tools function as add-ons to popular spreadsheets, so data can be extracted from the warehouse and loaded into a worksheet for analysis. These third-party tools are feature-rich, providing such functions as:

- "Drill-down" navigation (i.e., moving from summary information to supporting detailed information)
- Multidimensional "views"
- Rotation of dimensions
- Charting and trend analysis
- Ranking
- Exception reporting
- Data mining
- Row/column matrix and cross-tabulation

Most OLAP and ROLAP tools are web-enabled, so queries can be run from a standard Internet/intranet browser. The resulting data can be published as simple web pages accessed by any Internet/intranet user.

There are a few vendors who claim to provide an end-to-end data warehouse solution, but most data warehouses involve cooperation between multivendor products.

Pressure to Distribute Data

In service for the last twenty-five years, large relational databases manage the information of many corporations such as banks, insurance companies, health maintenance organizations, and reservation networks. Some have even been organized into data warehouse structures. It was originally thought that collecting all the data into a single relational reservoir (Figure 1-2) would simplify data access. Using the toolkit of relational services such as data definition languages (DDL), data manipulation languages (DML), referential integrity checkers, constraint monitors, and structured query language (SQL), technologists hoped to provide open access to everyone, in-

Figure 1-2. Data warehouse as a data reservoir.

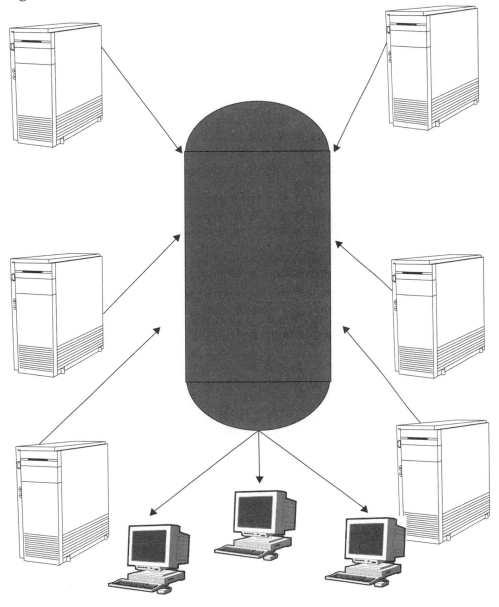

cluding the user community. Even if this approach could not entirely remove programmers from the access path for all data, it was thought that it would at least speed up the query process.

However, many years of experience with this approach has taught that, while it was certainly acceptable for some users, few got anything like optimal service. There were even a certain percentage of users who had no service because SQL proved too difficult to learn or ad hoc SQL-based queries were too costly and time-consuming to process. Even when functioning optimally, data structures cannot be dynamically altered to fit individual needs without formal data processing intervention. As a side effect of centralized processing, owners lost control of their data stores and found data maintenance complicated by the centralized system. While the organization as a whole may have benefited from these data reservoirs, they are obviously not the ideal solution.

As companies grow, so does user frustration if data remains centralized. With the advent of the more recent generations of powerful personal computers, users in many organizations "voted with their feet" and opted for de facto decentralization. They bypassed their own data processing departments and acquired and installed local departmental databases and local area networks (LANs) suited to their group's needs. Difficulties arose in maintaining consistency between the central and local systems, and there were constant problems with data transfer between locations. For example, many users acquired data for their local systems by keying in data from reports generated by the centralized computing system. Not only is this a waste of time and labor, it opens the local system to keypunch errors and virtually guarantees that the local system will be behind the central system because of the time lag between printing the report and keying in the data. So pressure started to grow for formal decentralization of databases and database functions (Figure 1-3) while maintaining integration and perhaps some centralized control.

Often quoted in the early days of data processing to justify centralization, Grosch's Law stated that "the power of a computer is proportional to the square of its cost." But this principle was repealed in the late 1970s by the onward march of technology—notably, the advent of "cheap memory." New legislation—Moore's Law—took effect when Gordon Moore, the cofounder of Intel Corp., was able to say

Figure 1-3. The user in a decentralized environment.

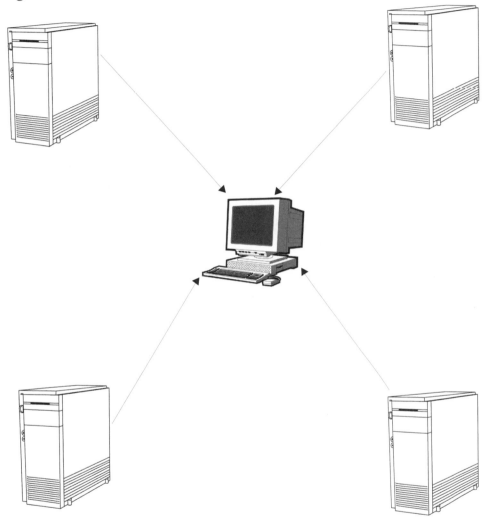

that "every eighteen months computing capacity doubles and price halves." At about the same time this shift in pricing structure was occurring, reliable and affordable communications network facilities opened the door to data distribution.

While the "user pull" for distribution was occurring, these hardware advances opened the door to a "technology push" to distribute data. There are other very good technical reasons for distributing data, such as:

- Security concerns
- Capacity planning
- Recovery issues

Distribution can, in some ways, make security simpler. The surest way to protect data is to deny access to it. If the data to be secured is stored on a departmental server, access to it can be limited by denying requests for information originating outside the department. Increasing the capacity of a centralized computing system is a difficult task, often requiring the replacement of the central processor and downtime for the entire computing system. In a distributed environment, a new server added to the network often solves capacity problems without any interruption in service. For disaster recovery and backup purposes it is clear that having data and processing at various locations is desirable; if one processor fails, another picks up its workload and continues on.

Decentralization of data brings several benefits to a business:

- It simplifies systems evolution, allowing improved response to user requirements.
- It allows local autonomy, giving back control of data to the users.
- It provides a simple, fault-tolerant, and flexible system architecture, saving the company money.
- It ensures good performance.

A number of objections can be raised to counterbalance these advantages, some sufficiently troublesome that they might prevent the adoption of the distributed information systems idea. Technological problems currently occupying the attention of developers are:

- Ensuring that intersite accessing and processing are carried out in an efficient manner
- Distributing processing between nodes/sites
- Distributing data to best advantage around the various sites of a network
- Controlling access (i.e., security) to data linked by networks
- Supporting disaster recovery efficiently and safely

- Controlling transaction processing to avoid destructive inter-ference

Some design issues are:

- Estimating capacity for distributed systems
- Predicting the traffic in distributed systems
- Designing effectively to maximize data, object, and program placement
- Minimizing competition for resources between nodes/sites

While it is important to recognize and address these difficulties, the basic advantages, both technical and business, of distributed processing give it a decided edge for large-scale projects such as data warehouses.

At the same time this pressure for distribution was mounting, a quite different pressure was also building—to use the new technology to integrate, with as little disruption as possible for the users, data systems that were already distributed (and perhaps incompatible). Many of these systems were founded by users dissatisfied with the services provided by centralized computing and were designed and installed without the aid or approval of the enterprise's data processing department. Hence, they vary widely in platform chosen, communications protocols used, and software installed. Having been at the forefront of the distributed data trend, these users will not be satisfied if they are left behind when the rest of the organization is interconnected.

The advent of decentralized systems is well justified. But arguments in favor of decentralization have much less force if the integration of already-distributed systems is not addressed (Figure 1-4). Developers are currently tackling the issue of stitching together heterogeneous systems as well as incorporating the more manageable homogeneous ones.

The need to integrate disparate data can arise from many sources. Data may be stored at several locations within an organization for historical reasons, but managers at the parent company require summary data from local sites. Integrating the local sites into a global network is only practical. Also, there is often a driving need for integration to handle change. Departments and divisions within

Figure 1-4. Isolation caused by failure to integrate.

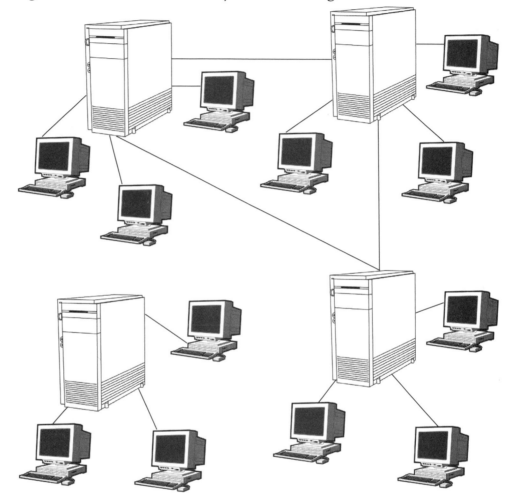

an enterprise reorganize, and companies merge or split apart. Any of these actions requires reconfiguration of the computing systems to best serve the resulting organization's needs.

Applications are continually being developed in response to changing user needs, changes in local or global standards, new government regulations, or simply to tune their performance. Therefore, management of change is of central importance in database systems for both business and technological reasons.

To accommodate change, a database may have to be converted from one logical data model to another. Several databases, each using a different logical data model and a different database management system, may have to be integrated for any number of technology-related reasons, such as:

- A desire to exploit new database-related technology
- A desire to get a better match from among the available database systems for a given application profile
- A desire for greater flexibility or better services

These technological issues compound the user pull for change.

With almost overwhelming business and technological reasons for integrated distributed systems, it is a foregone conclusion that they must happen. However, just installing communications networks to link computing systems is not by any means a complete answer to distributed systems. Programmers and others who want to make a query using two or more networked databases must:

- Know the location of the data to be retrieved.
- Split the query up into bits that can be addressed in single nodes.
- Resolve, where necessary, any inconsistencies between the data types, formats, or units as stored at various locations.
- Arrange for the results of each single-site query to be accumulated at the originating system.
- Merge the data acquired from all sites.
- Extract the details required.

When it is considered that data must also be kept current and consistent and that failures in communications links must be detected and corrected, it is clear that system support services are badly needed. For several years, the issues raised while trying to provide this type of service have been the focus of many in the database community.

It is important to avoid the mistake of treating the distribution of data under the umbrella of a data warehouse as providing the ultimate answer to all data handling problems. The systems introduced in this book must be seen as just one tool in the future array of information handling products (Figure 1-5). For now and in the near future, distributed data warehousing offers the best in decision-support

Figure 1-5. A variety of information handling systems.

services; there are, however, other business needs and new products that promise to fulfill them.

Data Mart Issues

Business issues may influence the construction of a distributed data warehouse. All companies keep a careful eye on the bottom line, and the political environment in some organizations can be a formidable factor. The politics of data warehousing center on data ownership, user refusal to share data, and users' hidden agendas. Like old-fashioned librarians of legend, some users think that they own the data entrusted to their care. They view data not as a resource whose value increases when shared, but rather as a matter of personal property to be defended against outside encroachment. The basic tenets of data warehousing are anathema to these users, and they will resist warehousing with all their resources. Large data warehouse projects often involve millions of dollars and thousands of worker-years to produce anything useful, a serious expenditure for even the largest of corporations. The scope of a warehouse project is difficult to estimate, and deadlines are hard to set and even harder to meet, leading to cost overruns and missed deadlines. Only rigid control and excellent management can keep a warehousing project from becoming a financial black hole.

There are also technology issues that may influence warehouse construction. Performance problems frequently arise in large warehouses because there are difficulties handling many simultaneous requests. With a distributed warehouse design, this problem is ameliorated, but does not completely disappear. Also, the length of time it takes to produce a warehouse often discourages potential users. They argue that, by the time the project is finished, their requirements will have either changed or disappeared altogether.

For these and other reasons, data marts, which are smaller subsets of the data warehouse specifically designed to meet departmental needs, have come into fashion. There are two basic types of data marts: dependent and independent. For the dependent data mart, data is loaded from production systems into the centralized warehouse and then extracted, enhanced, and loaded into the data marts (Figure 1-6). This type of data mart eliminates many performance problems and even helps resolve a political issue by returning control of some data to the users. It does nothing, however, for the financial problems. If anything, it exacerbates them because the data warehouse must be built before the first data mart can be implemented.

With independent data marts, an organization can start small and move quickly, often realizing limited results in three to six months. The data marts are developed one at a time, as need dictates and finances allow, independent of any data warehouse project. The data necessary to populate the independent data mart is extracted directly from the corporate production systems. Issues of political parochialism are ignored by this approach, although they tend to come up later on, whenever someone suggests networking the independent data marts into a distributed data warehouse.

Figure 1-6. Dependent data mart.

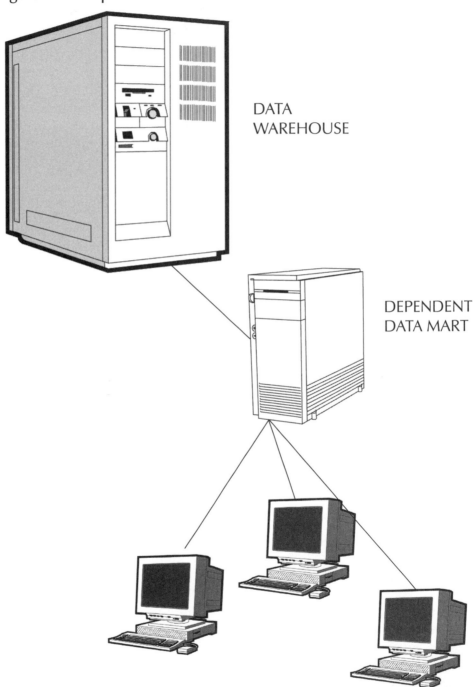

DATA
WAREHOUSE

DEPENDENT
DATA MART

Proponents of this approach argue that after starting with a single, small data mart, other marts can proliferate in departments that have the need (Figure 1-7). Eventually, by satisfying the various divisional requirements, an organization can build its way up to a full-scale distributed data warehouse. This approach, like any other, has consequences. The independently devcloped data marts may not be exact duplicates, in terms of hardware and software, of one another and could be difficult to network and jointly manage. Also, multiple data marts developed without reference to each other require multi-

Figure 1-7. Independent data marts.

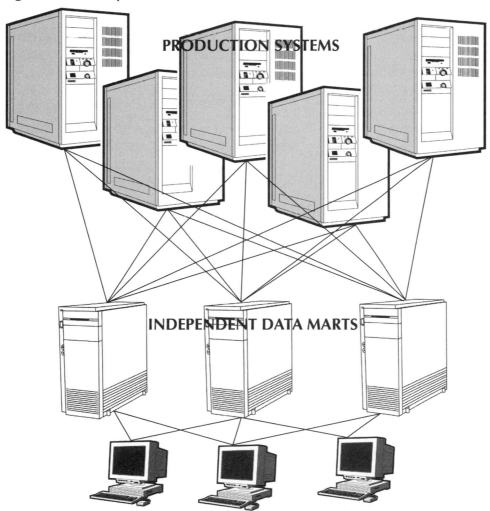

ple (and sometimes redundant) data extracts from production systems.

And populating data marts or data warehouses even once with usable data is a serious challenge. To avoid the "garbage in, garbage out" syndrome, a number of issues surrounding the acquisition and utility of data must be resolved. The greatest problem is the number and diversity of the existing legacy systems. Many legacy systems are, by virtue of their age or design, relics from a bygone computing era. The antediluvian remains are usually constructed around flat files or hierarchical data structures. Some are EBCDIC and others are ASCII encoded. Even within the classification of hierarchical, there are numerous products and packages used to construct the data, including the ubiquitous COBOL homegrown files. Of course, newer generations of systems have implemented SQL-based relational structures, which prove no friendlier to data extraction than their older COBOL cousins.

As if extracting data from numerous internal sources was not enough, external sources of data are being added at the request of business-line users who want to enhance the value of the information in a data warehouse. These sources come in different formats and must be matched, or converted to match, to internal sources of data. Each of these generations, products, and homegrown systems has its own unique quirks with regard to data storage and the best mechanism for wresting the data from them.

Diversity is also a challenge in the data mart arena, especially when using independent data marts. If the system architect is not vigilant, each mart will have its own independent extract from each production system. The jumble of lines in Figure 1-7 indicates the duplication of uploads and extractions to the various data marts when this occurs. Each extraction and cleaning process is costly, and doing similar things multiple times wastes corporate resources. The extraction process also takes time and system resources, placing a drain on the production systems. Too many extractions will adversely affect production system availability. Eventually, the production system could be so busy feeding the data marts that it has insufficient time or resources to perform the processing for which it was designed. Alternatively, reducing production availability to the data marts creates obsolete data marts.

Further adding to the challenge is the fact that the independent data marts are often created with no overall enterprise data model in mind. The result is that any given data element may be extracted and transformed into multiple different versions of itself, depending on the point of view of each specific data mart requesting the data element.

Data consistency problems are not confined to the data marts alone. The legacy systems may each capture and process similar information (e.g., gender, marital status, or order information). However, their isolation from one another leads to the legacy systems utilizing dozens of different mechanisms for structuring that data syntactically and semantically. Data may be captured using a variety of different units of measure (e.g., pounds versus tons). One legacy system may encode gender using a single-letter designation, while another may use binary designators; a third system may have a full word, and yet the fourth system may have two data elements (one each for male and female). Marital status and conventions for capturing names (e.g., Jr., Dr., Mr., Mrs., Ms.)—all are candidates for yet another form of diversity that presents problems in data consistency.

Once consistent semantics and syntax are established, there is the not-so-minor problem of data content. Is the data in the legacy systems accurate? Are there misspellings of proper nouns that will cause multiple records when there should be only one? Have poor data-entry validations allowed such anomalies as dummy social security numbers or blank customer account identifiers, so that there are people with the same SSN or multiple customers with the same customer numbers? Are there ZIP codes missing in one system, or some that do not correlate with the city/state in the address fields? To avoid these kinds of issues, the data architect must develop mechanisms for ensuring that both consistent and correct data enters the data marts or warehouse. Incorrect data—bad data—is very costly to a company. Imagine paying the accrued yearly profits for a money market account to a customer based on an average deposit of $800,000.00 instead of $800.00. It can and has happened, when a programmer thought he knew that the data in the balance column of a table was kept in thousands of dollars (10^3 instead of 10^1), and there should not have been any balance less than one (1). Or, how many sales are missed because a query to locate all customers in a certain geographic area, as defined by ZIP code, fails to locate the 40 percent of potential clients whose ZIP codes are wrong. Unfortunately, the examples are almost endless, and corporations lose millions annually due to bad data.

The Web and Other Emerging Technologies

Today's businesses are operating in a very different environment from that of only a few years ago. Information is proliferating at dizzying rates. Data marts and data warehouses are springing up everywhere to accommodate the mounting stores of facts that are the lifeblood of business. More important, technologists and business-line users alike are under intense pressure to quickly transform the "straw" of raw data into the "spun gold" of meaningful information upon which key business decisions can be based.

Partially responsible for this change, the Internet and World Wide Web make fast, easy, global communications a reality. The Web has opened the door for global commerce, engendering a community where everyone moves quickly and makes decisions fast. The advantage goes to the organization that can do it better and faster than the competition. In this environment, finding an effective way to place knowledge in the hands of the people who need it, when or before they want it, wherever they are, is a major business challenge.

Data warehouse systems are the primary technological tool enabling a business to respond more quickly and in a more intelligent manner in this rapid-paced environment. Warehouses provide to analysts and all levels of management the information they need to understand customer preferences and buying habits, product performance, and the success or failure of marketing efforts. Many companies have made competitive gains in the marketplace as a result of using data warehousing technology.

But any data warehouse is only as good as its data. For a warehousing project to be successful, its designers must:

- Extract data from existing systems (i.e., legacy systems, transaction-based systems, relational databases, and external data sources).
- Cleanse and validate the data.
- Integrate the data into a logically and syntactically coherent whole, in accordance with the enterprise data model.

The delivery of data warehouse information to decision makers throughout the enterprise has been an expensive and challenging task. Once data has been extracted and organized for user access, analytic software has traditionally been loaded on each user's workstation. Users are then trained, and ongoing user support staffs are recruited. User requirements and even the users themselves change constantly, resulting in "moving target requirements" and a significant support burden.

The Internet, the World Wide Web (WWW), emerging object-oriented (OO) technologies, and web-enabled decision-support tools offer at least partial solutions to some of these issues. In addition to simplifying the installation and upgrade of data warehouse access tools, an intranet can introduce a new level of collaborative analysis and information sharing among decision makers. Moreover, the OO technologies can speed applications development and allow the by-products to be reused. The Internet/intranet and World Wide Web play four major roles in a distributed data warehouse with great advantage to the corporation. These network technologies permit:

- Data transfer, via a corporate intranet or other private network, from source systems within the company to the warehouse and data marts
- Access to data sources, via the public Internet and WWW, located outside the company and the transfer of that information to the warehouse
- Data transfer, via a corporate intranet or other private network, between the distributed components of the warehouse and/or between the warehouse and data marts
- End-user access, via a corporate intranet or other private network, to data stored in the warehouse and data marts

Each of these functions places a different kind of stress on the corporate network, which must be explicitly managed to ensure acceptable service levels for the users. In the future, additional network considerations will come into play to support expanding cooperation among distributed warehouse components.

Most data warehouses will be sourced, at least in part, from mainframe databases for years to come. Many legacy systems house corporate data, often in transaction-based or production systems that are best included in the data warehouse by means of data extraction and transfer. Other mainframe-based systems, often using relational technology, could ideally be included, as is, becoming a component part of a distributed data warehouse, if communications and cross-system management facilities are available.

High-speed access to these mainframes is necessary for efficient transfer of data to the warehouse and/or data mart environments. While the mainframe can attach to multiple networking services, high-speed interfaces ensure a practical way to transfer data into the warehouse. Most local area networks do not have the bandwidth for large data transfers to a data mart without seriously impacting service levels.

Many mainframe suppliers have embraced IBM's Enterprise Systems Connection (ESCON) standard. ESCON provides inherent advantages for the distributed environment, with data transfers rates up to 17 megabytes per second and extended distances up to 60 kilometers. For system success, new distributed warehouses must coexist with mainframes and maximize the speeds and feeds of data between these two critical components.

The implementation of LAN technologies is also undergoing a radical change. With the focus on higher-bandwidth connections internally and externally and on commodity components, the near future offers even faster networks and lower LAN startup or replacement costs. As LAN communication technologies strain to reach the "magic" 100 Mbps (megabits per second) mark, the traditional constraints of network bandwidths will fall, enormously simplifying support for small data marts within a LAN environment. These changes encourage corporate use of data marts as a cost-effective way to move to data warehousing.

Businesses' growing reliance on network-centric computing environments, and the variety of different technologies and network protocols used, makes systems management critical and more complex than ever. In addition, performance monitoring, backup, and disaster recovery must all adapt to support the new environment. Adaptability to emerging technologies and changing concepts must be built into any systems management strategy.

A network-centric computing environment is a corporate necessity if the potential of a data warehouse is to be realized. As with the advent of most new technologies, it not only provides better service, it is more economically efficient than traditional data access methods. The inclusion of an intranet should cause the enterprise to rethink its computing strategies—from the desktop to the local area network to the division server to the mainframe. Entire architectures can change when methods of networking, protocols, bandwidth considerations, and most important, software must be considered when making design and implementation decisions. An intranet allows a company to take advantage of web-enabled applications. They can play a critical role in ensuring the success of information access within an organization.

How does an organization choose its distributed warehouse tools? It must look for solutions that can handle all aspects of user computing from designing and building reports to deployment, administration, and management of decision-support applications. Depending on resources available and the skill level of the user community, a company may want to look for a solution that is truly user-friendly, requiring no programming or scripting.

Web-enabled decision-support tools have come a long way in a relatively short time. However, the level of sophistication of the solutions can vary widely. Web-enabled decision-support tools can be roughly grouped into four categories:

- *Web Client-Based Tools.* Such tools deliver the ability to publish static information in HTML format so that it can be accessed and read by browsers. They provide basic file distribution services, saving or converting reports and documents into HTML files that can be stored on the web server so they are available to all.

- *Web Client and Server Shared Functions.* These tools deliver the ability to publish static reports on a scheduled basis, deliver on-demand reports, or initiate a report for dynamic execution from the desktop browser. They provide dynamic HTML publishing (i.e., HTML documents are created on the fly in response to user requests), with an HTML page or document as the output. These tools implement a four-tier architecture (web browsers, web servers, application servers, and databases) and most use the Common Gateway Interface (CGI) to link web servers to external programs.

- *Interactive Web-Enabled Environments.* These tools deliver the ability to execute applications in a browser environment, and they can have some application components written in Java or ActiveX. They provide Java-assisted publishing, adding Java applets or other client-side programs to enhance the interface between the user and the Web, and also provide support for localized processing.

- *Dynamic Use of Java and OO Technologies.* These technologies provide dynamic Java publishing. These programs are designed, maintained, and executed entirely on the Web using Java code. This method uses a classic three-tier architecture (Java applets, a Java application server, and a back-end database or resource manager) and is not constrained by HTML and HTTP (see Chapter 5).

These definitions provide a useful starting point for evaluating the hundreds of web-enabled decision-support tools and web configurations available today and in the near future.

To be most useful and effective, web-enabled decision-support tools should support Internet standards such as HTML output, hotlinking, and CGI scripts. The tools should also take advantage of JPEG and GIF formats for images (to extend HTML's output capabilities) and may have Java applets and ActiveX controls in place. Deployment of Java applets, in particular, can allow a product to provide interactive and content-rich decision-support environments. Whatever the tools chosen, be certain that the vendor has a strategy for the future, allowing an easy migration path to emerging technologies and standards as they mature.

According to many industry experts and analysts, server-based processing is key to successful web-enabled decision support. Web-enabled products that lack server-based processing, including many of the popular user-centric query and reporting tools, are going to be at a distinct disadvantage when it comes to delivering complete, web-enabled decision support. Without server-based processing capabilities, users will not be able to take advantage of the benefits of automated scheduling and on-demand reporting.

It is also important that the product support server-based processing on both UNIX and Windows NT platforms. Being able to use the tool with both UNIX and NT network operating systems increases scalability and ensures that the medium-size to large organizations that use both platforms can deploy a single seamless solution to all their users. It is very important to understand what level of support for server-based processing a product is actually delivering.

Some products have the ability to perform all of their processing on the server. Others offer only partial implementations, with only a portion of the processing (e.g., scheduling) actually being performed on the server. Since the Internet/intranet is a server-based environment, if a product requires any processing to be executed on the user's desktop (e.g., SQL generation, calculations, sorting, correlation of result-sets, or formatting), it may not be satisfactory either in terms of performance or functionality.

Whether organizations choose to deploy their web-enabled decision-support solution within UNIX or Windows NT environments or both, it is essential that they have complete flexibility in mapping to back-end data sources. This includes access to data warehouses, data marts, and corporate, departmental, and personal databases.

In Brief

As we begin the twenty-first century, our world is experiencing the unprecedented growth of a technology that promises to bring people closer together in both business and society.

Corporations recognize that information placed in the hands of decision makers is a powerful tool. To meet decision makers' nearly insatiable appetite for information, data is being extracted from operational systems and placed in warehouses. Eventually, every enterprise will implement some type of data warehousing solution, be it a full-fledged, comprehensive distributed data warehouse, a virtual data warehouse, or a simple departmental data mart. The options and potential are limitless.

Most large corporations already have databases, workstations, and access to the Internet. Many of them have also developed private intranets and recognized the need to employ emerging technologies to improve decision support.

This book explains how to leverage World Wide Web technologies in the construction of a successful distributed data warehouse. It analyzes key technical issues such as distribution of data and functions across systems, web-enabled decision-support applications, web-assisted information flow throughout the distributed environment, and object technologies and their interrelationships. This book also discusses how to store data to best meet an organization's decision-support needs, and how to provide users with common, simple, transparent access to information, regardless of where it resides. Finally, it contains suggestions for successful warehouse implementation, such as when a split between operational and informational databases is necessary and how to accomplish it, and how web and data warehousing technologies combine to fulfill decision-support needs.

2

Data Warehouse Architecture

Corporate data represents a valuable strategic asset for any firm; its value becomes tangible, however, only when that data combines into actionable information. The information technology (IT) industry has been talking about delivering data to knowledge workers and providing them with decision-support systems for two decades.

In the late 1970s, relational database management systems (RDBMS) were introduced and gained acceptance as production systems. One of RDBMS's biggest selling points was its relative ease of direct query, without the aid of a program. The RDBMS proved so easy, in fact, that many business users learned SQL (structured query language) to take advantage of the new systems. This opened a completely new market to vendors to provide easy-to-use, SQL-based query and reporting tools. The SQL query products simplified database access to the point where almost any knowledge worker could go directly to the RDBMS production system and retrieve the exact data the user wanted, when the user wanted it. The revolution had begun; users would never again be satisfied with their data processing departments deciding what data they would have and when they could have it.

Of course, there was a big drawback to this situation, and it showed itself almost immediately. As soon as knowledge workers started to issue ad hoc queries against production data in significant numbers, the production system developed horrendous performance and availability problems. In the worst case, users who were not trained in using SQL could submit queries that would tie up the entire system for hours, locking out not only other users but also mission-critical production applications. Even when users were knowledgeable in SQL, their queries impeded production applications. The technologist's answer to this problem was to severely curtail, or in some cases forbid, ad hoc queries to production data.

Once the jinn was out of the bottle, business users were not about to let the data processing department force him back in. Users would not quietly return to the old world of rigidly scheduled reports constituting their only access to corporate data. To answer the surging demand for information, businesses were forced to invest resources in building databases, separate from the production systems, for housing and retrieving query data. IBM Corp. dubbed this concept of a separate database to support the knowledge worker the "information warehouse." Later, Bill Inmon would coin the phrase that stuck—the "data warehouse."

Like all major technology trends, data warehousing should enjoy a long life cycle with three main stages: introduction, deployment, and maturity. Today, warehousing is just entering the deployment phase of its cycle. However, many leading practitioners see a roadblock along the way to its reaching the next stage, maturity, when a technology is universally adopted.

In one way, the problem is that data warehousing has proven to be too successful for its own good. The more useful the data warehouse, the more the users want to enhance its functionality even further by adding more data. The size of the typical data warehouse is growing so rapidly that 100 gigabyte data warehouses are becoming commonplace and 100+ terabyte monsters are not unheard of. The building, maintenance, and administration of such large traditional data warehouses are very complicated and enormously expensive. If there is no change in either the current trend toward larger warehouses or in the way those larger data warehouses are structured, a substantial segment of the market will not be able to afford a data warehouse, and the technology may never fully reach the mature stage.

If building a data warehouse is so time-consuming and expensive, why have corporations been willing to do so? It is certainly not a task any business will undertake unless it can expect great benefits. Information access for all, not just a handful of users, is the promised reward for the expenditure of thousands of worker-hours and a price tag upwards of $3 million. In a successful data warehouse implementation, thousands of users can access and analyze the warehouse's data, share information, and collaborate in the decision-making process. If the data warehouse only meets the needs of a small group, it is a failure, viewed as a technological "black hole" sucking resources from the company's coffers.

Corporations today must respond to a rapidly changing marketplace, dealing with pressures such as a newly energized global economy, deregulatory changes, and occasional mergers, acquisitions, and megacorporate breakups. Just to stay current, companies must access external databases, creating a demand for web-enabled applications to navigate the Internet. To reduce costs and remain competitive, many corporations have had to downsize, placing pressure on the knowledge worker to become more productive. Increasingly, corporations worldwide are adopting the data warehouse as the architectural foundation for making better decisions and responding faster in a quicksilver business environment.

If the end user is not included in the architectural process, their requirements will never be fully met. Lack of user input limits the effectiveness of the data warehouse project and can even undermine it completely. Employees from all business areas want enterprisewide information access to make more intelligent business decisions. Whether it is to identify business trends, analyze customer buying profiles, formulate marketing strategies, perform competitive cost analyses, or support strategic decision making, the properly architected data warehouse can deliver the information the business user needs to accomplish these tasks. However, users will benefit most when the processes and tools for collection and distribution of information have been chosen with their needs in mind.

Architecture is a high-level description of the organization of functional responsibilities within a system. It is not a prescription that cures a specific problem or a road map for successful design. The goal of architecture, in this book, is to convey information about the general structure of systems; it defines the relationships among system components. Client/server is an architecture in the sense that it defines a relationship. It should be kept in mind that architecture is not "the solution" to a business or data processing problem. It is a powerful framework within which the developer can craft any number of different solutions.

Just like any construction, building a data warehouse requires an overall plan—an architecture. Actually, two separate architectures should be devised, a technical architecture and an information architecture. The technical architecture provides a blueprint for assembling hardware and software components, defining what and how tools and technologies will be used. It may include middleware and primary database structures as well as which development and access tools to use. It outlines how these components will be integrated to provide a complete support environment for the data warehousing project.

The information architecture deals with the warehouse's data; it describes the content, behavior, and interaction of the business objects. Information architecture provides a structure for the information components of the business: subjects, events, roles, associations, and business rules, and, in doing so, it prescribes the building blocks for applications development. Most applications development occurs outside of information architecture. Developers are free to create the application as though it were the only one they, or anyone else, will ever develop, with no design detailing which technologies should be employed or why, no thought given to how information should be encapsulated and accessed, and no common framework for interaction with existing applications. The intersection of technical and information architectures brings order to this chaos. Business objects, defined by the information architecture and manipulated by the application, use the services of the components defined by the technological architecture. Computing architectures, however, do not address the details of an application design. It is still the responsibility of the programmer to create the best application design possible. Without a coherent architectural plan, any data warehousing project is predestined to disaster.

Role of a Data Warehouse

The goal of integrating data to provide accurate, timely, and useful information to a company's decision makers is not new. Businesses have been seeking to create corporatewide information centers that would enable them to better understand their customers, products, and markets for twenty-five years. Now, business conditions and exciting new technologies, such as the Internet, are creating a new wave of interest in decision-support systems, giving rise to an explosion in the growth of data warehousing.

Today's highly competitive marketplace has caused companies to fundamentally alter the way they do business. Centralized markets and competition have created pressure to speed up product cycles and lower costs. Rightsizing, the Internet, business process reengineering, and shorter time-to-market cycles are forcing companies to do more with less. All of these pressures have combined to accelerate the pace of business, requiring organizations to recognize and adapt to change more rapidly. Good strategic planning and timely decision making have become critically important as companies seek to cut costs and gain an advantage over their competition. In this environment, businesses need constant access to useful information.

As the need to make quick decisions has gained importance, the data available to support the decision-making process has proliferated. The overwhelming market acceptance of relational databases, the Internet as a data source, and the availability of inexpensive platforms combine to allow corporations to accumulate and/or access a massive amount of data. This data can help companies to understand customer patterns, to know who buys what, when, where, and why.

There are several technologies that are of significant value for analyzing all this data. Online analytical processing (OLAP) software has matured, providing a significant performance boost and delivering data to users in a form suitable for decision support. Some OLAP products are based on popular relational technology (i.e., ROLAP tools). Others are multidimensional online analytical processing (MOLAP) tools that are based on more recent database technology called multidimensional databases (MDD). Among the technologies showing great promise for data warehousing are the Internet and the World Wide Web. The mere existence of the Internet has revolutionized thought processes. These technologies, when adapted to corporate use, have the capacity to provide every employee throughout a global organization with easy access to company and Internet data. The question still remains as to how these masses of nontechnical but business-savvy knowledge workers will find what they need in a web-enabled distributed data warehouse. Although the inclusion of the Internet exaggerates the problem, the solution is the same for all levels of distributed data warehousing.

Data warehousing must not only provide data to knowledge workers, it must also deliver information about the data that defines content and context, giving real meaning and value. This data about data is called metadata, and it is of critical importance to achieving the potential of a data warehouse. Another key component to successful data warehousing is architecture. This architecture must be flexible enough to provide for the inevitable inherent changes the data warehousing environment will require as it matures within a company, and rigid enough to provide a solid framework for warehouse development.

Data Warehouse Definition

The goal of data warehousing is to create competitive advantage for the company that builds one. It does this by tapping and organizing the huge quantities of raw data being captured by operational and other systems. Corporations know that the databases servicing all of the various departments (i.e., marketing, distribution, sales, and finance) contain information that, if properly extracted, analyzed, combined, and stored, can dramatically increase the effectiveness of the decision-making process. A well-designed and accessible data warehouse can provide a company's knowledge workers with the information they need to ensure corporate success.

It is hard to find an organization that is not implementing some kind of a data warehousing solution. Many corporations, however, refer to data warehousing with different terms. And nearly every company implementing a data warehousing project is doing so in a unique way. This diversity is possible because a data warehouse is an architecture, not a product or a database. It is an architecture that defines what information will be delivered to users, how the information will look, and what tools users will employ to access the information. This architecture can assume many forms.

Data warehouses assemble data from all over an organization—from legacy systems, desktop databases, spreadsheets, credit reports, sales calls, and more. This collective data structure makes a larger amount of summarized data available to a wider group of users than would be possible with any of the underlying systems. It can be mined or queried in ways that are useful for decision making through a common, centralized database or through distributed databases and easy-to-use query software.

How do data warehouses differ from operational systems? Quite simply, operational systems have different structures, needs, requirements, and objectives than do data warehouses. These variations in data, access, and usage prevent organizations from simply co-opting existing operational systems as parts of the distributed data warehouse. For example, operational data is short-lived and changes rapidly, whereas data warehouse information is historical in nature and has a long, static life. Operational systems feature standard, repetitive transactions that use a small amount of data; warehouse systems feature ad hoc queries and reports that access a wide range of data. High availability, rapid response, and real-time updates are critical to the success of operational systems, but are not nearly as important to the data warehouse.

The architecture of a data warehouse differs profoundly from the design and structure of an operational system. An operational system has clearly defined input, strict processing requirements, and clearly defined output. It is assumed that the system requirements will remain constant throughout its life cycle. In designing a data warehouse, there are no precisely stated requirements. There is, however, a variety of source data to choose from, many different possible ways to organize and aggregate the data, and an almost infinite variety of possible outputs. An organization must assess not only its current informational needs but also likely future needs. This requires a flexible architecture that ensures the data warehouse can adapt to a changing environment.

Operational systems are typically developed by first determining and then defining the business processes in conjunction with the users. With this complete, application code can be written and databases designed. Since the primary goal of an operational system is efficient performance, the design of both applications and databases must be geared to provide the best online transaction processing (OLTP) performance. Operational systems often handle high volumes (i.e., hundreds of thousands of transactions per hour) and must return information in acceptable user-response timeframes, often measured in fractions of a second.

By contrast, data warehouses start with a wide variety of data and vague or unknown usage requirements. Data warehouse users seldom know the specifics of any of their queries ahead of time. In fact, as users learn more about the available data and how to use it for decision making, the designer will need to tailor the warehouse to improve performance in view of usage patterns. Typically a user does not know the second question he or she will ask until the first question has been answered. In the area of data mining, which looks for statistical trends and anomalies, users do not even know what the question is until they get the answer.

Both operational and warehouse systems play an important role in an organization's success. They need to coexist as equally valuable corporate assets. This can be done by carefully designing and architecting the data warehouse to exploit the power of operational data while meeting the unique needs of the company's knowledge workers.

Tons of data are captured by operational systems, but accessing the data and gleaning anything useful from it can be difficult, time-consuming, expensive, and nearly impossible. Most companies are trapped under a deluge of unintelligible data. To break out of this logjam, businesspeople demand ease of access to predigested data, analytical tools, and summary information. Results from the initial implementation of a data warehouse often show a favorable return on investment, and the competitive advantage gained from a full-scale data warehouse will be far more valuable.

To construct a data warehouse, there must first be business interest in the project, a core of potential users with a critically perceived need, and corporate sponsors. To lock in critical business buy-in, find the company's worst "pain" and present the data warehouse as the curative for that pain. Real business pain does not have to be life-threatening and usually is not, but it is truly annoying. Make sure the first stage of warehouse implementation eliminates the pain: Automate the production of manually scheduled reports; reduce error rates across systems by scrubbing data before queries; organize data from the business users' perspective with summarized views and drill-down queries for various analysis; or do whatever else it takes to prove the value of the data warehouse.

Data warehouses organize business data to answer questions about why things happen, not just what things happened. The real value of the data warehouse architecture is not just in providing answers to questions but also in encouraging the knowledge worker to formulate even more questions. Focus the data warehouse architecture on getting from what to why as quickly as possible for the best results.

How is it possible to design a data warehouse to answer questions about *why* things happen when all the source data has been collected about *what* happened? Dimensional modeling is the name of a technique for organizing data in databases in a simple and understandable fashion. When a database can be visualized as a "cube" having three dimensions, or as a geometric solid with four or five or even more dimensions, people can imagine slicing and dicing that figure along each of its axes.

Dimensional modeling gives the user the ability to visualize data. The ability to visualize something as abstract as a set of data in a concrete and tangible way is the secret of making the abstract understandable. Try a simple example. Imagine a business where the CEO describes what the company does as follows:

> We sell products in various markets, and we measure our performance over time.

The data warehouse designer listens carefully to these words and adds the appropriate emphasis:

> We sell PRODUCTS in various MARKETS, and we measure our performance over TIME.

Most users find it easy to think of this business as a cube of data (Figure 2-1), with labels on each of the edges of the cube. Any point inside the cube is at the intersection of the coordinates defined by the edges of the cube. For this example, the edges of the cube are labeled as Products, Markets, and Time. The points inside the cube are where the measurements of the business for that combination of Products, Markets, and Time are stored.

Compare the dimensional model of the business with a data dependencies model as shown in Figure 2-2. This is the same business, but instead of talking to the CEO, the warehouse designer spoke with a sales representative and was given an invoice. The designer has drawn a detailed data entity chart that describes how every item on that sales invoice relates to every other item and what all of the many-to-many and many-to-one relationships between data elements are. The picture certainly reveals more detail about the data relationships than the dimensional approach does. However, does it

Figure 2-1. "Dimensional" representation of data.

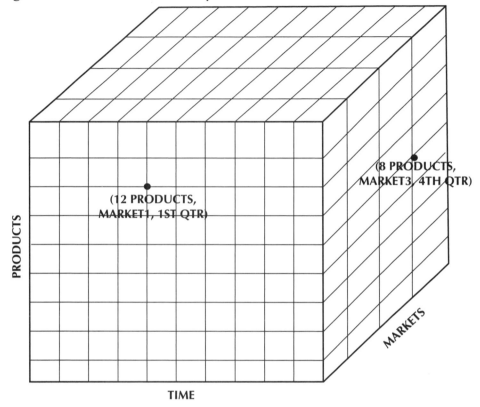

contribute to understanding the business? Unfortunately, most people cannot hold a diagram like Figure 2-2 in their minds and cannot understand how to navigate it even if they can remember it.

Both the dimensional model of a business and the data dependencies model of a business are capable of storing exactly the same data and are capable of supporting exactly the same final business analyses. It is just that they present the data differently. The dimensional model enables the business user to understand the data and see the *why* as well as the *what*. The dimensional model is a top-down model (the designer started by speaking with the CEO), and the data dependencies model is a bottom-up model (the designer started with a salesperson).

The data warehousing effort is primarily directed toward building an enterprise data warehouse organized into categories or subjects that are meaningful to business users. The data is defined in a

Figure 2-2. "Data dependencies" representation of a sales order.

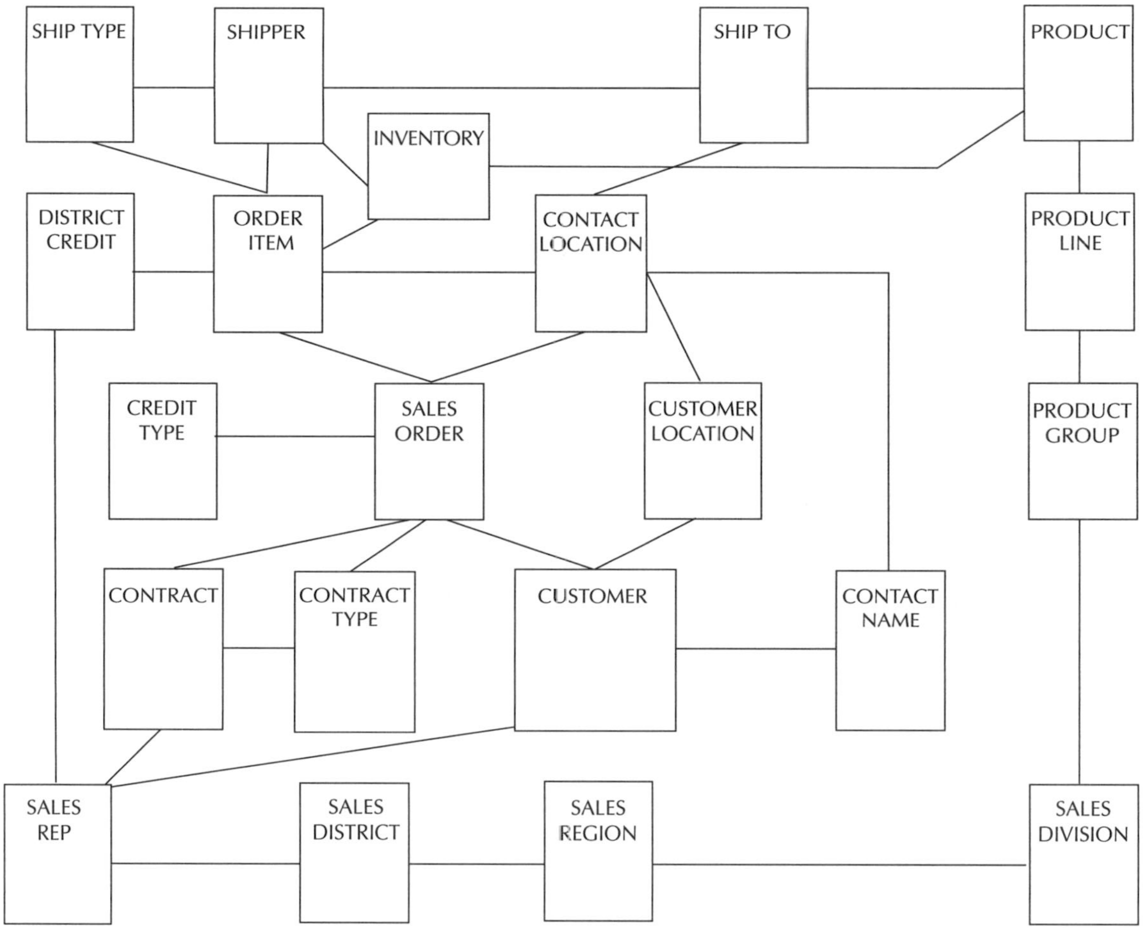

single integrated model (normally a dimensional model) that attempts to meet the needs of the entire enterprise (Figure 2-3). In most data warehouses, data is extracted from operational files and other systems and stored in the warehouse's databases that cannot be changed or deleted. Frequently, the data is timestamped and organized into historical files. A directory is provided to manage the metadata, or the data about the data. Metadata gives the description of and meaning to the data in the warehouse so the user can understand what data is available and where it is housed. The data is then organized into subject areas and provided to the business analysts and executives in a read-only environment.

The data warehouse so created is a combination of operational and historical data, repackaged to accommodate knowledge workers who want to report, analyze, or drill down without having to access operational files directly. Like any data warehouse, it has four major architectural components:

- Data extraction and transformation facilities
- Data movement and triggering facilities
- Database management systems
- Decision-support and analysis tools

Most of the effort in building a data warehouse revolves around data integration—making sure that the data has the quality and the structure necessary for inclusion in the warehouse. Several steps are involved in this process:

- Extracting data from the source systems
- Transforming data
- Matching and consolidating data
- Eliminating data redundancies
- Validating and cleansing data
- Loading the data structures
- Managing the metadata

These steps are critical in ensuring that the data populating the warehouse has the accuracy, reliability, and business logic that are absolutely necessary. Inattention to any of these points can spell disaster for the warehousing project. From the business user's perspective,

Figure 2-3. "Enterprise" model.

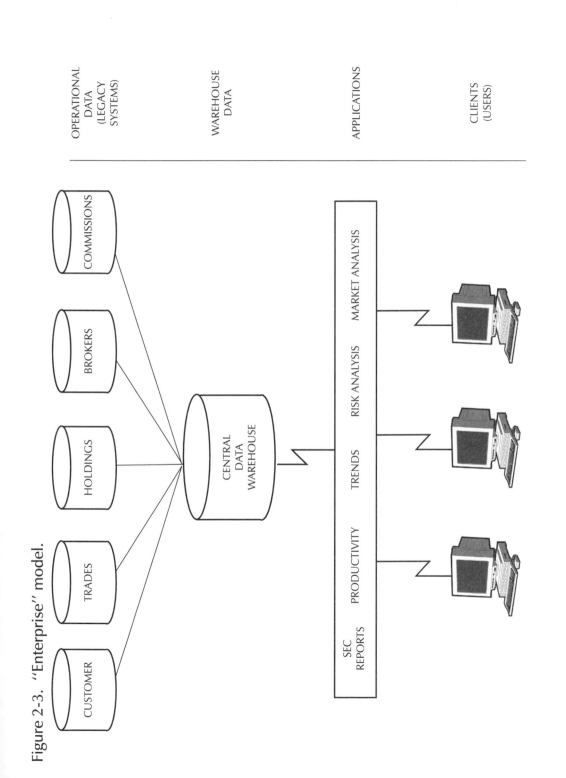

OPERATIONAL DATA (LEGACY SYSTEMS)

WAREHOUSE DATA

APPLICATIONS

CLIENTS (USERS)

CUSTOMER

TRADES

HOLDINGS

BROKERS

COMMISSIONS

CENTRAL DATA WAREHOUSE

SEC REPORTS

PRODUCTIVITY

TRENDS

RISK ANALYSIS

MARKET ANALYSIS

the only thing worse than no information is inaccurate information leading to false conclusions; and poor data integrity will inevitably lead to inaccurate information.

Reengineering data for warehouses requires careful planning and design to ensure that the business lines get meaningful information. This planning not only requires that data architects understand the business-line information requirements, they must also understand the structure and meaning of the data elements in the source systems. The appropriate source data must be selected, transformed, integrated, cleansed, and stored in the warehouse, available for the business lines to use.

The use of middleware, also called data integration tools, can be very helpful in managing these data problems. It can reduce the time, complexity, and costs involved with both the initial population and the ongoing maintenance requirements of a data warehouse. Most of the middleware products available today have filtering capabilities and are driven by business-line rules. These tools are especially useful if both a warehouse and data marts are in use, because they can populate both at the same time, ensuring consistency of data across multiple systems.

Like many seemingly simple tasks, the actual construction and implementation of a warehouse that meets the objectives defined here is more difficult than it first appears. Figure 2-4 demonstrates the basic architectural constructs required to develop a data warehouse system.

The systems on the left in Figure 2-4, titled Comptrollers, Trading Desk, and Investment Bank, represent standard, individual OLTP systems that are designed to process transactions in each department. In this configuration, data from each of these systems is uploaded into a data warehouse. Along with the data itself, there is information about the data, or metadata. The metadata is available throughout the enterprise and is used to manage the data in the warehouse for decision-support applications. A brief description of each of the architectural components follows.

Enterprise Data Model

The enterprise data model attempts to define the data requirements for the enterprise as a whole. It includes data relevant to the entire

Figure 2-4. Architectural components of a centralized data warehouse.

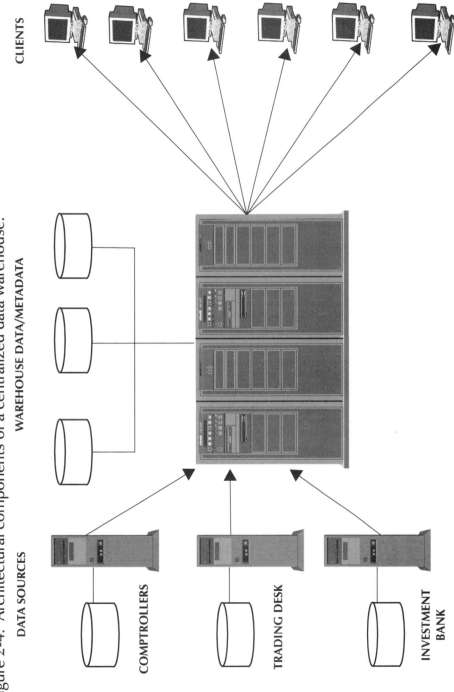

organization, as well as data peculiar to individual areas. The enterprise data model is the foundation of the data warehouse, since its constructs will control what information is available to the end user.

Metadata

Since the data warehouse will store and aggregate data from many sources within the organization and sometimes from sources outside the company, it is necessary to gather information about the data being stored. This helps clarify the definition and the significance of the data more fully. For example, is the data sourced from only one place in the organization, or is it a composite from multiple sources? How current is the data? Is it refreshed daily, weekly, monthly, or less frequently? If the data is summarized, where are the individual transactions that were used stored? What formulas were used in calculating the summaries? The metadata is an integral part of the enterprise data model and, in the author's opinion, should be developed in conjunction with it for a data warehouse to be successful.

Data Integration/Upload

Large organizations today can be characterized as an information Tower of Babel, with systems of every sort distributed across the many departments of the organization. The data warehouse, in providing a single point of consolidation for this divergent data, will need to transfer, or upload, the salient data elements on a regular basis to ensure that the warehouse reflects the current information available to the organization.

Information contained in these disparate systems is often redundant, and since the systems were likely designed before the enterprise data model was assembled, the redundant data is usually maintained according to different data dictionaries. This means that even though both the Investment Bank and the Trading Desk know and do business with a Mr. John D. Rockefeller, they likely will have differing data definitions. The duplications and differences in individual data definitions will have to be rationalized, or cleansed, during the uploads. Often small differences in seemingly innocuous data can lead to a significant amount of work in achieving this goal.

Warehouse (Database)

The collective data must be stored somewhere, usually in a central repository. From an architectural perspective, data warehouse developers have to determine the physical storage dimensions of the warehouse (e.g., how big it is and how it should be partitioned) as well as the logical dimensions of the warehouse (e.g., the database technology that should be used). To date, most warehouses have been built using parallel or traditional relational technology.

OLAP

Online analytical processing refers to the ability of the system to support decision making. This technology allows users to view information from many angles, drill down to atomic data, or roll up into aggregations to see trends and historical information. It is the final and arguably most important piece of the data warehouse architecture.

Management

Managing and coordinating the successful integration of disparate source systems into a consistent data model requires a significant management component, as does the warehouse itself. The warehouse must provide current data and ensure the availability of the system, which means managing the scalability of the hardware and software as the dimensions of the system (size of database, number of users, number and complexity of queries) grow.

Traditional Data Warehouse Architecture

The basic model that makes up a centralized data warehouse needs to be flexible to provide for the business needs of the future. The data warehouse must constantly evolve in response to increasingly sophisticated queries. The introduction of new data sources into the warehouse architecture requires an ongoing, elastic approach to design.

Building a data warehouse is always an iterative process. A company does not take all of its systems and put them in a warehouse overnight. Typically, construction of a data warehouse starts with one or two data sources, with additional data added gradually, over time. So too, the tools and products that enable companies to implement data warehousing change. New products will be developed and existing products will mature in time to meet new data warehousing requirements. As these new or improved products are incorporated, the data warehouse will change.

Business users know they need access to data, and they may even know the first few queries they will place, but the nature of a data warehouse prevents users from knowing everything they will eventually need from it. As users become more familiar with the data contained in the warehouse, their understanding and use of it will change. This evolution may require more data, different data, and/or new data formats. As this feedback loop from users to the designers is established, the data warehouse will change.

The company itself will change, too. The business environment in which it functions is changing every day, and the enterprise needs to accommodate new markets, reorganizations, mergers, and right-sizing. As business changes, the data warehouse must change to keep pace.

Previously, it was stated that a data warehouse can be defined as an architecture for delivering information to knowledge workers. It is not a product, but is often instantiated as a collection of products and processes that, working together, form a delivery system for information. As discussed earlier, to be meaningful, this information must be composed of both data and metadata. Together, these elements provide understanding of the data warehouse.

To understand how these two elements, data and metadata, flow from the operational systems through the data warehouses and to the knowledge workers, examine an architectural template of a data warehouse. This is called a template because, in the author's experience, no two data warehouses are ever the same. A full-blown architecture, such as described here, will evolve to a mature state over time and with considerable effort, as dictated by corporate necessity.

Figure 2-5 depicts an implementation of a data warehouse architecture. Data flow is the main focus of data warehousing. The data is extracted from the source operational systems (on the left), scrubbed, integrated, and transferred into the data warehouse's data structures. Along with operational systems, external data and data from other

Figure 2-5. Data warehouse architectural implementation.

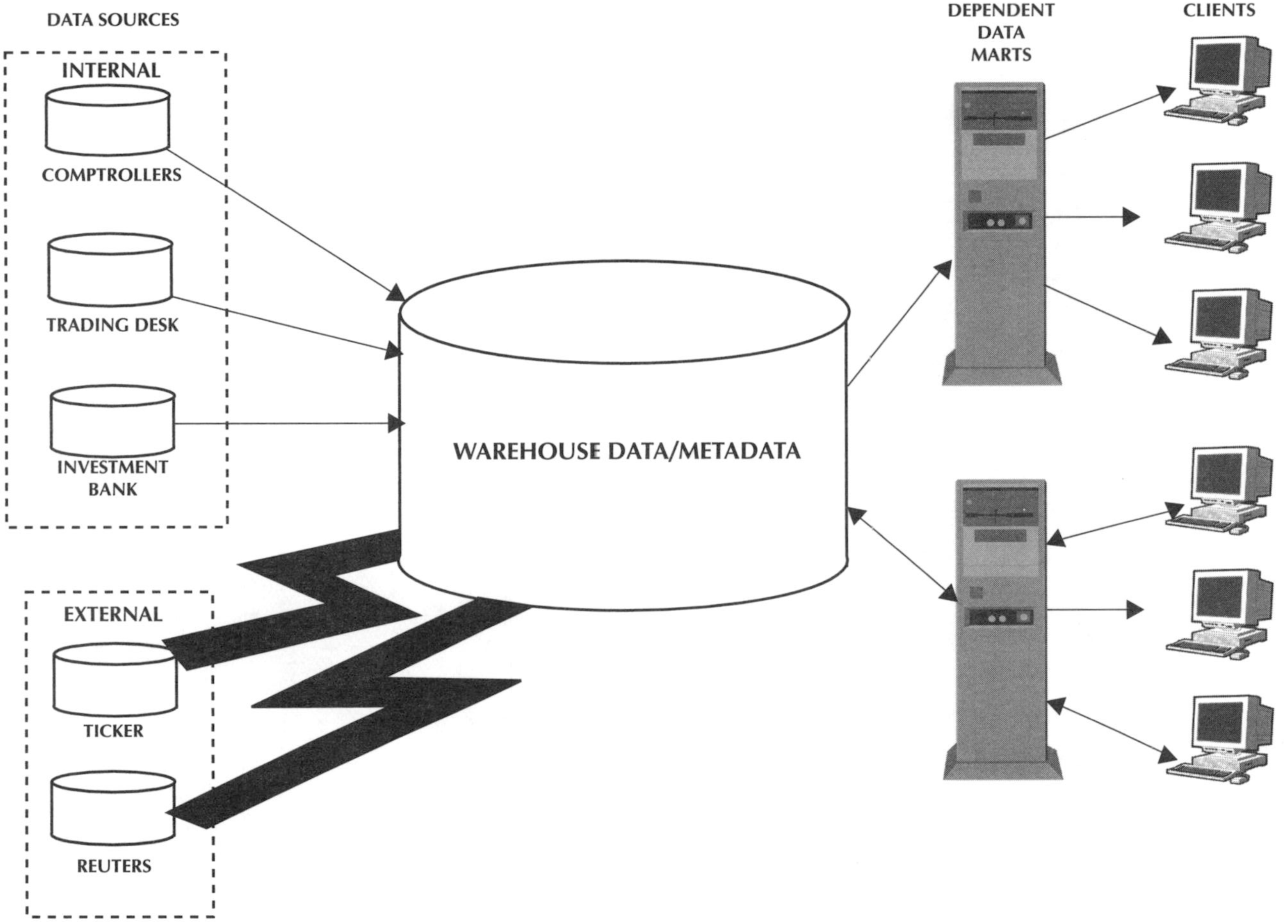

internal locations (e.g., spreadsheets, departmental databases, and packaged applications) may be supplemental sources of data. A data warehouse of this sort uses a relational database for the warehouse's data structures. In this case, the physical data warehouse acts as an archive and staging area for delivery of the data through focused channels, depicted in Figure 2-5 as departmental data marts.

Subsets of data are extracted, by subject area, and loaded into the data marts. They are specifically designed to provide departmental users with fast access to large amounts of topical data. These data marts often provide several levels of aggregation with drill-down capabilities and employ physical dimensional design techniques suitable for use with OLAP tools. An enterprise's data warehouse architecture may include many data marts. Using sophisticated tools, users can extract information from departmental data marts and easily manipulate the data to perform specific analysis.

The metadata from the multiple data sources is integrated into a single enterprise data model. This logical model is not tied to any particular product or implementation of a physical data storage structure. Instead, the model provides data warehouse architects with an overview of the business that enables them to understand the type of data available to the warehouse, the origin of the data, and the relationships among the data elements. It also helps the architects to provide more suitable names for the data elements than those used in the operational systems.

From the starting point of this enterprise data model, the physical databases can be designed and the actual data warehouse implemented. This logical business model also serves as a basis for the physical design of any dependent data marts. The actual design and physical implementation of the data warehouse and data marts may be radically different, with varying degrees of data normalization, different levels of aggregation, and even different types of physical data storage. But the logical data model serves the same purpose for both warehouse and marts; it preserves business relationships and data origins and links to the source systems.

The metadata contained in the logical model can be made available to specialized data warehousing tools for use in analyzing the data. The data and metadata are thus kept in sync as both flow through the data warehouse distribution channel from source to target data mart to customer.

Metadata can be defined as "data about data," but this definition is sometimes difficult to understand. An example may help to clarify the situation. Any database contains both data and metadata. As an example, a CLIENT table has the following entry:

John D. Rockefeller, 100 Park Ave., New York, NY

This information is data in the table. However, these column names are the metadata:

customer_name,customer_add,customer_city,customer_st

The metadata is kept to identify the source of the entry (i.e., these four data elements were all extracted from the Trading Desk client table), and the relationships among the data elements (i.e., customer_st is the state in which the client, identified as customer_name, resides). Metadata is essential to bind together the database, the source system, and the application programs that access and update the data.

A helpful analogy is found in contrasting arithmetic and algebra. The expressions

$$5 + 5 = 10$$
$$3 + 4 = 7$$
$$2 + 6 = 8$$

are all arithmetic statements that are data to the algebraic formula

$$a + b = c$$

All respond to the same rule. The same is true of data in a database, whether it is from an operational system, a spreadsheet, or a data warehouse. The data is defined, controlled, and accessed through the formula of the metadata.

In the most advanced forms of the traditional data warehouse architecture (Figure 2-6), there are many source systems, multiple extract and load utility programs, a single data warehouse database, and then many more extract and load utility programs to move data

Figure 2-6. Traditional data warehousing architecture.

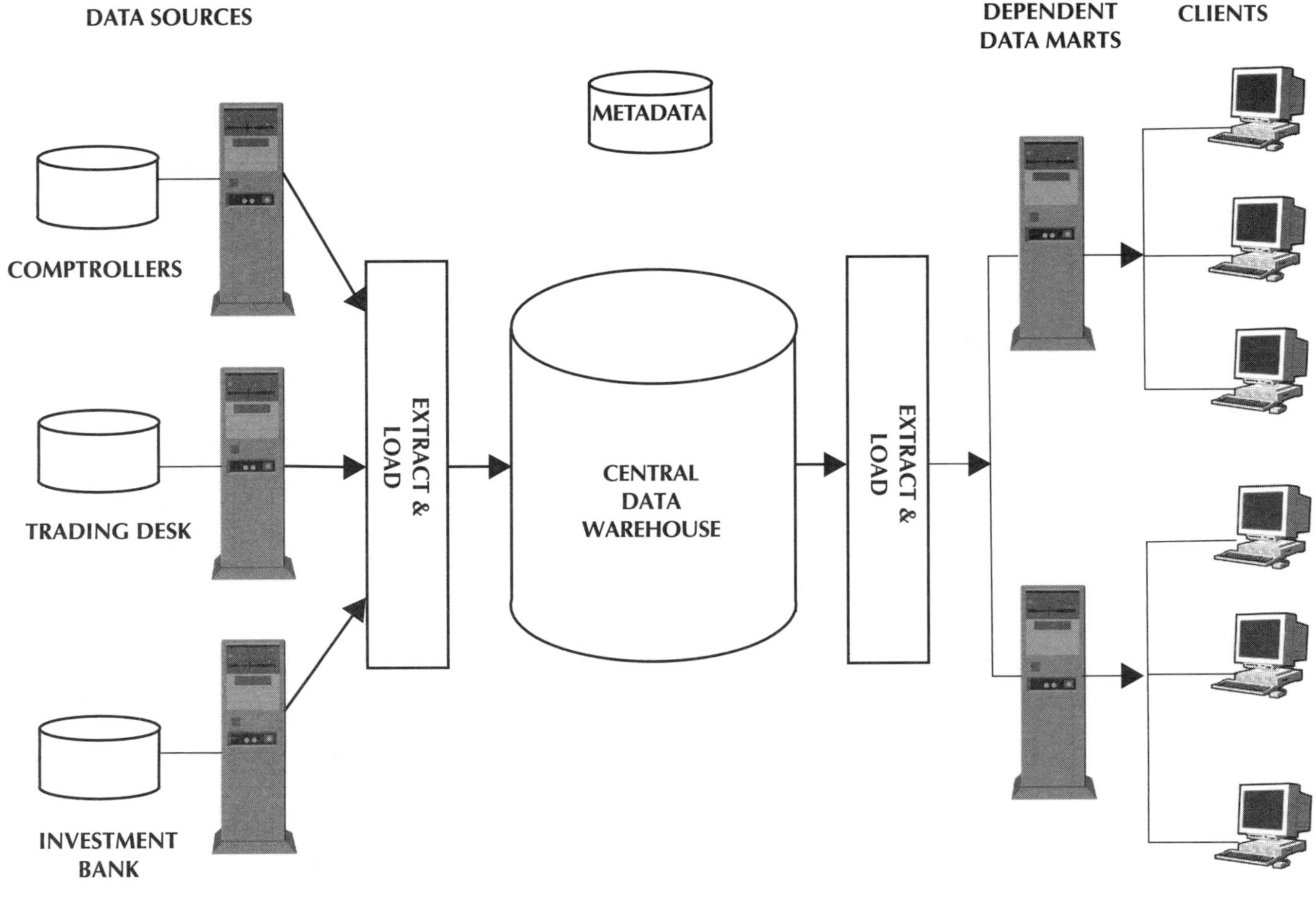

DATA SOURCES

COMPTROLLERS

TRADING DESK

INVESTMENT BANK

EXTRACT & LOAD

METADATA

CENTRAL DATA WAREHOUSE

EXTRACT & LOAD

DEPENDENT DATA MARTS

CLIENTS

from the data warehouse to the dependent data marts. Managing the metadata in this circumstance is a real challenge that can require assistance. In addition, while the metadata defining the warehouse's database and the extract and load utility programs is mainly of interest to data processing professionals, business users are interested in the metadata relating to the data marts to help them construct queries and establish data mining activities.

In Figure 2-6, a logical model/metadata exists for each specific stage of the data warehouse: source system, physical data warehouse, and data marts. In fact, each stage may have multiple sets of models/metadata if the designer is working with individual data models for each of the source systems and unique models for each data mart. Although this is a curious instance, representing one of the more unusual examples of data warehousing, data warehouse architecture needs to accommodate multiple sets of models/metadata and the mapping between them.

For many companies, their on-line transaction processing (OLTP) is the basis for decision support. To facilitate this, the OLTP data is copied to other systems or RDBMS. Refreshed regularly, the data may be a limited subset of the OLTP elements, and might include summary tables, but actually is mapped one-on-one to the OLTP data. Although some would not classify this as data warehousing because of the absence of the traditional "data warehousing process," it is a common mechanism for providing users with the access to operational data they need.

Once started on this course, the next step in the process is to recognize that OLTP issues are not applicable to the data warehouse. Data warehouse data is time-dependent, aggregated, summarized, tuned, and usually named differently than the OLTP data elements. Business users' queries frequently span the application boundaries of the OLTP systems, placing greater emphasis on standard names and representations of replicated data. Initial data quality assessments should be made and quality controls instituted where needed prior to loading the data warehouse. Some data may be acquired from non-OLTP sources.

Examine a brokerage as an example. The designer recognizes the inherent differences between the OLTP data and data warehousing, but also knows that the business users primarily want access to the OLTP information. The designer uses an existing corporate data model (built from and synchronized with the OLTP systems) and re-engineers it to the new DBMS (database management system) environment. The database administrator (DBA) implements, indexes, and tunes the design based on anticipated usage.

In this situation, the concept of source-to-target is very important, and therefore the metadata and mapping gain importance. More emphasis is placed on the metadata, as it is used for utilitarian activities (e.g., unloading source data, transforming the source data, and loading the warehouse). Data sources that are non-OLTP are recognized, mapped, and used.

As the differences between the data warehouse and the OLTP metadata grow, it becomes imperative to maintain the relationship between the two. To abandon the mapping between OLTP systems and the data warehouse would make the logic in proprietary applications in both source and target systems difficult to maintain and leave them with little or no chance for reuse.

In summary, the data models/metadata serve at least three roles in any warehouse:

- They facilitate automated transformations.
- They aid the developer to navigate and tune the system.
- They help users understand what they have to work with.

In all stages of the data warehouse architecture, companies that design with updates and changes in mind build better systems. In this environment, the role of data models/metadata and records of changes and transformations are vital to the success of the data warehouse.

Another Approach

Business buy-in for a centralized data warehouse is not always easy to obtain. As seen, a full-scale implementation requires the construction of a data model, selection and extraction of data from source systems, data integration, loading and maintenance of the warehouse's data structures, installation of user-oriented data access tools, and perhaps several dependent data marts. All of this requires time and money—thousands of worker-hours, often spread over three or more years, and an investment in excess of $3 million. The idea of "starting small" on a data warehouse makes a lot of sense from the company's perspective, allowing it to minimize risk while deriving benefits from the system as early as possible. After all, what is an independent data mart (Figure 2-7) but a "small" data warehouse.

However, as the project to build a single independent data mart is launched, it is important to have an overall plan in place to propagate this technology to other departments in an orderly, timely, and integrated fashion. Doing so not only will help to reduce the time and expense of successive installations, but it will also help reduce costs and increase productivity in the operation of the data warehouse itself, should one be eventually built.

An integrated architecture should be developed to tie the data marts together to facilitate cross-functional analysis and maintenance. This is, after all, only common sense: It would be wasteful and foolhardy not to adopt as many elements of the first successful implementation into the subsequent data marts in other departments. Some of the elements to be considered in an overall architecture include:

- Common data model
- Extraction tools
- Transformation tools
- Processes
- Data dictionary
- OLAP tools

This raises the thorny question of the enterprise data model. Certainly, it is better to have completed the data model before starting work on the independent data marts. The data model is, after all, an overview of the business and would greatly assist the architect and designer in formulating their plans for the data mart. However, a comprehensive enterprise data model is an expensive and time-consuming project, and the corporation may not be willing to spend either the time or money before seeing some tangible return on investment. Often, the designer is forced to proceed without the benefit of any data model. While it is possible to successfully design and implement a data mart without a model, this brings an element of risk to the project that it would be better to avoid. At the very least,

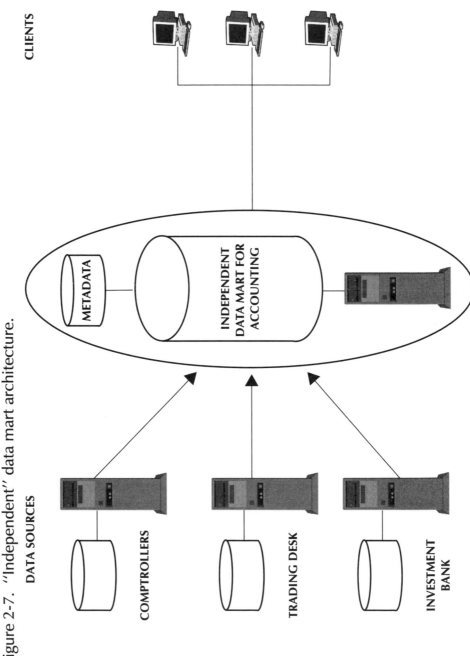

Figure 2-7. "Independent" data mart architecture.

the enterprise data model/metadata must be developed concurrently with the data marts' projects.

When the decision is made to construct individual data marts for use by specific business areas, an important shift in architectural perspective occurs. The centralized warehouse concept takes a back seat to the individual application. This creates a position where the business application drives the technology, rather than having the technology drive the business application.

If data warehouses and data marts are truly tools for management, then economics must be one of the primary factors in determining which to deploy. The success of data warehousing projects depends on a number of factors:

1. *Technology.* Technology choices are a major factor in the decision to deploy full-scale centralized warehouses or application-specific data marts. For example, roughly one-third of the initial cost of any warehousing or data mart project is spent on hardware and another third on internal development services. Each business must decide what combination of hardware and software best suits their circumstances.

2. *Buy-In.* A second factor, important in achieving payback, is corporate acceptance of the finished product. Most businesses measure the return on their investment in terms of increased productivity and market gains that can be credited to the use of the warehouse or mart. Therefore, organizations whose warehouse/mart goes unused have incurred the same costs as those whose warehouse/mart is well used, but they have realized much smaller, or nonexistent, benefits.

3. *Adoption Rate.* An economic death knell for a data mart/data warehouse project is slow corporate adoption of the product. This makes it imperative that the initial stages of the project, even if it is the prototype, be usable and that its availability and utility be well publicized. In fact, prudent use of pilots/prototypes can go a long way toward ensuring continuing funding and corporate acceptance of the overall project. Of course, the subject area should have corporate visibility, the tools must be well suited for the application, and the successful results need to be communicated to the rest of the organization

4. *Business Strategy Impact.* Perhaps the most important factor is the impact the data warehouse/data mart has on business strategy.

The real and most far-reaching benefit of this type of project lies in the solid decision support it offers; therefore, the company's chief decision makers need to be made aware of the impact the project is having.

5. *Economics.* The economics of data marts versus data warehouses is an almost-too-obvious-to-mention point. In most organizations it is far easier to fund at the departmental level than it is at the enterprise level. This is especially true given the fact that there is no guarantee that the project will succeed, and thus a smaller risk (the data mart) is easier to sell.

Regardless of whether a business chooses to construct a global centralized data warehouse or a single independent data mart, it will find itself in need of an *n*-tiered, or multitiered, computing environment. *N*-tiered implies a hierarchy with several levels, but it does not exclude a networked data mart layer within the hierarchy. Because even one data mart tends to breed more data marts (which, in turn, usually grow to include a distributed data warehouse), a sound data plan must be in place to provide a strong foundation. It makes no difference whether a corporation starts at the bottom of the hierarchy, with a data mart, or at the top, with a full-scale centralized data warehouse—the corporation must have a goal in mind and a plan for relating the various levels and networks. The data plan cannot be easily constructed or effectively managed without an active metadata catalog.

If a company begins its information architecture with a centralized enterprise data warehouse, it will quickly realize the need for subsets of the data and summary information. The easiest way to meet these needs is to spawn dependent data marts, by subject area, from the enterprise data warehouse. This is referred to as top-down development and is the approach recommended by most warehouse gurus.

The other approach is to construct an independent data mart first to meet the needs of a specific user group (see Figure 2-7), but this mart must be built according to a data plan and with rollup as a goal. Additional subject-area data marts will be added until finally, the need will arise for the marts to participate in a hierarchy in which detailed information from each mart is extracted and consolidated into an enterprise data warehouse. This method of construction requires very careful thought, planning, and management, but is probably the faster method of arriving at an enterprise view than starting with the centralized data warehouse.

Since *n*-tiered data warehouses can encompass the best of both worlds, enterprise data warehouses and data marts, they are more than just a solution to a decision support problem. They are an important part of an information architecture. This information architecture exists today in nearly every corporation, just like the operational architecture has existed for some forty years. To support this information architecture, along with robust metadata, a tool that reverse engineers the various data marts' data models into logical units would be of tremendous value. However, the data model/metadata is not the only critical factor; there are other components that are just as necessary. The information side has some of the same requirements as the operational, such as data transfer mechanisms, and some different ones, such as automated data type conversions.

A peer-to-peer, secure transport system is a requirement to move large amounts of data safely between the levels of the warehouse. Scheduling becomes paramount in the information architecture to automate the loading, extracting, moving, and delivering of data everywhere. As an infrastructure for the information architecture, there must be a management facility that is able to deploy work to multiple servers, execute the tasks concurrently, automate the execution of multiple dependent tasks, and log, audit, and perform recovery and alerts. Key features of *n*-tiered data warehouse architectures are:

- Bottom-up or top-down information strategy
- Robust, single catalog that not only holds the model/metadata but manages the spawning and rollup
- Groupware capabilities for sharing information
- Client/server model with servers located in the business units or departments
- Distribution and deployment across the Internet and intranet
- Data distributed to the user in the desired format on a user-defined schedule
- Subscription service allowing users to request information from any component of the data warehouse

- Action scheduling by calendar and event
- Transformation engine that can be run concurrently and on multiple servers
- Management engine for deployment of tasks, recovery/restart, logging, and load balancing

After trying out these different architectures, many companies may come to the conclusion that they need an enterprisewide view of corporate data as well as a focused, single application view. An option is to consider building a total information infrastructure, either a top-down data warehouse architecture with a centralized enterprise data warehouse first and then the dependent data marts later, or a bottom-up solution, where the independent data marts are built first and rolled up to the warehouse. In either scenario, the corporation will eventually settle into a framework of an n-tiered data warehouse.

Challenges of a Centralized Data Warehouse

So far, centralized data warehouses have failed to meet users' needs. A major part of the problem is the sheer size of the project. The attendant challenges of trying to track and supervise something as gargantuan as the construction of an enterprisewide consolidation warehouse are outside the normal range of managerial experience. According to industry surveys, fully half of the centralized data warehousing projects fail within their first year, and less than one in twenty ever reach their envisioned conclusion. This says that most "successful" warehousing projects end somewhere well short of the hoped-for enterprise data warehouse, leaving the knowledge workers to work with an incomplete view of the business. This section focuses on the challenges of centralized data warehouses and how they can affect the project.

Data Model/Metadata

Just the thought of undertaking a single data model for the entire corporation is enough to make the author, a battle-scarred veteran of many data modeling projects, get weak-kneed. The road to a single useful model is tortuous, demanding, and above all, long. It is so long, in fact, that even working with a team of experienced modelers, it may take eighteen months or more to complete—too long for most corporate timeframes. Many data warehouse projects end here, at their very start.

Building the enterprise data model must begin with an understanding of the combined information needs of all users who might access the warehouse for decision support, whether they are in research, finance, marketing, sales, or senior management. This is followed by a through analysis of all existing data processing systems and any previous data models (most of which are nonexistent except as embodied in the working systems). Finally, after running these two gauntlets, designers are faced with the task of rationalizing all of the existing models into a single model, filling in the many holes, and ensuring that the metadata is accurate and complete. The importance of the metadata cannot be overemphasized; the eventual success or failure of the data warehousing project will hinge on the metadata's reliability. The finished model needs to fit the needs of all identified uses, and concessions may be needed. Often, these compromises are so drastic that the resulting product is universally panned.

Parochialism

In every organization, there are users and even data processing workers who will try to refuse access to the data they control, or who do not want to cooperate for political reasons. This is especially true in departments that have gained some measure of autonomy from their information technology (IT) department. They have installed local area networks and quasiproduction systems on their own, using their own budget, without the approval, support, or assistance of data processing. It can be very difficult to get the data owners' buy-in to the project so that they will make their documentation and designs available. It is also difficult to gain access to their data and systems if they believe their autonomy and/or their ability to perform their jobs without IT interference is threatened by the data warehouse project.

Political agendas are even more difficult to understand and overcome. The data warehousing project will bring change to the organization, and far too many employees view any change as a threat—to their job security, political power, or their position in the corporate pecking order. These employees, business users and technologists alike, will obscure, obfuscate, and outright misinform to maintain the status quo. The best approach is to sell the data warehouse as a personal opportunity to this group. The best insurance against political agendas for a warehouse designer is to always validate all data information.

Implementation Challenges

Another challenge faced during the construction of a centralized data warehouse is the actual implementation. Here, the challenges focus on translating the enterprise data model into a successful prototype and then into a full-blown functional system. Typically, these challenges break down as follows:

- *Implementation Time Frame.* The development cycle for a typical centralized data warehousing project is at least three years. The implications of a three-year time frame are significant to any corporation. When a company starts a data warehousing project, it is because decision makers need help now, not three years hence. In three years, a business typically experiences two or more market cycles, the introduction of new products, several reorganizations, and the turnover of a quarter of the staff. Its information needs will have changed significantly. It is almost a certainty that the warehousing project will either deliver little real value or will have been redirected frequently, thereby pushing the end date even farther out. Fully half of the currently completed centralized warehouses are considered failures for just this reason.

- *Database Size.* The average data warehouse is based on a substantial subset of the enterprise's operational data that, taken together, affords the business user the current view of the corporate position. The data storage requirements do not stop here; many iterations of this daily data need to be kept to provide a historical record. Most businesses want five or more years of data readily available. Even if monthly or quarterly summaries are kept instead of daily records for historical purposes, the storage requirements are huge. However, the designer can anticipate this requirement and make appropriate plans.

What is more difficult to anticipate are all the summary tables, indexes, and other structures that will be needed for decision-support activities. The "completed" data warehouse must be refined to meet the needs of its users, and the enhancements add to the database size without adding any new data. As the need for new reports and summary tables grows, the centralized data warehouse can explode to several times the size of the designer's original estimate.

It is virtually impossible to tell before implementation how popular the system will be—to anticipate the number of users, the type and volume of user queries, and the stress they will place on the system. If the project is a successful one, users almost always demand the addition of yet more data and summary tables. As the size of the database nears 100 gigabytes and its complexity increases, it becomes harder to tune and response times slow. Also, as the volume of queries becomes larger and they become more elaborate, response times lengthen. The situation can become so bad that response times are measured in minutes, not seconds. It is almost as if the success of the system leads to its own demise.

- *Data Model Transformation.* As mentioned earlier in this chapter, the enterprise data model is a complex construct. When the centralized warehouse is actually constructed, this model must be transformed into the physical storage structures of the warehouse (when an RDBMS is used, as is most common, those structures are tables). Tables and their indices must be built, primary keys chosen, foreign keys defined, and partitioning schema instantiated. Even a perfect data model, should one exist, cannot be implemented directly. Some data redundancy, absent in the model, is necessary in the physical system to avoid costly joins.

Oftentimes, because compromises were made in the design phase, the concepts defined in the data model are found not workable in the implementation phase. Therefore, the model must be revisited by the design team. The more complex the model, the more difficult these situations will be to correct, since interrelationships among data elements often mean that a change in one element propagates changes throughout the system.

- *User/Data Interaction.* Implementing directly a complex data model with star or snowflake schemas can lead to another problem. The business users are experts in their own areas, not in data model navigation. Faced with an almost incomprehensible star schema, users get frustrated. They were hoping that the warehouse would allow them to decouple their work from IT, not cause them to require help every time they want to place a query. Even worse, users can misinterpret results if they do not know exactly what data they are getting back from a complex query.

A centralized data warehouse is intended to serve everyone in the company and therefore has to contain a complete set of enterprise data. However, no single user has need to access anywhere near the entire scope of data contained within the warehouse. Users can find the abundance of data available disconcerting, and coupled with their confusion about the table schema, the result often is that they are unable to locate the information they want. They have data overload. In other cases, users think they are getting the information they need, but in fact they are working with the wrong data and therefore come up with erroneous results. Since the object of a data warehouse is to provide users with decision support, these particular situations are subversive to the very foundation of the warehouse.

• *Maintenance.* Once built, the centralized data warehouse, like any data processing system, must be maintained. The physical size of the database can complicate this routine effort. A warehouse of any size must be reindexed and repartitioned on a regular basis, all of which takes time. The larger the warehouse, the more time these routine tasks require. Denormalization of tables, coupled with extensive use of indexing and summarization to allow users rapid access to the information, can push large data warehouses well into the hundreds of gigabytes and even the multiterabyte range. Not only does this place demands on the number and capacity of disk drives and controllers, it also stresses the processor itself.

Some large centralized warehouses reach a point where the amount of time required to upload the integrated data from source systems and update the data warehouse exceeds the available downtime of the system (e.g., overnight or weekends). Companies in this situation are faced with a devil's choice: They might update the data during working hours and, at best, seriously impact response times or, at worst, lose several hours a day of productivity. Or they can reduce the frequency of updates, thereby losing accuracy, currency, and other opportunities.

The size of the database also affects the backups and preparations for disaster recovery, both of which are critical if the company intends to protect its investment in the warehouse. These are activities no business can afford to forego, regardless of time constraints.

Further exacerbating all of these implementation challenges is the fact that businesses functioning in today's climate are not stable and constant entities. Competition is cutthroat and successful management is always trying to respond rapidly to changing business conditions. Knowledge workers demand new information and changes in existing reports, as well as new kinds of reports. As queries mutate, DBAs must respond by building new indexes and summaries, constantly tuning the system to support the changing demands. The data warehouse must keep pace with the business or even a stay a step ahead to remain useful.

Distributed Data Warehouse Architecture

The purpose of any database is to integrate and manage the data relevant to a given activity, such as check processing for a bank or securities clearance for a brokerage. The motivation for establishing a centralized data warehouse is to get the data relevant to all of the operations of the corporation gathered together in a single reservoir, so all of the problems associated with decision support in the enterprise can be serviced in a uniform manner. This is to be done through a consistent set of languages, physical data structures, constraint checkers, consistency checkers, development tools, and other data management functions.

However, as demonstrated, centralized warehouses are beset with problems that cannot be solved without radical revision of the operating system and/or the basic concepts of data sharing. These issues, and the emergence of the independent data mart as the cost-effective entrance into warehousing, lead the author and others to embrace a distributed data warehouse concept.

The distributed data warehouse architecture involves the merging of two diverse concepts—namely, integration through the database element and distribution through the networking element, as shown in Figure 2-8. However, it was the "desktop" computer revolution of the 1980s and the availability of reliable data communica-

Figure 2-8. Data integration and distribution.

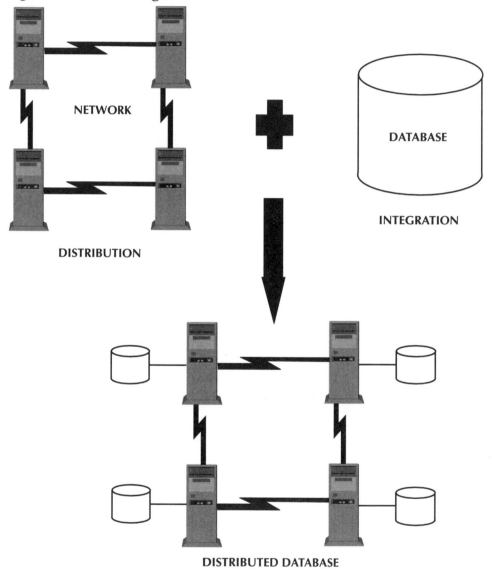

tions facilities that have made the distributed data warehouse possible.

A distributed data warehouse (DDW) can be defined as a logically integrated collection of shared data that is physically distributed across the nodes of a computer network. The terms *global* and *local* are often used when discussing a distributed system in order to distinguish between aspects that refer to a single site (local) and those that refer to the system as a whole (global). For example, the local database refers to the database stored at one specific site in the network (a data mart), whereas the global DDW refers to the logical integration of all the local databases onto a distributed data warehouse. Note that the DDW is a virtual concept, since it does not exist anywhere physically.

Three- and four-level architectures for centralized data warehouses have gained widespread acceptance, and most data warehouses adhere to one of these schema. There is no such equivalent for distributed data warehouses. The concept is relatively new, and the few products that exist to facilitate distributed warehousing do not follow any one architectural model.

Distributed data warehouses can be divided into three separate groups, based on totally different philosophies, which are suited to quite different needs:

- Homogeneous distributed data warehouses (Figure 2-9)
- Heterogeneous distributed data warehouses (Figure 2-10)
- Single DDBMS distributed data warehouses (Figure 2-11)

The term *distributed data warehouse,* as used throughout this book, refers to any and all of the different types, and they will only be differentiated when necessary. Most of the concepts discussed are applicable to all three forms.

A homogeneous distributed data warehouse has multiple data collections; it integrates multiple data resources. The homogeneous system resembles a centralized data warehouse, but instead of storing all the data at one site, the data is distributed across a number of sites in the network. Each of these sites can have its own autonomous database and is capable of functioning as an independent data mart. The same type of database structure (i.e., database product) is used at each site, usually relational technology. These independent databases are joined together by a network through a distributed database management tool (Figure 2-12), logically uniting them into an enterprise data warehouse. Users' queries to databases outside of their LAN are managed by the distributed database management tool. It is possible to include a non–data mart database within this system (i.e.,

(text continues on page 70)

Figure 2-9. Homogeneous distributed data warehouse.

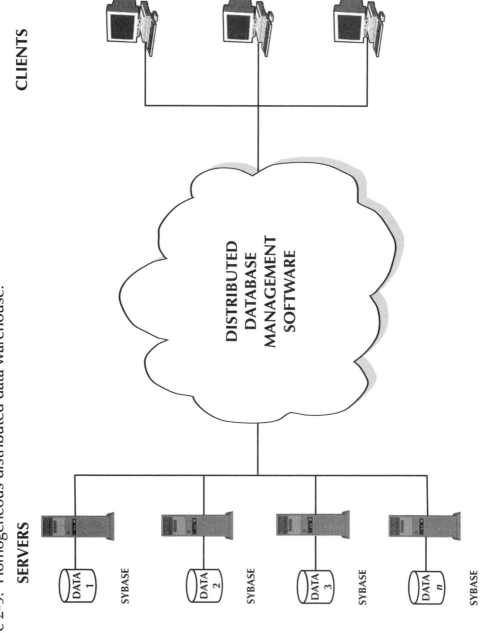

CLIENTS

DISTRIBUTED
DATABASE
MANAGEMENT
SOFTWARE

SERVERS

DATA 1   SYBASE

DATA 2   SYBASE

DATA 3   SYBASE

DATA n SYBASE

Figure 2-10. Heterogeneous distributed data warehouse.

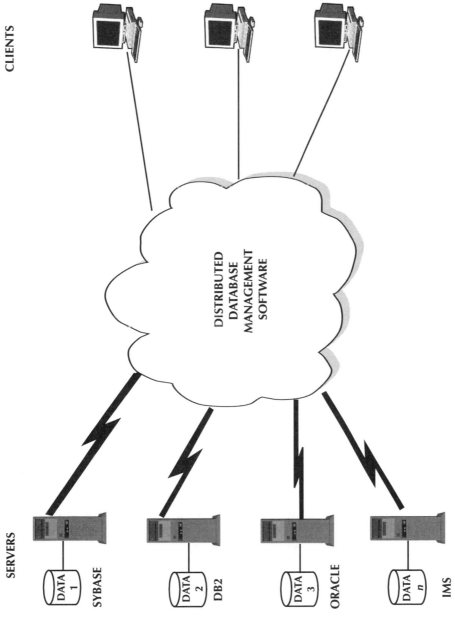

Figure 2-11. Single DDBMS distributed data warehouse.

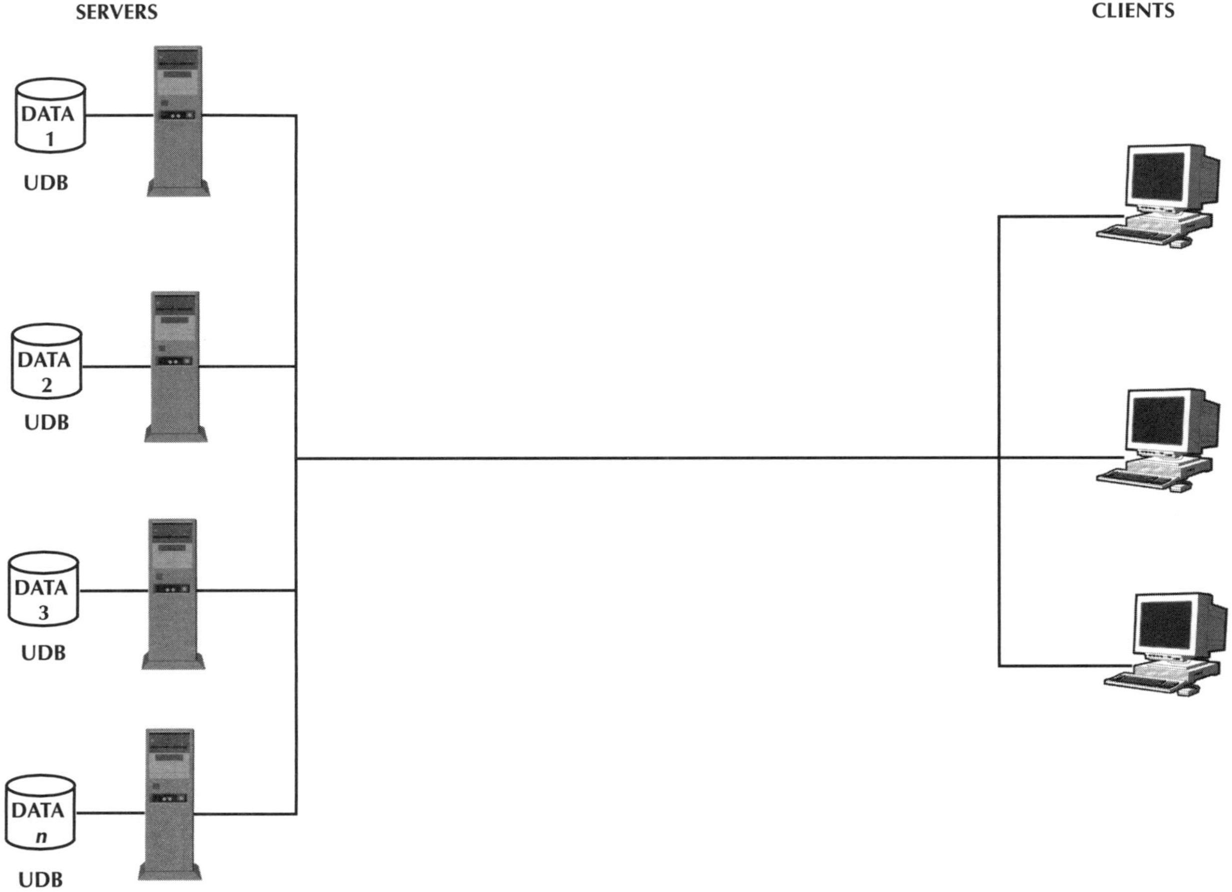

Figure 2-12. Distributed database management tool.

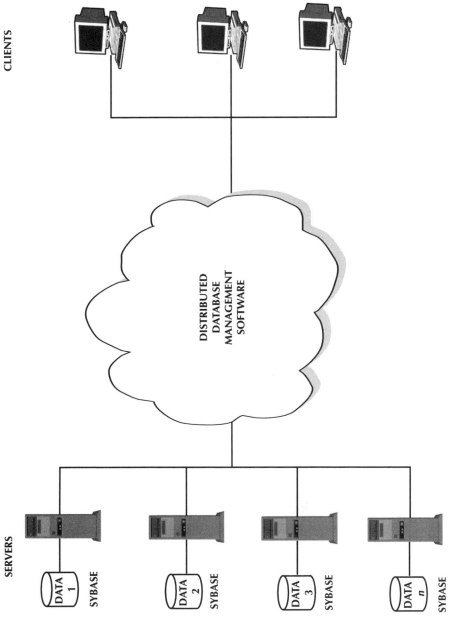

a relational production system), provided it uses the same database management system as the other included databases.

However, care must be taken in the design of the individual participating databases. They must all have used the same database management system and implemented it in exactly the same way. For example, all must store monetary amounts in the same way (e.g., decimal, 2) and utilize the same rules for null values. A homogeneous distributed system has no facility for data conversion and transformation.

This architecture has a number of advantages. Since most of the business users' queries are satisfied by their local data mart (by some estimates, as much as 95 percent), they enjoy all of the advantages of an independent data mart, including rapid response times, local control over the data stored in the mart, and a database tuned to their query pattern. Because they also have access to information stored on other data marts, they enjoy the advantages of an enterprise data warehouse, such as the ability to query across departmental lines, and a good overall view of the business.

The architecture of the distributed database management tool is key to the function of a homogeneous DDW (Figure 2-13). To handle the distribution aspects of the system, two key elements are required beyond the normal relational services—namely, the fragmentation and allocation schemas. The fragmentation schema describes how the global relationships are divided among the local databases. It can be thought of as the "locator" for the information stored across the systems.

Figure 2-14 demonstrates an example of a relationship, a "completed trade," which is composed of five separate fragments, each of which could be stored at a different site. To reconstruct the completed trade, the following operations are required:

"COMPLETED TRADE" = (A JOIN B) UNION (C JOIN D) UNION E

where JOIN and UNION have their normal relational meaning (it must, of course, be possible to reconstruct the global relationship from its fragments using standard relational operators). In practice, this means that the "key" of the relationship must be included in all fragments. Also, A and B, and C and D must be joinable, and the products and E all union compatible.

Figure 2-13. Architecture of distributed database management software for a homogeneous distributed data warehouse.

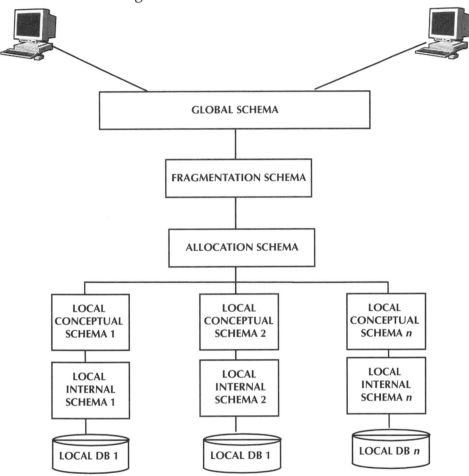

Any discussion of the fragmentation schema points out the importance of, and absolute requirement for, a global data model/metadata in a distributed homogeneous system. Without current data models of the individual data marts and an unconditionally reliable global data model, the queries across systems are not possible.

The allocation schema is also necessary for a cross-system query. It specifies the location of each fragment, functioning as a "router" for the distributed system. It supports the possibility of data replication within the system by allowing the fragments to exist at more than one site. When replication is present, an optimizer selects the most efficient access path.

Figure 2-14. A "completed trade" relationship.

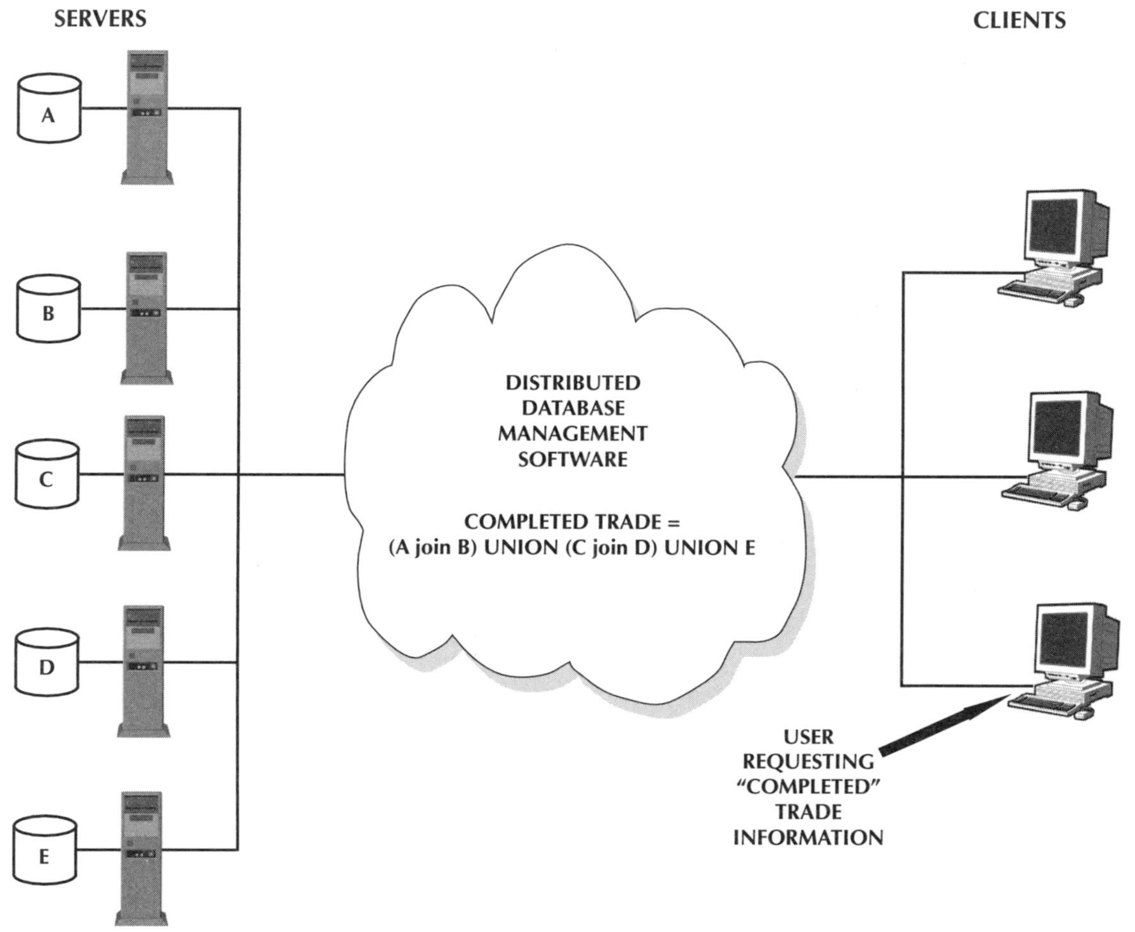

CLIENTS

USER REQUESTING "COMPLETED" TRADE INFORMATION

DISTRIBUTED DATABASE MANAGEMENT SOFTWARE

COMPLETED TRADE = (A join B) UNION (C join D) UNION E

SERVERS

A

B

C

D

E

The heterogeneous distributed data warehouse system (see Figure 2-10) is characterized by the use of different DBMSs at the local sites. While most of these locations function as independent data marts, it is possible to include other data sources, even external ones (via the Internet). Users enjoy the same advantages with a heterogeneous distributed data warehouse as they do with a homogeneous one: rapid response times for most queries, local autonomy, and the ability to query the global warehouse. Because different data sources can be included in the heterogeneous system, users may have enhanced access to corporate data.

Again, the architecture of the heterogeneous distributed management tool is key to the functioning of the system. The same two devices, the fragmentation and allocation schema, are employed for fragment location and routing. However, some additional services, which are built around the global data model, are required because of the heterogeneous nature of the system.

The global data model/metadata is a logical view of the data within the heterogeneous distributed data warehouse. In this case, it may be only a subset of the union of all the local data models, since local DBMSs are free to decide what portion of their data they wish to contribute to the global data model. An individual node's participation is defined by means of a participation data model, which is imposed on top of the local data model. The participation data models must include the rules that govern the mappings between the local and global levels. For example, rules for unit conversion may be required when one site expresses volume in hundreds and another in thousands. Rules for handling null values may be necessary where one site stores information that is not stored at another.

The third, and in many ways most attractive, of the distributed systems in the single DDBMS data warehouses. Using this approach, the warehouse's database "looks" like a centralized data warehouse—that is, from the point of view of the user or developer, there is only one database. All access to the warehouse is handled through the distributed database management system (DDBMS). There are no independent data marts per se in this system. However, it is possible to start small, with the DDBMS installed at a single site, which temporarily functions as a data mart (Figure 2-15). Additional sites are brought online as the need for additional data and the number of

Figure 2-15. "Starting small" on a DDBMS data warehouse.

SERVERS

CLIENTS

DATA
1

UDB

users grows (Figure 2-16). As databases are added, the data is distributed, by placement, replication, or partitioning, across the network.

The users enjoy the benefits of a centralized warehouse (a truly businesswide perspective) and the advantage of a distributed warehouse (rapid response times). The single DDBMS is a centralized data warehouse without the extravagant hardware and development costs. It offers the additional advantage of development in small, incremental stages, reducing the risk level of the project while providing payback within a short period of time. This increases interest in the project and improves the funding possibilities.

Because of the nature of the single DDBMS data warehouse, there is no distributed database management tool. The architecture is similar to that of a single database management system, only the data physically resides at multiple locations. No fragmentation schema is necessary, but the allocation schema is of increased importance. There are no individual data models; there is only the global data model/metadata, and it is an absolute requirement.

The allocation schema once again contains the physical location of the data stored in the warehouse. It supports the use of data replication, to improve data availability, and table partitioning, to speed response times. When replication is employed, an optimizer chooses the appropriate iteration to provide the best access path for each query.

Each of these distributed data warehousing schemes offers advantages to the business that embraces the distributed paradigm. With a distributed data warehouse, it is possible to start with a single data mart and gradually grow into an enterprise data warehouse. Entry costs are low, and even the full-scale distributed warehouse is dramatically less expensive than its centralized counterpart. In some instances, existing databases can even be added as is, without costly extractions and loads. This combination of flexibility and cost-effectiveness makes distributed data warehousing the preferred method for the foreseeable future.

Challenges of a Distributed Data Warehouse

The distributed data warehouse is a relatively new concept. While many organizations have implemented multiple independent data

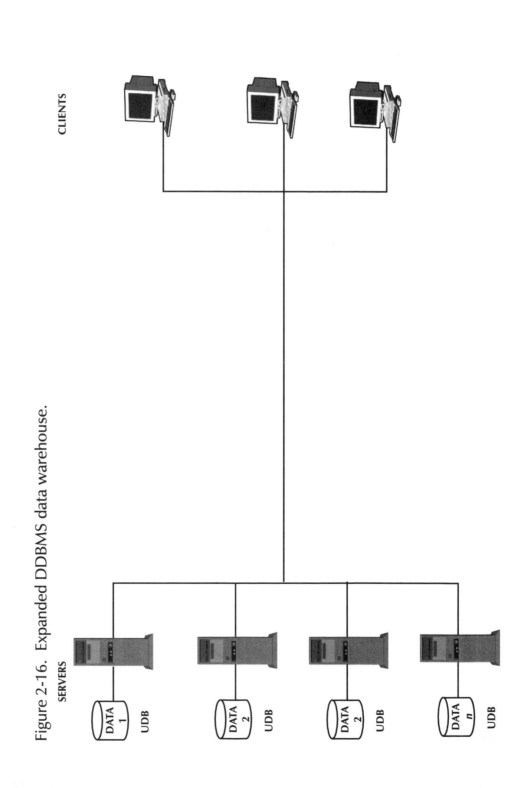

Figure 2-16. Expanded DDBMS data warehouse.

CLIENTS

SERVERS

DATA
1

UDB

DATA
2

UDB

DATA
2

UDB

DATA
n

UDB

marts, few have taken the next logical step of joining them together. There are several reasons: lack of technical expertise in distributed systems; reluctance to try out new technology; and most important, the limited number of distributed data management tools and systems in the marketplace, none of which can be considered a mature product. In addition, many technologists are unaware of the few tools that are available.

A handful of organizations have taken the next step and constructed a distributed data warehouse. Unlike centralized warehouses, which have been well studied, no numbers are available concerning the success or failure of the DDW. Judging by anecdotal evidence and the author's own experiences, DDWs have a high probability of success and, even if they never reach completion, the business has gained one or more functional data marts from the project.

However, as with any data warehouse project, there are challenges and pitfalls. This section addresses them and how the decisions made during the project, especially in the design phase, can affect the overall success of the effort.

Distributed Database Management Tool/System

The key component in the interconnected architecture of the distributed data warehouse is, of course, the distributed database management tool or system, depending on the type of architecture employed. It allows the warehouse's data to reside in multiple locations joined together by a network and enables cross-site queries. Use of any of the distributed database types creates a number of challenges common to them all. For example:

- The distributed database should be transparent to the users while it simultaneously delivers high levels of performance, reliability, and availability.

- The distributed database must accommodate the heterogeneity of the physical environment. Mix-and-match hardware, differing network protocols, and diverse operating systems are all part of the problem.

- The distributed database must include systems management tools that will accommodate all the diverse software products and function over the network infrastructure.

- The distributed database must include facilities for managing (or at least interfacing with) the communications network to ensure security, reliability, availability, and consistent high levels of performance.

Choosing an architecture before the first data mart is begun is certainly the best approach. It will eliminate, or at least ameliorate, many of the problems just stated. However, the warehouse designer does not always have that luxury. Frequently the designer must deal with one or more data marts already in place, with their existing hardware, operating systems, DBMS, and attendant software. The designer must then select the best distributed database management tool for the circumstance, keeping in mind the challenges outlined previously.

Distributed databases alter the database implementation paradigm, raising some concerns not present with a conventional DBMSs. Some implementation issues are:

- Capacity planning
- Predicting the traffic patterns between node sites
- Maximizing data, object, and program placement
- Minimizing competition for resources between nodes/sites
- Supporting disaster recovery efficiently and safely
- Controlling transaction processing to avoid destructive interference

The database administrator charged with resolving these issues should be trained in distributed system management and must work closely with the architect, designer, and chief modeler to achieve success.

Finally, there are issues with the management tools/systems themselves. The distributed database management tools/systems are at best immature products and do not always provide the highest levels of performance. Some of these issues are sufficiently troublesome that, if steps are not taken to avoid the problems, they might cause the warehouse project to fail:

- Intersite accessing and processing is not always carried out in an efficient manner.

- Processing may not be distributed properly between sites.
- Data might not be distributed to best advantage around the various sites of a network.
- Access (security) may not be adequately controlled to data linked by networks.

Skilled DBAs and system programmers can handle all of these problems by manually redistributing data and processes, careful tuning, and when necessary, using each of the individual DBMS's own internal security facilities. A distributed data management tool/system requires a much higher degree of vigilance on the part of its support personnel than does the conventional DBMS to ensure its success.

Data Model/Metadata

Having an enterprise data model at the start of a distributed data warehousing project would be very useful. Unfortunately, this is almost never the case. What the company usually does have instead are models of the existing individual data marts. These need to be carefully reverse engineered into a global data model, resolving all inconsistencies. This "global" data model may be very different from an enterprise data model; it contains only the data and metadata about the existing data marts. For the success of the warehousing project, it is not immediately necessary to extend this model to include the remainder of the business, but it is a useful exercise that aids in the design of additional sites. At the very least, the global model must be kept current, incorporating new data/metadata as sites are added to the warehouse.

Data/User Interface

Like the centralized data warehouse, the distributed warehouse is intended to eventually serve everyone in the company. However, using either a homogeneous or heterogeneous distributed database approach, users have access to a local data mart and access to the entire warehouse. This greatly simplifies things for them; most of their queries require department-specific information and are directed to the local data mart. There is no confusion about which data is needed. It is only when the users venture into the warehouse that there is a chance for trouble. There it is a possibility that they cannot find the correct data or they choose the wrong data and come up with erroneous results.

The single distributed database management system looks just like a centralized warehouse to the users. All queries are directed to the warehouse as a whole and, without some assistance, users are likely to get lost while searching for the data they need. Good metadata can function like a roadmap for the users, guiding them to the right locations.

Maintenance

The distributed data warehouse, like any processing system, must be maintained. Here, the physical size of the databases is almost never a consideration. Rather than allow any one site to become overcrowded, a new site is added. However, DDWs do have some system-specific maintenance concerns. Restarts and recoveries must be planned for each individual site and then for the warehouse as a whole. Because identical data is often stored at two or more sites, consistency can be a problem if not constantly monitored.

Tuning is also an issue for a distributed data warehouse. Each individual data mart must be tuned, and then the entire warehouse adjusted to ensure adequate performance. Tuning includes more than just indices and summary tables; selected data and even entire tables may be relocated to a different site or duplicated across sites. Static queries should be explained to check for maximum performance and alterations made to the query and/or in the warehouse where necessary. In extreme circumstances, whole processes (e.g., programs, stored procedures, and data) may be moved to improve timing. The company that initiates a distributed warehousing project faces many challenges, venturing into poorly charted waters. However, the entry cost is modest, the issues are manageable, and the potential rewards well worth the risk.

What to Choose

The arrival of new technologies, the prevalence of the Web and intranets, and the experiences of those who pioneered data warehousing have brought about a new and better way to build a data warehouse. This new architectural approach starts with a limited-scope independent data mart that simultaneously introduces the new technology to the organization, proves the value of the warehousing concept, and produces a substantial return on investment. In parallel with the initial implementations, the business can be developing both an enterprise data model and the appropriate architecture to ensure that the subsequent data mart implementations will blend with the first and that the completed whole will form a corporatewide distributed data warehouse.

As the data warehouse market developed over the past fifteen years, many different philosophies and methodologies have evolved, some requiring extensive resources and some with a quick-fix approach. Today, it is apparent that no single architecture is right for every situation. If data warehousing technology is to reach the next stage of its life cycle, universal development, corporations must be allowed to examine their information needs, data source structures, and timelines and requirements and have the freedom to apply whatever warehousing architecture best suits their needs. A few organizations will choose a traditional centralized data warehouse; some will select a single system distributed warehouse, with the remainder opting for homogeneous or heterogeneous data marts joined together to form a distributed data warehouse. All will likely come to the conclusion that an *n*-tiered architecture, supported by an intranet, will bring the best results and most flexibility for the future.

Once requirements are gathered, a strategy outlined, and architectural approach selected, the organization should begin work on its data model/metadata. The data model gives organizations the tool they need to maintain the architecture of the data warehouse. Changes in data warehouse content, physical implementation, available technologies, user requirements, and the business environment can all be addressed in the data warehouse through the logical model. Although modeling is time-consuming, if the process starts with one subject area at a time, the payoff will be many times the effort in the end.

A data warehouse at all stages of development needs to provide not only data but also metadata to be successful. In data warehousing, success is not defined by the quantity of data, but by the users' ability to understand, locate, analyze, and act on the warehouse's contents. Metadata is the key to user/data interaction.

The shortest, quickest, and most cost-effective approach in most circumstances is to build from the bottom up, creating independent data marts to meet specific departmental needs, but with the forethought to remain in line with the corporate information strategy. This will yield early, quick success by giving departmental information to a selected group of business users and encourage the enterprisewide information effort. The n-tiered architecture employed in this effort has the flexibility and scalability to support both short-term and long-term objectives. A distributed data warehouse thus begun can deliver better information throughout all its phases to business users and enable informed decisions based on accurate, timely, and precise corporate data.

3

Data Placement in Distributed Warehouses—Distribution and Transformation

One of the greatest challenges facing the organization that chooses to implement a distributed data warehouse is data handling in this relatively new environment. All distributed systems based on relational technology, and warehouses in particular, have the ability to store extremely large quantities of data (100+ terabytes if necessary) at an attractive cost per megabyte. It was likely this cost benefit that lured the company to the distributed warehouse paradigm initially. Along with an almost unlimited storage capacity comes the mixed blessing of multiple processors that are capable of functioning in a truly parallel fashion. These benefits lead to the question of how to distribute data around the various sites in order to take advantage of the "natural" parallelism inherent in distributed relational systems while still preserving the advantages of the individual data marts.

Another fundamental issue in distributed warehousing is one of providing automatic methods of transforming access to data that is stored in an "alien" access language into requests that can be dealt with by the local DBMS. While this is normally only a problem in heterogeneous systems, its resolution has implications important to any distributed warehouse with World Wide Web connections.

The Data Placement Problem

Most distributed data warehouses appear suddenly, overnight in fact, when two or more independent data marts are joined together. The majority of these warehouses are of the homogeneous or heterogeneous type, although some use a single distributed database management system approach (see Chapter 2). Since it was conceived as the union of a group of separate systems, the distributed data warehouse at "birth" already has a built-in data store residing at several different locations. The data objects are predistributed in a fashion that best suits the needs of the independent data marts, normally along departmental lines. There is a great deal of duplication of data across the systems, with key elements, such as customer names and addresses or a product list, resident at all sites.

However, the arrangement of data objects that matches the requirements of the data marts might not suit the best interest of the warehouse. One of the easiest ways to understand this is to consider an example—say, a full-service brokerage house doing business as a fifty-person partnership. This brokerage house interconnected its four independent data marts to form a distributed data warehouse. The data marts were constructed, using RDBMSs, in the following fashion:

Data Mart 1, Trading Accounts. This first data mart contains the stock (local and foreign) trading activities of all the firm's clients.

Data Mart 2, Money Market Accounts. The brokerage makes a money market fund available to its clients for short-term investment of liquid assets. All client monies held by the brokerage, whether for future investment, to cover margin calls, etc., are deposited temporarily in this fund. This data mart holds the record of activities for the money market accounts as well as the "master" client file and its attendant data.

Data Mart 3, Bond Accounts. The brokerage also acquires and holds bonds for its clients, and the record of these transactions is kept in this data mart. In terms of total assets, the bond department is as busy as the trading desk and insisted on its own data mart.

Data Mart 4, Internal Accounts. This data mart contains the in-house records—brokerage expenses (e.g., rent, utilities, transportation, data processing costs, and accounting services), in-house trading account, in-house bond fund, payroll accounts (brokers are paid a percentage of funds under management or a percentage of each transaction), and partnership accounting, etc.

Each of these data marts functions well, providing its users with excellent decision-support capabilities. The brokers and bond traders are especially pleased with their systems, Data Marts 1 and 3, for the instant access to a client's account they provide. However, now that these four data marts have been joined into a data warehouse, the users are expecting more from it. The brokers still want to see the stocks owned by their clients, but they also want to see any bond holdings and their clients' cash position, too. Bond traders are also making similar queries—for clients' complete portfolios. With the distributed data warehouse this access is possible, but it requires three queries to three different systems. Using the relational system, the query for the client, "John D. Rockefeller," would be:

```
SELECT
    Client_Name (Table A), Client_Stock (Table B)
FROM
    Client Data (Table A), Client Stocks (Table B)
WHERE
    Client_Number (Table B) = Client_Number (Table A) and
    Client_Name (Table A) = "John D. Rockefeller"
                            +


SELECT
    Client_Name (Table C), Client_Balance (Table D)
FROM
    Client Data (Table C), Client Balance Table (Table D)
WHERE
    Client_Number (Table D) = Client_Number (Table C) and
    Client_Name (Table C) = "John D. Rockefeller"
                            +


SELECT
    Client_Name (Table E), Client_Bond (Table F)
FROM
    Client Data (Table E), Client Bond Table (Table F)
WHERE
    Client_Number (Table F) = Client_Number (Table E) and
    Client_Name (Table E) = "John D. Rockefeller"
```

Note: Tables A, C, and E all contain the same type of data, Client Data:

> Data Mart 1 houses Tables A and B.
> Data Mart 2 houses Tables C and D.
> Data Mart 3 houses Tables E and F.

While this arrangement of data worked fine for the independent data marts, it is not ideal from the perspective of the new distributed warehouse. There must be a better way to arrange the information to facilitate queries.

One possible approach is to combine the stock and bond accounts into a single table and eliminate one of the two copies of the client table. If the resulting combined account structure is too large to be conveniently stored at one site, it can be horizontally partitioned (by account number or client name) and reside at two or more locations (in this example, Data Marts 1 and 3). This redistribution of data yields at least two benefits to the warehouse as a whole: It eliminates the storage of one set of client names and addresses, and it allows the broker and trader requests for portfolio information to be fulfilled with two queries and access to only two systems. With the account records combined and redistributed across two sites, the brokers and traders can have complete portfolio information in one-third of the time it used to take.

The portfolio example was relatively easy to solve. The situation is more difficult when it is necessary to distribute the components of more than one relationship across multiple sites. To illustrate this concept, consider an example using the same brokerage house. Only this time, a bond trader knows of a new municipal bond offering by Trenton, New Jersey, about to come to market and would like to alert some clients to the opportunity. Because the bond trader's time is limited, he decides to notify only those people who have purchased municipal bonds in the past; he feels that they will be the ones most inclined to buy a new offering. Also, municipal bonds give the greatest tax advantage to those purchasers living in the community offering the bonds, so he should confine his initial phone calls to only those people with a home address in Trenton or the surrounding area. Using a relational system, the bond trader needs to do the following:

```
SELECT
    Client_Name (Table 4), Client_Phone_Number (Table 4)
```

From
  Client Securities (Table 1), ZIP Code (Table 2),
  Bond Table (Table 3), Client Data (Table 4)
WHERE
  Client_ZIP_Code (Table 4) = ZIP_Code (Table 2) and
  ZIP_Code (Table 2) = City_Name "Trenton" (Table 2) and
  Client_Bond (Table 1) = Bond_Name (Table 3) and
  Bond_Name (Table 3) = Bond_Type "Municipal" and
  Client_Number (Table 4) = Client_Number (Table 1)

As can be seen, to fulfill this query the bond trader will need data from four tables located at three sites to find the clients he seeks:

Data Marts 1 and 3	Client Securities (Table 1 now contains the combined customer accounts for the warehouse) and Client Data (Table 4 contains the combined customer data file for the warehouse)
Data Mart 3	Bond Table (Table 3 contains all bond names and their type, such as corporate, Treasury, and municipal)
Data Mart 2	ZIP Code Table (Table 2 contains all U.S. ZIP codes and their location)

To maximize the join between the ZIP Code Table and the Client Data Table, the ZIP Code Table could be duplicated and repositioned to reside in both Data Marts 1 and 3, instead of its original location in Data Mart 2. This would simplify the join and take advantage of the natural parallelism of the distributed environment. The local RD-BMSs at both locations could then process their half of the Client Data Table with the ZIP Code Table simultaneously. By just duplicating and repositioning the ZIP Code Table, total query time is reduced by about 30 percent.

The disposition of the Bond Table is somewhat more difficult. It is a very large table containing all the bonds issued in the United States for the past twenty years, as well as some older active issues, and is indexed by bond number. While storage in a distributed system is inexpensive, it is not so cheap that it is practical to duplicate everything everywhere. Horizontal partitioning of the Bond Table would be possible, with the partitions residing in different locations, Data Marts 1 and 3 in this example. However, just because it is possible does not make it the best solution. Some benefit would be derived from the dual processing made possible by the split, but that would be negated by the cross-system traffic it would create.

Another approach to the Bond Table is possible. It is currently indexed by bond number, a unique number assigned to each offering of bonds when it is issued. It serves to identify and track the issue during its life cycle. An index could be added to the Bond Table on the Bond Type column, and then the table partitioned in such a manner that all bonds of the same type fall within the same partition (i.e., treasuries and corporate in partition 1, municipal and state in partition 2). Assuming two partitions, the Bond Table could be distributed between Data Marts 1 and 3. Now, only one partition of the Bond Table would participate in the join with the two partitions of the Client Data Table, and the cross-system traffic would be half of what it was before. Processing time for the Client Data/Bond Table would be cut in half. With both improvements in place (ZIP Code Table duplicated and repositioned and Bond Table partitioned and distributed), the total query time is reduced by nearly 80 percent. Of course, this example assumes that these improvements in no way conflict with other queries made to the data warehouse.

From these rather contrived and simplified examples it is clear that data placement within a distributed data warehouse can indeed have a significant impact on performance. The technique is made more complex by allowing redundancy (i.e., two copies of the ZIP Code Table), but this "extension" can bring compensating rewards. A methodology, or even a general approach, to solving the data placement problems of a distributed warehouse would be a great help.

A Practical Approach to the Placement Problem

It would be very convenient to have a mathematical solution to these data placement situations. But allocation problems are difficult to solve—it is unlikely that an algebraic expression (an algorithm with polynomial time complexity function) can be formulated to solve them. In fact, C. C. Chang and Phil Shielke demonstrated as early as 1985 that it is almost impossible for an algorithm to provide a complete solution to any of these problems, given realistic-size data structures and an acceptable timeframe. Unfortunately, their work was almost completely forgotten by many in the scramble to find a quick fix to the data placement problem. As of this writing, no such solution exists, nor is one likely to be forthcoming in the foreseeable future.

This does not suggest, however, that efficient problem-solving methods should not be sought. Rather, the focus must be on using heuristic methods to unravel the data placement issues. To this end, the author proposes one possible approach for determining data placement in a systematic manner. This methodology has been road tested on several unsuspecting major clients, always with (thankfully) successful results. After all, what is any good theory but the fortuitous outcome of trial and error?

When building the data marts/data warehouse, the design team first developed an architecture that served as a guide to the selection and arrangement of the various parts. So, too, with data placement: There needs to be an architecture or at least a general approach that functions as the framework for problem resolution. Like any architecture, this is not the solution to the problem or the blueprint for successful design, but it does act to focus energy into a step-by-step methodology that maximizes the opportunities for success.

This architecture can be broken down into two parts, with the first focusing on tuning and data placement to maximize user access and the second part focusing on techniques to minimize load times.

Maximizing User Access

Composed of twelve practical steps, this portion of the architecture should be applied sequentially. It is not that step 1 is more important than step 4; rather, the information acquired in step 1 influences the decisions made in the subsequent steps. Not all steps will apply equally or at all to every distributed data warehouse, but each step should be considered in light of the individual circumstances and the type of distributed system in use.

Step 1: Learn the fundamental goals of this particular distributed data warehouse. No two data warehouses are ever physically exactly the same, and no two ever have exactly the same objectives. Physical differences are easily discerned; philosophical differences and sometimes even a practical direction are slippery territory. Of course, the company intends to use the warehouse for decision support, but what decisions and who is supported? Is the warehouse primarily a collection of independent data marts, destined to serve individual divisions as a replacement service for monthly and quarterly reports? Does it support the firm's knowledge workers, opening new avenues of investigation for potential products or different marketing approaches? Or is it to function chiefly as the tool of upper management to provide an overall view of the business? The warehouse usage patterns will evolve over time, as will the warehouse itself, but there should be a starting point that establishes the warehouse's biases. Data placement is primarily a tuning device, and it is not possible to tune any system to maximize performance for all (actually, it is possible to tune a system to treat all users more-or-less equally, with the result being equally unacceptable to everyone). It is disastrous to distribute data to support individual data marts in one instance and then redistribute it again to support an overall warehouse function for the next circumstance. A clear direction must be chosen and adhered to consistently, to avoid working at cross-purposes.

Step 2: Design to suit the individual database management systems first. This advice applies only to homogeneous and heterogeneous distributed data warehouses (for a single DDBMS, you obviously must design to that product's requirements). Just because the environment is new, a distributed warehouse is not an excuse for the designer forgetting everything she ever knew. The distributed data warehouse is a confederation of stand-alone systems, and the requirements and rules of those systems must be respected in the distributed environment. For example, most of the systems participating in distributed warehouses use a relational database management scheme. Large tables are frequently partitioned for performance reasons in an RDBMS; if a table would normally be partitioned in the stand-alone system, it will still be partitioned in the distributed warehouse. One of the worst mistakes made by novice designers is to violate the rules governing data handling in the local DBMS while tuning the warehouse as a whole.

Step 3: Tune the local data marts next. Most queries in a distributed data warehouse are processed locally—by some estimates, as much as 95 percent of all inquiries are handled by the individual data marts. For this reason alone, the performance of the individual systems is extremely important. If users have excellent response times on 90 percent or more of their queries, they will be satisfied with their warehouse. However, in the process of tuning the warehouse as a whole, it is often easy to overlook the denigration of response times in one location. No thought is given to the principle that poor performance at the level of the individual system is magnified by cross-system queries. If one of the data marts involved in a multisystem query is responding slowly, the entire warehouse must wait for it to return the requested information before processing can be completed. What was a localized problem is now a warehousewide issue that can best be resolved by paying attention to the ailing data mart. Always maximize performance at the local level before making the decision to redistribute data.

Step 4: Make certain that the local "physical house" is in order. The importance of regularly scheduled data structure reorganizations and a refresh of statistics cannot be overemphasized. In the author's experience, even competent database administrators (DBAs) sometimes overlook this basic necessity or fail to perform it frequently enough, allowing performance to deteriorate as a result. As with step 3, proper data handling in a distributed data warehouse begins with maintenance at the local level.

Step 5: Optimize the query language. This is the simplest of the steps and the most frequently overlooked. It is easy for the warehouse designer and the DBAs to assume that the programmers and the interface products employed by the users (SQL when the data storage system is an RDBMS) are producing good code. And, in fact, they might be generating excellent code for local processing and terrible SQL for the extant distributed warehouse. Writing a query for cross-system processing is very different from crafting a single-system inquiry, and programmers and DBAs need training to learn to function efficiently in this new environment. While the various forms of the EXPLAIN command available are useful, most have a single-system bias. At least initially, all static and a portion of dynamic distributed SQL should be checked and improved by someone experienced in multisystem processing and very familiar with the data warehouse. If the local DBMS is equipped for stored procs (procedures), their use should not be overlooked in the distributed system. A stored proc can be called by a query that originated in another system, and they should be used whenever possible to maximize performance. Do not make the mistake of blaming the warehouse for improperly written queries.

Step 6: Apply standard optimization techniques. If the query language has been optimized and response times are still slow, apply standard optimization techniques to the data in-place before considering more drastic measures. Often the addition of an index or the partitioning of a large table will make a remarkable difference in query performance. Anything that improves the performance of a portion of a complex inquiry generally improves the entire query.

Step 7: Position data to be near "complementary" data. Data forms "natural groupings" whose elements are frequently requested together. All members of the group should reside at the same location to avoid the expense of constant cross-system queries. There are two ways to determine which data belongs together: Either have an extensive knowledge of the business the data supports, or understand the interrelationships among the data storage structures (e.g., tables in an RDBMS). Ideally, the warehouse designer has both, but it is often sufficient to just understand the physical table structures. Using an RDBMS, the tables of crucial importance to one another all share a common primary key. Those that are related, but are of lesser importance to one another, have a foreign key relationship. Tables having the same primary key should be stored together. Separating them will create intersystem traffic, a step taken only for the most compelling reasons (see step 9). Foreign key relations, while not as important, should be preserved whenever possible.

Step 8: Evaluate "static" tables. Nonvolatile tables are those data that change infrequently, if at all. Make certain that these tables are located at the site where they are most often used—that is, where they have a foreign key relation to one or more of the other tables stored at that location. If they are needed at more than one node, do not hesitate to duplicate them unless they are extremely large. In the second brokerage example examined earlier in this chapter, it was useful to have the ZIP Code Table resident in both Data Marts 1 and 3 to avoid cross-system queries. While intersystem inquiries are expensive, data storage is relatively cheap, and multiple copies of static tables are easy to maintain because they change so seldom.

Step 9: Make vertical partitioning work for the warehouse. Data storage structures that share a primary key can be viewed as being vertical partitions of one another; they could be united, by removing some duplicate data, to form one giant table. They all contain information about the same entity, the one identified by the primary key (assuming a business key is used). While this violates all the basic rules of data modeling and table design, it is a helpful logical construct when used to aid in data distribution decisions. In the first brokerage example discussed earlier in this chapter, the Client Data Table, the Client Balance Table, the Client Securities Table, and the Client Bond Table all had the same primary key, Client_Number, and contained data about the firm's customers. Any or all of them could possibly be merged into one structure. To improve performance in the example, the Client Securities Table and Client Bond Table were united to form the Client Data Table. This new table suited the query pattern much better than the old table structures. An occasion may also arise in distributed warehouse design where it is helpful to split apart, or vertically partition, an existing table. This is accomplished by dividing the existing table vertically, moving a portion of the attributes to a new table. Both of the new tables thus created have the same primary key as the original and the same number of rows. These new tables can then be located in the data marts where they are needed.

Step 10: Use horizontal partitioning to take advantage of the natural parallelism of the distributed system. Horizontal partitioning is the practice of dividing a large physical table into several smaller sections, or partitions, using a key range to define partition members. It is commonly used in almost all RDBMSs to improve system performance, speed up reorganizations, and shorten image copy times, for example. It is also useful in a distributed system to improve performance in an additional way; the various partitions can be positioned at different nodes so they can be queried simultaneously. This technique creates cross-system traffic as the result sets are assembled at a common location and should only be used when the "gain" from the concurrent processing outweighs the "loss" due to intersystem traffic.

Step 11: Introduce data redundancy to minimize cross-system traffic. As seen in step 8, duplication of static tables across nodes is an easy implementation of this rule. Duplication of other data can be "expensive" in terms of system resources; duplicate tables must be carefully updated and maintained to protect data integrity and concurrency. For this reason, duplication of "volatile" or "active" tables should be attempted only when the resulting savings in processing costs (i.e., intersystem traffic) justify the additional expense. In this chapter's brokerage examples, there are multiple copies of the Client Data Table. While the solution to the first example included the elimination of one copy of the Client Data Table and the horizontal partitioning and redistribution of another duplicate, there were still two copies of the table available after tuning. Each data mart continued to have all or part of the Client Data Table available to it to reduce cross-system traffic.

Step 12: Redistribute data and processes to reduce bottlenecks. A situation can arise where some nodes in the distributed warehouse are much busier than others. In fact, one site may be so busy that it adversely effects response times and/or system availability. If this happens, the problem can be ameliorated by load balancing, or relocating part of the data stored at the overworked site to another underutilized node. The data should be moved in groups (see step 7) along with its attendant processes (e.g., updates, queries, stored procs, archival activity) to produce the maximum benefits. If the distributed data warehouse uses the data mart architecture, the network might also be reconfigured to move certain users to the new site to minimize cross-system traffic. In some instances, relocating the data is not sufficient; it must be duplicated across nodes and the user population divided to alleviate the problem.

It is important to remember that all distributed warehouses change over time; this flexibility is one of their most attractive features. New data marts come online, additional information is acquired, the store of historical data continues to grow, and user requirements change in response to shifts in the business environment. The warehouse designer and DBAs must remain alert to these changes and constantly be ready to adjust the warehouse's configuration to suit the business needs. An unattended warehouse soon becomes obsolete, even useless.

Minimizing Load Times

The second half of the data placement architecture attempts to minimize load times. Almost all data warehouses acquire their information from production systems and other sources, with data transfers occurring on a regularly scheduled basis (e.g., once a quarter, month, week, day, or several times a day, depending on circumstances and the warehouse's purpose). It can happen that there is so much data to transfer, the load time exceeds the available batch window at one node or another. This in turn reduces the availability of part or all of the distributed warehouse.

Like tuning for availability, there is no quick fix for minimizing load times. Once again, the proposed solution architecture is presented as a series of steps to be considered in order. Not all steps apply to every distributed warehouse in each circumstance, but all should be reviewed before formulating and implementing a solution.

Step 1: Determine what facility is used to accomplish the load. Data loads come in all types: change programs that merely enhance the existing records in a table, load programs that add new records in a table, update programs that both load and enhance a table, and load utilities. The trick is to make certain that the fastest method is chosen for a particular job. Generally, load utilities are the most efficient way to build a new table or add records to an existing one. In some cases, third-party products are more efficient than the utilities that come included with the RDBMS; these products should always be tested before altering the load process in their favor. Changes are best accomplished programmatically, with attention paid to optimizing the query statement. Wherever possible, the same program should not be used to both change and add records; preprocess the data feed to separate the deltas from the new records and use a program for changes and a utility for loads. So too, for maximum efficiency, a program should not update or load more than one table at a time. While every RDBMS is somewhat different, several of them process loads much more rapidly without indexes, which can be built after the load process is complete.

Step 2: Determine if the data feed has been preprocessed. All data, before entering the warehouse, has undergone some preprocessing to cleanse, convert, and/or transform it. In some cases, this is not sufficient for optimal loads. The data might also need to be sorted into table sequence, or divided by partition key into multiple files, or split into two or more loads for different tables, and/or checked for referential integrity. Whatever processing can be done outside the warehouse saves time on the loads.

Step 3: Assess whether loads can process concurrently at one site. Most RDBMSs offer parallel processing, or the ability to run two or more processes concurrently. At a multitable site, several data loads may be able to run concurrently without fear of lock contention because they access different groups of tables. This technique alone can radically reduce elapsed clock time, but the local RDBMS must be retuned to support parallel processing. Some loads, however, cannot be run concurrently because of referential integrity constraints—either the foreign key tables must be loaded first, imposing a sequence on the loads, or several tables access the same foreign key table while loading to ensure referential integrity, and parallel processing would lead to lock contention.

Step 4: Determine whether foreign keys are necessary during load. Referential integrity is extremely important in any system, but it can be very expensive in terms of the time it adds to the load process. Wherever possible, check for referential integrity during the preprocessing phase and then drop the foreign keys during loading. This technique removes the artificial "load sequence" barrier and the "foreign key table" contention associated with parallel loads. Also, determine just how critical foreign keys are to the warehouse in general. While they do ensure referential integrity, is the warehouse paying too high a price for correct data? If the warehouse requires absolute accuracy (i.e., the corporate year-end statement is generated from the warehouse), then foreign keys are a must. However, if the warehouse is a decision-support tool, then the very small percentage of error introduced by preprocessing the data instead of depending on foreign keys might be tolerable.

Step 5: Assess whether large tables can be partitioned to allow concurrent processing. Often, the load process bottlenecks at a very large table. This can be resolved by horizontally partitioning the table in such a way as to permit the individual partitions to be loaded concurrently. Where there was once one enormous load there are now several smaller, faster loads, reducing elapse time by as much as 90 percent.

Step 6: Determine how aggregation and summary tables are built and loaded. Often, as a part of the regularly scheduled load process, summary and aggregation tables are constructed. There are several ways to do this, with some methods more efficient than others, in part dependent on the RDBMS used. Generally, it takes less time to perform mathematical computations programmatically than to use the services provided by the RDBMS (this should be tested using the chosen RDBMS before modifying any code). The most time-saving approach is not to build the summary and aggregation tables at load time; instead, create them using VIEWs. While this approach saves a great deal of time during the load process, it drastically slows user access to these tables and should be used cautiously.

Step 7: Determine how tables are arranged on the physical storage devices. The application of this technique is completely dependent on the RDBMS chosen and the type and configuration of the physical storage devices. For each given combination of hardware/software there are preferred methods of data distribution across the available storage devices that can be exploited to minimize load times (i.e., placing two tables that load concurrently on different devices). Since the potential savings in elapse time can be substantial (in some cases as much as 70 percent), it is well worth the effort to explore this avenue for load tuning.

Step 8: Consider moving some tables to an underutilized site. After applying the other, site-specific techniques for tuning, some nodes could still be overworked. With a distributed system, it is possible to relocate some of the processing to another, underutilized site in the network. To do this, a group of tables (see step 7 in the section on Maximizing User Access) must be moved, along with all their attendant processes. Care must be taken to relocate all the complementary tables together to avoid adversely affecting data access. Often, the network must be reconfigured in support of this data redistribution to keep users and their data together. If the distributed warehouse is based on the data mart paradigm, relocating data outside its home mart will increase network traffic substantially. As a result, this is a last-resort solution.

Step 9: Consider partitioning a large table and distributing the partitions across sites. Partitioning extremely large tables and concurrently processing the loads can drastically reduce load times (as outlined in step 5 of Minimizing Load Times). This basic technique can be taken one step further by relocating the partitions across the nodes of the network. Although this technique offers some savings over the traditional single-site method (just how much depends on the hardware and software in use), it definitely increases network traffic. Every access to the distributed table generates a multisite query and the extra processing costs of assembling the responses at the local node. Of course, query times might improve because of the parallel processing (see step 10, Maximizing User Access), but this depends on factors such as the number and type of JOINs, the location of the JOINed tables, and network speeds, for example. This technique must be applied cautiously, with thought given to the impact it will have on total data access.

As seen, there are circumstances when improving load times degrades data access. With a distributed data warehouse, the designer and DBAs are constantly working to balance the needs of the warehouse with the needs of the users. The warehouse team must be constantly aware that the changes they implement will affect the entire system—there are no insignificant changes. That is why it is so important to understand the overall goals and purpose of the warehouse; this knowledge guides the warehouse team to make the choices best suited for the individual warehouse.

No methodology can guarantee success to its practitioners. However, by utilizing both aspects of the data placement architecture described, the designer can be assured that the changes she makes to the distributed system will improve, not denigrate, overall warehouse performance. The steps should be applied in order: Try the basic, or simple, solutions first and progress to the more complex and expensive remedies only when absolutely necessary. Remember, for any warehouse data placement problem there are multiple acceptable solutions, and the best solution is almost always the simplest.

Integration of Diverse Database Systems

Another of the major challenges in distributed warehousing primarily affects only one of the three major types in use today, the heterogeneous system (Figure 3-1). However, most of the homogeneous and single DDBMS warehouses built also have a heterogeneous component—they have World Wide Web interfaces and utilize their Internet connections to acquire at least some data for the warehouse. Because they are reliant on external data stored in DBMSs not of their choosing, these warehouses, like their heterogeneous cousins, must con-

Figure 3-1. Heterogeneous distributed data warehouse.

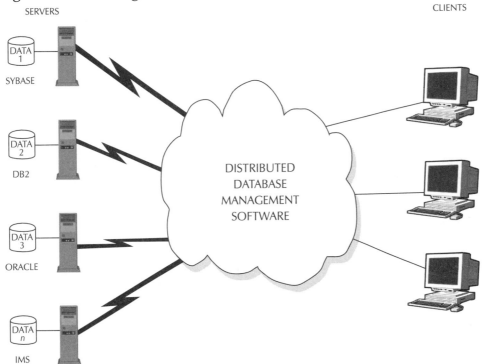

front the issues inherent in mixed-DBMS processing and find a way to resolve them.

   This challenge centers on cross-system queries. When users, connected by a LAN to a local data mart, wish to obtain data from a "remote" site within the warehouse, how do they go about it? Ideally, they just write their queries as if they were asking the question locally; after all, that is the idea behind a data warehouse. The user should not have to know, or even care, where the data is located or how it is stored in order to obtain it. For the distributed data warehouse tool to automatically transform the query written for one data mart into a query, or series of transactions, understandable by another data mart using a different DBMS, it needs to know how the two DBMSs in question relate to one another.

   The key component in this transformation is the "map" that tells the distributed data warehouse tool how the various data marts interrelate. This map is referred to as the global data model. It is constructed by integrating the component heterogeneous databases into a DBMS-independent universal schema. The global data model provides a virtual representation of all the data structures in the distributed data warehouse and, along with its attendant metadata, provides the backbone for query transformation. Without the global model, access to data in a warehouse is severely restricted.

The global data model cannot contain more information than the sum of the information contained in the contributing local schema. Frequently, it contains less, as the local systems choose to make only a portion of their data available to the distributed data warehouse. If individual data models of the contributing local systems exist, they must be melded into a unified whole. This requires a series of data abstractions and transformations to ensure consistency in the unified global model.

Abstractions

The first of these abstractions is aggregation, where a relationship between entities is represented as a higher-level object. For example, an "appointment" entity could be used to represent a potential relationship among a customer, a broker, and the brokerage company; a "derivative" might be a complex trade involving stocks, bonds, and interest rate swaps. Another abstraction is generalization, where a set of generic entities is considered to be a single entity (i.e., "client" might include individual customers as well as corporate entities). Restrictions can be placed on the generalized object or on a class of objects to obtain a subset of particular interest—for example, "bond traders" are a specific group within the generalized "employees."

Transformations

There are other conversions and transformations that must be performed to unite the individual data models. Most are needed for syntactic reasons, such as when items are stored at two or more locations using different measures (e.g., price per unit versus price per hundred). A different type of syntactic transformation would be used where the record structure differs among the various local databases. This can be very simple, as when in one local data mart stores the client's telephone number in the format "area code + telephone number." In another data mart, the area code and telephone number are kept separately. To reconcile the differing record structures, a syntactic transformation is needed. In a more extreme example, the customer data in one data mart may be kept in a database "root" segment, and the securities trades in dependent "child" segments of the same database. The same data is stored in three separate relational tables in another data mart. Here again, a syntactic transformation can resolve the differences.

A final example of transformation involves in the resolution of cross-system record duplication. Consider the brokerage business discussed earlier in this chapter where a securities sale is represented by an entry in the Client Stock Table in Data Mart 1. The same sale is also recorded as a credit entry in the Client Balance Table in Data Mart 2. It is not obvious from any syntactic considerations that these records represent the same transaction. The distributed database management system in use would have to "figure out" the meanings of the different structures from syntactic information furnished by the system designer.

Mapping

In addition to aggregations and transformations, special techniques are needed for mapping between the preexisting heterogeneous data models. One of the most important goals of such a mapping is that both the information stored in the local data model and the operators that can manipulate it be "preserved." When the mapping process is complete, the ideal outcome would allow everyone using the warehouse to have access to all the data represented in the local model. They would also be able to use every method of data access supported by the local DBMS without knowing anything about that DBMS (the use of this capability is subject, of course, to the logical and physical constraints of the finished distributed warehouse).

The methodology most commonly used for transforming data models is an old and reliable one; a source data description is mapped onto a target data description, in accordance with the rules of the source and target data models. This means that the local data model is mapped, one-to-one, onto the global data schema, with all aggregations and transformations carefully noted in the metadata. These data models, local and global, are considered equivalent if actual physical databases can be generated from them that are "one-to-one" and "into" (i.e., nothing left out).

Database states in the source and target data models are said to be equivalent if they can be mapped to the same state in some abstract metamodel. What this actually means is that they both represent the same view of the real world. Formal methods of establishing this equivalency depend on agreement to employ an abstract metamodel. While the concept of the metamodel is generally acknowledged, it has not yet been sanctioned by the modeling community. Therefore, more informal criteria are discussed here to establish the equivalency of states.

So, how can the data modeler be certain that the global and local models are really equivalent without generating real databases and comparing them? One way is to design the global model in such a way that any query that will "process" against it will also "process" against the local model (restated, if necessary). For this to happen, the set of operators available for each data model should be as complete as possible (i.e., for each of the objects in the data definition language of the data model, there exists a corresponding way to express it in the data manipulation language). Then, a sequence of events can be defined to transform the operators of the global model into the operators of the local data model. If both data models, global and local, are complete and one-to-one, then they can process the same queries because they are equivalent models.

To put the goal for data model transformation in more pragmatic terms, any transaction that runs on the database generated from the source (local) data model should be able to be rewritten to process on the database generated by the target (global) data model. Also, this rewriting of the transaction should occur automatically, performed by the distributed database management tool. Without a serviceable global data model, it is impossible to form a distributed data warehouse from heterogeneous systems.

The Global Data Model

Many methodologies and example schema have been proposed over the past fifteen years for reverse engineering a global data model from local ones. Some methodologies enjoyed brief periods of popularity before fading away, while others never gained even that small measure of acceptance. As diverse as these proposed approaches have been, they all agreed that three basic conditions had to be met to guarantee total inclusion of all kinds of heterogeneous systems into the global data model:

- The global data model, at any stage of its evolution, must be capable of absorbing new data models (if necessary by extending its DDL and DML using a system of axioms expressed in global data model terms).

- The information and operators from the local data models must be preserved after inclusion in the global data model (i.e., there must be commutative mappings between the schema and operators and a "one-to-one" and "into" mapping between database states, local and global).

- The local data models must be synthesized into a unified global data model, not just included as isolated submodels.

Methodologies

Today, most global data models are constructed using one of three generally accepted methodologies. The first such model, called UCDM or the unifying conceptual data model, was developed by starting with the relational data model and extending it incrementally by adding axiomatic extensions equivalent to various well-known data models. For example, to include the network data model in the UCDM, the axioms of uniqueness, conditional uniqueness, and obligation for unique, unique non-null, and mandatory attributes were added. While it is a useful methodology, UCDM is somewhat rigid and difficult to work with.

Another, more pragmatic methodology is DAPLEX. It is a special-purpose system designed to be used as both a language and the common data model to which each local data model maps. This system uses the functional model as a pivot representation onto which the heterogeneous systems map on a one-to-one basis. Real-world entities and their properties are represented as DAPLEX entities and functions. Separate views of the integrated model are provided to meet local requirements.

Mapping between most well-known data models, and even operating system files, is easy using DAPLEX. For example, a relational model can be included by representing each relationship as a

DAPLEX entity and each domain as a DAPLEX single-valued function. The network data model can be described in a similar fashion, and even sets are accommodated by representation as multivalued functions that return member entities. Even with all of its good qualities, DAPLEX is the distant second choice of most modelers because it is difficult to learn and works best only when used in conjunction with a distributed database product called Multibase.

By far the most popular methodology, the relational data model without axiomatic extensions, has become the backbone of warehousing systems in the United States. The majority of the data modeling community has judged it adequate for the combined representation of all database systems, and it is used as the underlying structure for the global data model in nearly 98 percent of all warehouses. In fact, it is so widely accepted that many data modelers learn only relational modeling without even knowing that alternatives exist.

The relational data model was first proposed by E. F. Codd and C. J. Date in the early 1970s as a new paradigm for representing interrelationships among data, and it was extended shortly thereafter to become the basis for a more efficient system of data storage/retrieval. The impact of the relational model on the data processing industry cannot be overestimated—it revolutionized the way people regarded data, bringing about the realization that properly organized and readily accessible data is a corporate asset. It has spawned dozens of database management systems, from DB2 and Oracle to Microsoft's Sequel Server, and changed forever user expectations.

To use the relational model as the basis for a global data model, there need to be relational views of the local systems (often nonrelational in structure) that can be blended together to form the global schema. The problems associated with construction of these local data models varies depending on the type of DBMS used by the underlying system. There are, however, some general considerations applicable to building a relational data model regardless of the base system.

First, all the data sources must be identified and categorized in the local system, and a relational equivalent established. It is normally not difficult to identify the data sources themselves; these are the files and databases used for storage in the local database management system. The data element definitions and formats are somewhat trickier, since so few systems have a functional data dictionary, and many nonrelational systems permit (and even encourage) the storage of duplicate data under the same or different names in several places with differing formats. A data type and length must be chosen for the data element to become a properly defined relational attribute and all its possible sources identified and documented and, where necessary, a conversion factor specified in the metadata.

Defining the data type and length ties into the second factor that needs to be established—integrity constraints for the data elements. Are duplicates allowed? Must a number fall within a certain range? Are only three possible values acceptable in a field; if so, what are they? The possible range of allowable values for each data element must be considered and defined. These should be based on the actual data stored in the local system, provided it is "clean" or valid. Considerable research is always required to establish the correct integrity constraints.

The relationships among the data elements must also be established and captured in the relational model, and this can be the most difficult task of all. Where the relational model is very good at recording many different kinds of relationships (e.g., one-to-one or one-to-many, foreign key relationships, the interrelationship of data stored in a "star schema"), the relationships in other systems are often vague or nonexistent. Instead, these systems frequently rely on the knowledge of the programmers to provide the necessary connections among the files and databases. This information too must be hunted down and incorporated into the relational model.

Every file or database in the local system that is to be mapped onto a relational model generates at least one relationship—a file or database is, by definition, a logically related group of records. They all contain the same type of information about the key elements and can be transferred to the relational model in the form of one or more normalized tables with the same primary key that, in the case of multiple tables, form a snowflake schema. The foreign keys illuminate themselves during the process of "normalization," or removal of data redundancy from records stored in the same table. In DBMSs with parent/child record relationships, there is a natural mapping of a one-to-many relationship between the "parent" table and any "children." The "invisible" relationships known only to the experienced programmers should also be sought and recorded to make the mapping

Figure 3-2. Global data model for brokerage example.

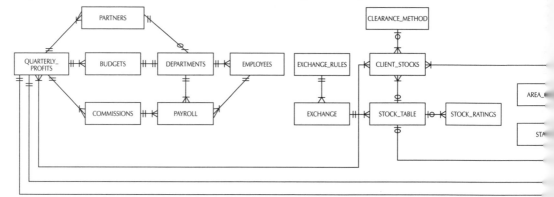

between the local system and the relational model as complete as possible.

Generally, relational attributes map to local data items, and relations are mapped to record types or programmer knowledge. Where the mapping is not one-to-one or has been derived from some other source, it must be noted in the metadata. This will allow the completed global data model to play a key role in query transformation. To illustrate how this might work, it is useful to consider an example. Using the same brokerage house as in the previous examples in this chapter, assume that Data Mart 1 has a DBMS that employs DL/I databases for its storage structures. In this case, instead of a Client Data Table and a Client Stocks Table, there is only a Customer database. The other Data Marts all remain the same, using relational database management systems. A global data model, based on a relational schema, has been constructed for the warehouse formed by uniting Data Marts 1, 2, and 3, as shown in Figure 3-2.

The same query is posed as in the earlier example, requesting portfolio information about the client John D. Rockefeller. It is written in SQL because it is based on the global data model:

```
SELECT
    Client_Name (Table A), Client_Stock (Table B),
    Client_Balance (Table D), Client_Bond (Table F)
```

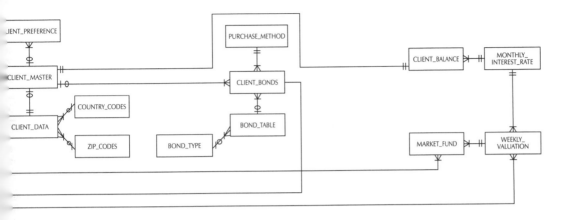

FROM
    Client Data (Table A), Client Stocks (Table B),
    Client Balance Table (Table D), Client Bond Table (Table F)
WHERE
    Client_Number (Table B) = Client_Number (Table A) and
    Client_Name (Table A) = "John D. Rockefeller"
        and
    Client_Number (Table D) = Client_Number (Table A) and
    Client_Name (Table A) = "John D. Rockefeller"
        and
    Client_Number (Table F) = Client_Number (Table A) and
    Client_Name (Table A) = "John D. Rockefeller"
        and
    Sale_Price (Table B) = " " and
    Last_Update (Table D) = "(today's date)" and
    Sale_Price (Table F) = " "

With assistance from the global data model, the distributed database management tool in use in this warehouse can break this query into three parts, to extract the requested data from each Data Mart. The most difficult transformation is the one addressed to Data Mart 1, which uses the nonrelational DBMS. The metadata for the Client Data Table and the Client Stocks Table indicates that they are actually one DL/I database, Customer, and that the attributes Client_Name and Client_Stock have the same name as the underlying data items. The metadata also indicates that there is a Client Data Table stored in both Data Marts 2 and 3. With this information from the global data model and its attendant metadata, the query can be rewritten as follows:

For Data Mart 1

    GU Client_name = "John D. Rockefeller"
    Check return code
    If return code not 0 then go to Customer_Not_Found
    Else Save Customer data.
    Loop:
        GNP
        If return code not 0 then go to terminate_loop
        Else if Sale_Price <> " " skip segment
            Else Save Stock data.
    End loop.
    Terminate_loop.

For Data Mart 2

    SELECT
        Client_Name (Table C), Client_Balance (Table D)
    FROM
        Client Data (Table C), Client Balance Table (Table D)
    WHERE
        Client_Number (Table D) = Client_Number (Table C) and
        Client_Name (Table C) = "John D. Rockefeller"
                and
        Last_Update (Table D) = "(today's date)"

For Data Mart 3

    SELECT
        Client_Name (Table E), Client_Bond (Table F)
    FROM
        Client Data (Table E), Client Bond_Table (Table F)

WHERE
  Client_Number (Table F) = Client_Number (Table E) and
  Client_Name (Table E) = "John D. Rockefeller"
      and
  Sale_Price (Table F) = " "

In this oversimplified example, the query transformation was straightforward—the Client_Name could be located in the root segment of the Customer database. The JOIN between the Client Data Table and Client Stocks Table was translated directly into the GNP (Get Next within Parent) command, which would return the "child" segments containing the stocks owned by the client. While not all query transformations are so easily accomplished, most have a one-to-one correspondence between the SQL statements and the commands in the local DBMS. If the global data model has been properly constructed with attention to the accompanying metadata, the transformation can be accomplished automatically.

What to Remember

The multiprocessor, multisite configuration of the typical distributed data warehouse makes it the perfect place to store extremely large quantities of data in a very cost-effective manner. However, along with an almost unlimited storage capacity comes the mixed blessing of multiple processors that can function independently of one another. This combination of many storage locations and many processing locations leads to the question of how best to distribute data around the various nodes. The desire to exploit the "natural" parallelism of the distributed systems must be carefully balanced with the advantages of the individual data marts.

Unlike the traditional data warehouse whose "birth" is a carefully scripted affair that occurs gently over a period of time, the distributed warehouse appears suddenly, when the network joining two or more independent data marts is enabled. Conceived as the union of a group of separate systems, the distributed data warehouse begins its existence with a built-in data store scattered around the different nodes. The data objects are predistributed in a fashion that is best suited to the needs of the independent data marts. Normally, no thought has been given to optimizing data placement for warehouse performance. How, then, should data be rearranged for a distributed warehouse? Unfortunately, there are no quick and easy solutions, no formula to follow that will lead to optimal data placement. Instead, the warehouse designer should focus on a heuristic approach as the most efficient problem-solving method available.

A heuristic approach to data placement can be viewed as the architecture for problem resolution. Like any architecture, it is not the solution to the problem in itself or even the blueprint for the solution. Instead, it provides the framework for a step-by-step approach that leads to success. The first part of this architecture focuses on tuning and data placement to maximize user access, and a series of steps (included in this chapter) that should be applied sequentially. While not all steps apply equally to every distributed data warehouse, each should be considered in light of the individual circumstances and the type of distributed system in use.

The second half of the architecture addresses the other side of the data placement problem, data loading. Almost all data warehouses exist as decision-support tools; they do not directly process the company's transactions. They acquire their information from production systems and other sources, with data transfers occurring on a regular schedule. Often, there is so much data to shift that the load process runs longer than the available "batch window" at one node or other. This in turn reduces the availability of part or all of the distributed warehouse.

Once again, the proposed solution architecture is a series of steps that should be applied, in order, to data placement problems. Not all steps apply to every distributed warehouse, but all should be reviewed before formulating and implementing a solution to reduce load times.

There are situations where improving transfer times degrade data access. With a distributed data warehouse, the designer and DBAs must constantly work to balance the needs of the warehouse with the needs of the users. The warehouse team must be sensitive to the fact that any shifts in data placement they make will create ripples throughout the entire system. Knowledge of the warehouse's purpose and objectives will guide the warehouse team, enabling them to make the best choices for the circumstances.

In addition to the data placement issues caused by lengthy data transfers and access requirements, there are placement problems that arise naturally as the warehouse evolves. The typical distributed warehouse will change over time with the addition of new data marts, supplemental information, and shifting user requirements. The warehouse team must remain alert to these changes and constantly be ready to adjust the warehouse's configuration to suit the business needs. Data warehouses must be adapted to serve their user community; the user community should never have to adapt to the warehouse.

No architecture or methodology can guarantee success to its practitioners—a poor implementation and inattention to detail can spoil the best architecture. However, the techniques outlined in this chapter will give the warehouse team a foundation on which they can build practical solutions to all their data placement problems. The steps should always be applied in order so that there is a progression from the basic, or simple, solutions to the more complex and expensive remedies. Remember, for any warehouse data placement problem there are multiple acceptable solutions, and the best is almost always the simplest.

Most of the distributed data warehouses built today have a "heterogeneous" component—they currently have or will soon add World Wide Web interfaces, allowing them to utilize their Internet connections to acquire at least some data for the warehouse. This reliance on external data, while very convenient, has its downside; it makes these warehouses vulnerable to the issues inherent in mixed-DBMS processing.

The challenge of heterogeneous processing centers on the need to provide automatic transformation of the access to data stored in a "foreign" language into requests that can be dealt with by the local DBMS. This transformation can be accomplished by using the services of the global data model, which is formed by integrating the various databases that compose the distributed warehouse into a DBMS-independent universal schema. The global data model acts as a virtual representation of the warehouse and allows manipulation of the local databases. Without a serviceable global data model, it is impossible to form a distributed data warehouse from heterogeneous systems.

The global data model must contain all the information the local systems choose to make available to the distributed data warehouse.

To blend the individual data models into a unified whole requires a series of data abstractions and transformations. Methods of mapping between different models must be developed so that all the information and its corresponding operators are preserved. When the mapping process is complete, the global data model should facilitate access to all the shared data using every method supported by the local DBMS.

Of the various methods proposed and tried for constructing a global data model from local ones, the relational data model has proven the most durable. It has gained such wide acceptance that it is virtually the only model used for warehouse development. Most data modelers in the United States learn only relational modeling.

To use the relational model as the basis for a global data model, the modeling team must first construct relational views of the local systems. These models can later be blended together easily to form the global schema. How difficult it is to build these models varies, depending on the type of DBMS used by the underlying system. There are, however, some general considerations applicable to building a relational data model regardless of the base system:

- Identify and categorize the data sources in the local system and establish a relational equivalent.
- Establish integrity constraints for the data elements.
- Establish the relationships among the data elements and capture them in the relational model.

Generally, local data items map to relational attributes, and record types map to relations. In some systems, entity relationships are not all expressed as record types—only the programmers know how the data items stored in different files relate. Care must be taken to include this specialized knowledge in the local data model. This will enable the completed global data model to play its key role in query transformation.

The structure of the typical distributed data warehouse confers many advantages: almost unlimited data storage capacity, true parallel processing capabilities, and great flexibility. It also has some drawbacks: slow and/or costly data access, long data transfer times, and difficulties translating queries to process at remote locations. If the warehouse team is aware of the issues, they can resolve them as part of the development process. The major problems inherent in distributed warehousing can be resolved when the team applies good modeling techniques during the design phase and follows a data placement architecture during the development phase.

4

Concurrency Control in Distributed Warehouses

All database management systems are more or less alike. That is not to say that they are "all created equal"—they most definitely are not. However, almost forty years of experience have taught the vendors that certain basic services are absolutely required of a database management system (DBMS), regardless of its type or intended platform. One of the most important of these basic services is the ability to support multiuser access to the data (i.e., several users simultaneously reading and writing to the database). While it sounds simple, concurrent access is not easily accomplished or regulated, and the problems associated with it are well documented and researched. Better methods have been sought since the introduction of the first true DBMS in the late 1960s, and improvements in concurrent "write" access are still extensively investigated. The recent introduction of new technologies such as distributed database management software and multiprocessor hardware adds new levels of complexity to the issue, elevating concurrency control into the data processing spotlight.

Distributed database management software, the engine that powers distributed warehousing, must be able to support multiuser access to data regardless of where the user or the data is located in the system. This is further complicated by the propensity, especially in warehouse implementations, toward maintaining duplicate copies of "popular" data at different sites. To ensure concurrency control, the DDBMS must not only decide which copy of the data will be accessed by a query, it must also find a way to update the other copies of that data if a change is made.

Most data warehouses today are implemented using multiprocessor hardware, either SMP (symmetric multiprocessing) or MPP (massively parallel processing). This is especially true for distributed warehouses that are equipped to take maximum advantage of the beneficial price/performance ratio and the massive data handling capabilities of the server-class SMP machines. A typical distributed warehouse might be composed of two to ten multiprocessor servers, each of which houses between two and sixty-four processors. Even the classic, centralized warehouse is probably running on mainframe hardware that utilizes MPP.

Sometimes, the SMP architecture is called "shared memory processing," because a group of processors operate cooperatively using a common memory pool. With a shared memory architecture, it is easy to add memory to a common pool, enhancing the flexibility of the architecture. SMP systems are comparatively inexpensive and ideally suited to situations such as distributed warehouses where initial requirements are modest but the developer knows that the environment will eventually need to be scaled up. SMP will be there, ready to accept more processors and/or memory when the need arises.

MPP technology is usually encountered in larger, mainframe-class hardware, and many centralized warehouses are beginning to take advantage of its features. Frequently referred to as "share nothing systems," MPP systems have large numbers of processors working in parallel, each with their own system resources. While they lack the easy scalability of SMP, MPP systems are generally faster than their smaller-scale rivals. With the new architectural enhancement known as NUMA (Non Uniform Memory Access), MPP systems, too, will be able to share common memory while they maintain their low latency.

All the major relational vendors are attempting to improve the performance of their products by adding parallel query capabilities that spread the work of a single query across several processors. This will reduce processing times, especially for large bulk warehouse operations that scan great quantities of data. Example of this might be report generation, data maintenance, and data mining operations.

Concurrency control, in either of these multiprocessor environments, becomes a very major concern. It is no longer just an issue of proper scheduling that will be handled by the DBMS. The warehousing team—architects, designers, database administrators (DBAs), and programmers—must all be aware of the potential problems and work together to ensure proper warehouse function.

Transactions

Of fundamental importance to concurrency control is the notion of a transaction. A transaction can be defined as the basic unit of work in a DBMS; it is a set of actions that must be carried out together. For example, the transfer of funds from a money market account into a personal checking account could be considered as a transaction; it is not complete until the money is debited from the money market account *and* deposited into the checking account. It is the DBMS's job to control concurrently executing transactions so they do not get in each other's way. The part of the database management system that performs that task is the scheduler. Serializability is the most common means of proving the correctness of these schedules. Communications between the scheduler and the program (or query) issuing the transaction are handled by the transaction manager, which coordinates database operations on behalf of the applications.

Transactions transform a database from one consistent state to another consistent state, although consistency may be violated during execution. As in the funds transfer example, the database is in an inconsistent state during the period between debiting the one account and crediting the other. If a system failure were to occur during this time, then the database would be damaged or inconsistent. It is the responsibility of the DBMS's recovery manager to ensure that all transactions active at the time of failure are rolled back or undone. The effect of a rollback operation is to restore the database to the state it was in prior to the start of the transaction, when there was consistency.

The four basic properties, sometimes called the ACID test, common to all transactions are:

1. *Atomicity.* The "all or nothing" property; a transaction is an indivisible unit.
2. *Consistency.* Transactions change the database from one consistent state to another consistent state.

3. *Independence*. Transactions execute independently of another (i.e., the partial effects of incomplete transactions are not visible to other transactions).

4. *Durability*. Also called persistence; the effects of a successfully completed transaction are permanently recorded in the database and cannot be undone.

An application program running in a database environment can be viewed as a series of transactions with nondatabase processing taking place in between transactions (see Figure 4-1). The transaction manager oversees the execution of the transactions and coordinates database requests on their behalf. The scheduler, on the other hand, implements a particular strategy for transaction execution. It tries to maximize concurrency without allowing simultaneously executing transactions to interfere with one another and, in doing so, compromise the consistency or integrity of the database. The transaction manager and scheduler are clearly very closely associated and their functions interrelate. How a transaction manager responds to a database request from an application will depend on the scheduler being used.

Transactions issued by concurrent users/programs can be interleaved in only two ways: Either they can execute in turn, end-to-end, in which case only one transaction is active at a time (Figure 4-2), or they can execute concurrently (Figure 4-3). The start of a transaction is signaled by a begin transaction command made explicitly or implicitly by the user/program. The transaction concludes with either a commit command to the DBMS, indicating a successful conclusion, or an abort command, indicating an unsuccessful termination. This abnormal termination (abort command) can be brought about by the transaction itself if it is unable to perform the required action (e.g., $2,500 cannot be withdrawn from the money market account and transferred to checking because there is only $2,200 available in the money market account). Or it can be the result of the execution of the concurrency control algorithm.

In an environment controlled by a distributed database management system, like a distributed warehouse, a transaction may access data stored at one or more sites. Each transaction must be divided into subtransactions, one for each storage site it will access. These subtransactions are represented by agents at the various sites. A com-

Figure 4-1. DBMS transactions in an application program.

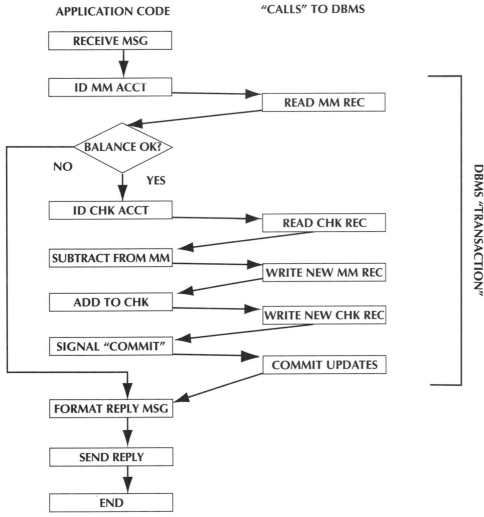

mon way of indicating a subtransaction, and the example that will be used in this book, is as follows:

- The agent of transaction T_1 at site A will be referred to as T_{1A}.
- The agent of transaction T_2 at site A will be referred to as T_{2A}.

A distributed version of the funds transfer example used earlier can be created by assuming that the money market accounts are stored at site A, and the personal checking accounts are stored at site

(text continues on page 122)

Figure 4-2. Serialized transactions.

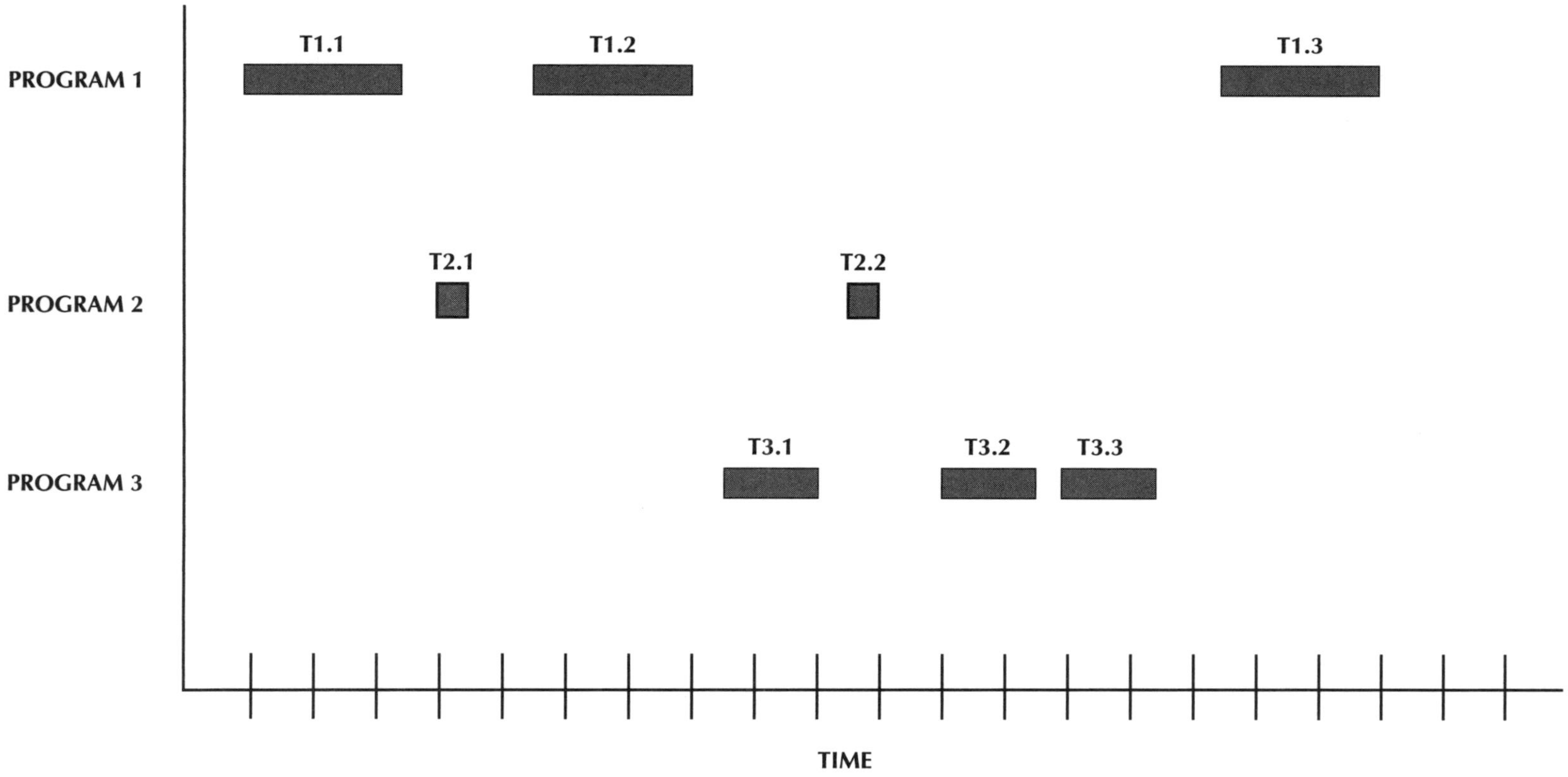

Figure 4-3. Concurrent transactions.

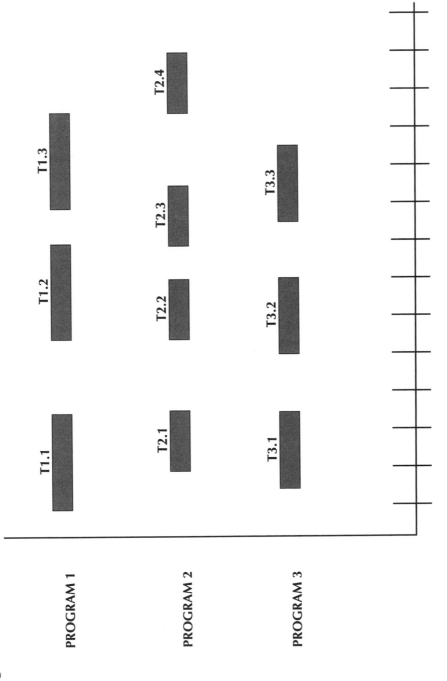

B. The customer wants to transfer $2,500 from a money market account (X) to a checking account (Y). While this is still a transaction (T_1) and is, by definition, an indivisible unit of work, it must be broken down into two subtransactions, or agents, that will be treated as indivisible transactions by their respective processing systems. In this example, the processing flow for transaction T_1 would be as follows.

EXAMPLE: TRANSACTION T_1 (FUNDS TRANSFER)

```
begin transaction T₁

    begin transaction T₁ₐ
        read balanceₓ
        balanceₓ = balanceₓ − 2500
        if balanceₓ < 0 then
            begin
                print 'insufficient funds'
                abort T₁ₐ
            end
        end − if
        write balanceₓ
    commit T₁ₐ

    begin transaction T₁ᵦ
        read balance_Y
        balance_Y = balance_Y + 2500
        write balance_Y
    commit T₁ᵦ

commit T₁
```

The subtransactions of the global transaction T_1 must not only be synchronized with the other purely local transactions processing concurrently at their site, but also with other global transactions active in the distributed system at the same or other sites. Distribution adds a new dimension to the complexity of concurrency control.

Interference between Concurrent Transactions

There are many ways concurrently executing transactions can interfere with one another and compromise the integrity and consistency of the database. Three major examples of such interference are:

- Lost updates
- Violation of integrity constraints
- Inconsistent retrieval

These problems apply equally to centralized DBMSs and distributed systems.

The first of these problems, the lost update, occurs when an apparently successfully completed update by one user/program is overridden by the processing of another. For example, transaction T_1 (from the funds transfer problem discussed previously) is processing concurrently in a centralized DBMS with another transaction, T_2, that is depositing \$1,000 to the money market account (account$_x$) of the customer.

Suppose that at the start of the two transactions, the balance in the money market account is \$3,000. The increase of \$1,000 by transaction T_2 could be overwritten by the decrement to \$500 by T_1, "losing" \$1,000 as shown in this example.

EXAMPLE: LOST UPDATE CAUSED BY TWO CONCURRENTLY PROCESSING TRANSACTIONS

Value of Balance$_x$
\$3000

		begin transaction T_2
begin transaction T_1	\$3000	**read** balance$_x$
read balance$_x$		balance$_x$ = balance$_x$ + 1000
balance$_x$ = balance$_x$ − 2500		**write** balance$_x$
if balance$_x$ < 0 then		**commit** T_2
begin	\$3000	
print 'insufficient funds'		
abort T_1		
end		
write balance$_x$	\$ 500	
read balance$_Y$		
balance$_Y$ = balance$_Y$ + 2500		
write balance$_Y$		
commit T_1		

The \$1,000 deposit to the money market account is lost because of the conflict between two concurrently processing transactions.

A different type of problem can also arise when two transactions are allowed to execute concurrently without being synchronized, which results in a violation of the integrity constraints governing the database. This can be easily understood by looking at another example. Using the brokerage business example (see Chapter 3), a stockbroker manages his clients' accounts by trading stocks in line with their overall preferences. He does not consult each client for every transaction; the stockbroker has a list of their instructions that he uses as a guide for purchases and sales on their behalf. This list is kept in the Client_Preference Table.

The stockbroker is aware of a technology IPO coming to market and decides to purchase 1,000 shares on behalf of his client, John D. Rockefeller, because Mr. Rockefeller has some spare funds in his money market account. The broker first checks his client preference list and, finding no objection to technological businesses, makes the purchase. Unknown to the broker, Mr. Rockefeller phones the brokerage that same morning and, unable to speak directly with him, leaves a message with his assistant stating that he does not want to invest any more money in high-tech companies. The assistant makes the change to the table. Unfortunately, the two transactions process at the same time with the following results.

EXAMPLE: VIOLATION OF INTEGRITY CAUSED BY TWO NONSYNCHRONIZED TRANSACTIONS EXECUTING CONCURRENTLY

```
begin transaction T₁
     read stock_type,                    begin transaction T₂
        preference,                           update Client Preference where
        company_name                             Client_Name = 'John D.
     From                                          Rockefeller'
        Client Preference where            stock_type = 'hi tec'
           Client_Name =                   preference = 'no'
           'John D. Rockefeller'           company_name = 'any'
        if not found abort T₁          commit T₂
     read balance From Client Balance
        where
        Client_Name = 'John D.
        Rockefeller'
        balance = balance − 50,000
```

```
        if balance < 0 then
    begin
        print 'insufficient funds'
        abort T₁
    end
end - if
write balance
update Client_Stocks where
        Client_Name = 'John D.
        Rockefeller'
    stock = SSY
    purchase_price = 50
    quantity = 1000
commit T₁
```

Note that neither transaction is aware of the actions of the other as they update different data.

The broker buys the IPO, thinking he is acting in accordance with his client's wishes when in fact, he is making the sort of investment his client definitely does not want. This may appear to be a trivial example, but for the stockbroker it can be very important. Should the IPO decrease in value and the broker sell it at a loss, the client would be able to charge him with mismanagement because he acted contrary to the client's instructions. This could result in the loss of the broker's license.

The two examples just discussed—the lost update and the violation of integrity—both centered on transactions that are updating a database. Most concurrency control concentrates on update because transactional interference can corrupt the data. However, transactions that are only reading the database can obtain inaccurate results if they are allowed to read partial results of an incomplete transaction that is simultaneously updating the database. This is often referred to as a "dirty read" or an "unrepeatable read." The simplest example of this sort of problem is a program that summarizes data in a database (e.g., totaling credits or debits). The program will obtain inaccurate results if it is allowed to process with a concurrent program that updates one or more of the fields included in the total.

All of the examples given so far pose a serious threat to data integrity and lead to incomplete or inaccurate answers to questions posed by the user/program. Obviously, a way must be found to prevent these types of interference. To this end, all DBMSs have a scheduler whose job it is to avoid concurrency control problems.

Schedules and Serialization

Almost all DBMSs use a concurrency control algorithm whose purpose is to determine the best transaction schedule for avoiding interference. Certainly, if the DBMS allowed only one transaction to process at a time there would be no problems and no need for a scheduler or algorithm. One transaction would have to commit before another could begin. However, to enhance efficiency, DBMSs aim to maximize concurrency or parallelism in the system. They allow transactions that can do so safely to process in parallel. For example, transactions that access completely different portions of the database can execute together. Finding ways to maximize concurrent usage has been the objective of much research in the database community for the past thirty years.

A transaction consists of a series of reads and writes to the database. The entire sequence of reads and writes of all concurrent transactions taken together is known as a schedule. A schedule S is generally written as follows:

$$S = \{O^1, O^2, O^3, \ldots O^n\}$$

where O^1 indicates a read (R) or a write (W) operation. O^1 precedes O^2, which precedes O^n, and so on. This ordering is denoted as:

$$O^1 < O^2 < O^3 < \ldots O^n$$

Thus, the schedule S for transactions T_1 and T_2 in the lost update example presented previously would be:

$$S = \{R_2(balance_x), R_1(balance_x), W_2(balance_x), W_1(balance_x),$$
$$R_1(balance_y), W_1(balance_y)\}$$

where R_1 and W_1 denote read and write operations by transaction T_1. Note that most concurrency control algorithms assume that a transaction reads data before it updates it (i.e., the constrained write rule).

The order of interleaving operations from different transactions is crucial to maintaining the consistency of the database. If the order of execution of the operators above were different:

$$S = \{R_2(\text{balance}_x), W_2(\text{balance}_x), R_1(\text{balance}_x), W_1(\text{balance}_x),$$
$$R_1(\text{balance}_y), W_1(\text{balance}_y)\}$$

then the outcome would be quite different. There would not have been the problem of transaction T_1 overwriting the update performed by transaction T_2.

The objective of the concurrency control algorithm is to generate schedules that are correct (i.e., to leave the database in a consistent state). Of particular interest are serial and serializable schedules. A serial schedule is one in which all reads and writes of each transaction are grouped together so the transactions run sequentially, one after another (Figure 4-4). A schedule S is said to be serializable if all the reads and writes can be reordered in such a way that they are grouped together as in a serial schedule, and the net effect of executing the reordered schedule is the same as that of the original schedule S. A serializable schedule will therefore be equivalent to and have the same effect as some serial schedule.

It should be noted, however, that a serializable schedule is not the same as a serial schedule. The objective of the concurrency control algorithm is to produce correct schedules so that the transactions are scheduled in such a way that they transform the database from one consistent state to another and do not interfere with each other. Serializability is taken as proof of correctness. If a concurrency control algorithm generates serializable schedules, then those schedules are guaranteed to be correct. Deciding whether a schedule is equivalent to some serial schedule is difficult. If the constrained write rule is applied, then the algorithm to determine serializability of a schedule is of polynomial complexity.

Intuitively, it can be said that two schedules, S_1 and S_2, are equivalent if their effect on the database is the same. Thus, each read operation on a data item in both of the schedules sees the same value, and the final write operation will be the same in both schedules. More formally, the rules for equivalency of schedules can be stated as follows:

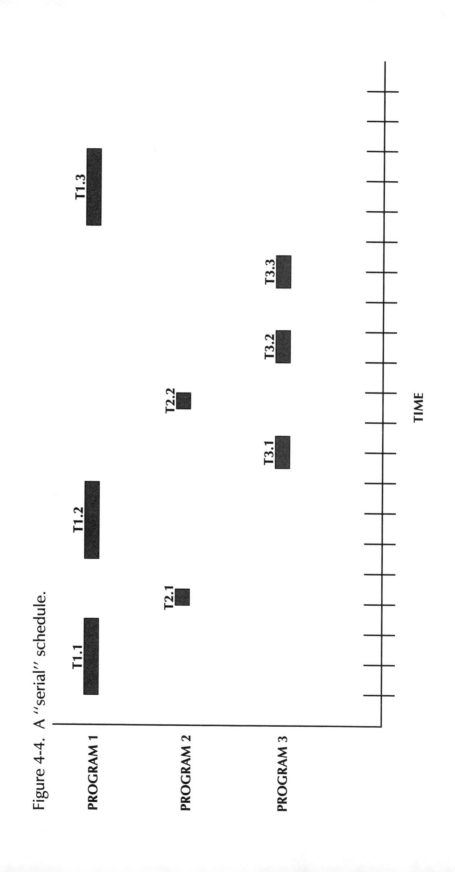

Figure 4-4. A "serial" schedule.

- Each read operation reads the same values in both schedules (for this to be true, the write operations must be equivalent).
- The final database state is the same for both schedules.

Read operations cannot conflict with one another, and the order of their execution makes no difference in a schedule. However, the execution order of read and write commands do matter, as do the order of write commands. In terms of schedule equivalence, it is the ordering of conflicting operations that must be the same in both schedules. The conflict between a read and a write operation is called a read-write conflict, and the one between two write commands is a write-write conflict.

The basic concepts of serializability are the same for both distributed and centralized systems, but with the added complexity imposed by distribution. For a simple example, imagine that two global transactions, T_1 and T_2, both process at two sites, A and B. Suppose that the transactions process serially with T_{1A} preceding T_{2A} at site A, and T_{2B} preceding T_{1B} at site B. The processing flow would be as shown in the following example.

EXAMPLE: SERIALIZABILITY

Site A	Site B
begin transaction T_{1A}	**begin** transaction T_{2B}
read x	read y
write x	write y
commit T_{1A}	**commit** T_{2B}
begin transaction T_{2A}	**begin** transaction T_{1B}
read x	read y
write x	write y
commit T_{2A}	**commit** T_{1B}

The schedules, S_A and S_B, would be:

$$S_A = \{R_1(x), W_1(x), R_2(x), W_2(x)\} \Rightarrow T_{1A} < T_{2A}$$
$$S_B = \{R_2(y), W_2(y), R_1(y), W_1(y)\} \Rightarrow T_{2B} < T_{1B}$$

Although their agents process serially at each site, the global transactions are not serializable. It is easy to envision how such a circumstance could arrive; if the global transactions T_1 and T_2 were launched simultaneously by different users, one at site A and the other at site B, then the schedulers operating independently at each site could schedule them this way. So, for distributed transactions, it is necessary to have serializability of all local schedules (both purely local and the local agents of global transactions) and global serializability for all global transactions.

Effectively, this means that all subtransactions of global transactions appear in the same order in the equivalent serial schedule at all sites. For the global transactions, T_X and T_Y, processing at sites A through N where they have agents, this can be expressed as follows:

if $T_{XA} < T_{YA}$
then
$T_{XN} < T_{YN}$ (local ordering at site N)
and
$T_1 < T_2$ (global ordering)

In a centralized DBMS, there is a single scheduler that is responsible for synchronizing transactions and for ensuring that only serializable schedules are generated. In a system using a single system distributed management tool, there is a global scheduler and transaction manager, and there may also be local schedulers and transaction managers, depending on the product used. Scheduling in a single DDBMS is very similar to that in the normal DBMS because of the centralized global scheduling facility.

In a heterogeneous or homogeneous distributed system, however, the DBMSs' schedulers and transaction managers themselves are distributed across the nodes in the network (Figure 4-5). At each node, there must also be a "global" scheduler and transaction manager to act as coordinator for those transactions initiated locally that need to process at more than one site. The alternative would be to appoint one site as coordinator for all global transactions. While this would simplify many of the problems associated with concurrency control in a distributed environment, it is a somewhat unrealistic approach because the site soon becomes a bottleneck. If it fails, becomes overloaded, or is disconnected from the network for any reason, no global transaction could process anywhere in the system.

Figure 4-5. Distributed DBMS schedulers and transaction managers.

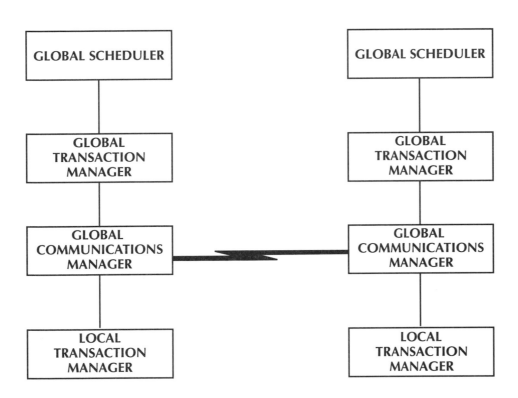

With distributed transaction control, the following sequence of steps is required to process a global transaction:

1. A global transaction is initiated at site A by the global transaction manager.

2. Using information about the location of data from the global data model/metadata, the global transaction manager divides the transaction into a series of agents at each relevant site.

3. The global communications manager at site A sends these agents to the appropriate sites.

4. Once all agents have completed processing, the results are communicated back to site A by the global communications managers.

Notice that the agents do not communicate directly with each other; they communicate through the coordinator.

This scenario ignores many issues, especially query decomposition and optimization. Each agent, from the point of view of the local transaction manager at its processing site, is itself an atomic transaction. It will terminate with either a commit or an abort operation. Still, the global transaction is also atomic, and its needs take precedence over the agents. When an agent is complete, it goes into a wait state and sends a message to the coordinating global transaction manager, indicating that it is ready to either commit or abort. The coordinating global transaction manager analyzes the responses from all the agents and then decides whether to commit or roll back the global transaction. It is only after that decision is made that the processing of the agents can be completed. The decision is broadcast to all agents, which in turn perform the processing as directed and notify the requesting site.

The global transaction manager can pursue a number of different decision strategies. The simplest is unanimity; if all agents return a commit, then the global transaction is committed. If all agents return an abort, then the global transaction and all agents are rolled back. However, if the agent responses are mixed, the decision is not as simple. The safest approach, of course, would be to abort all in this circumstance. If the database is highly replicated, a consensus approach might be taken, where the global transaction is committed if the majority of the agents "vote" to commit (and the unsuccessful agents abort). This technique must be applied with care and an understanding of how the result set may be affected.

Concurrency Control Techniques

There are three primary concurrency control techniques designed to allow transactions to execute safely in parallel:

- Locking methods
- Timestamp methods
- Optimistic methods

These methods were developed for centralized DBMSs and then extended to include the distributed environment. Both locking and timestamping are considered conservative approaches because they cause transactions to be delayed in case they might conflict with other transactions at some time in the future. Optimistic methods are based on the premise that conflict is rare, so they allow transactions to proceed unsynchronized, only checking for conflicts when a transaction commits.

Locking Protocols

Of the three, locking is the most frequently used method for concurrency control. There are several variations, but all share the fundamental premise that a transaction must claim a read (shared) or write (exclusive) lock on a data item before performing the operation. Since read operations cannot conflict, it is permissible for two or more transactions to hold a read lock simultaneously on a data item. A write lock gives a transaction exclusive access to the locked item. As long as a transaction holds a write lock on a data item, no other transaction can read that item or write to it. A transaction holds a lock until it explicitly releases it, and it is only then that the result of the write operation are made available to other transactions.

Some systems allow upgrading and downgrading of locks. So, if a transaction holds a read lock on a data item, then it can upgrade that lock to write if no other transaction holds any lock on that item. In effect, this allows a transaction to "inspect" an item before deciding what action it will take. In systems where upgrading is not supported, a transaction must seek and hold write locks on any data items it might update during the course of its processing. This has the effect of reducing the concurrency in the system. With downgrading, a transaction may downgrade a lock from write to read after it has updated a data item, increasing the concurrency in the system.

The size or granularity of the data item that can be locked in a single operation will greatly affect performance of the concurrency control algorithm. Consider the instance where a transaction needs to update one data element in a table or a field in a single record of a database. At one extreme, the concurrency control application might allow the transaction to take a write lock on just the data element or field in question. On the other hand, it might force the transaction to lock the entire table or database. In the latter case, no other transaction could process against the table or database until the first transaction was complete, which would clearly be undesirable. However, if a transaction were updating 90 percent of the data in a table, it would be better for it to lock the whole table instead of locking each individual data element, one at a time. Ideally, the DDBMS will support a range of granularity, with at least row-, page-, and table-level locking. Many systems will automatically upgrade locks, from page to table, when a certain percentage of data is being updated.

The most common locking protocol is known as two-phase locking (2PL). It is so-named because transactions using it go through two distinct phases during execution—a growing phase, when it acquires locks, and a shrinking phase, while it releases those locks. The rules for transactions that practice two-phase locking are:

- The transaction is well formed (i.e., it acquires a lock on an object before operating on it, and it releases all locks when processing is complete).
- Compatibility rules for locking are observed (i.e., no conflicting locks are held).
- Once a transaction has released a lock, no new locks are acquired.
- All write locks are released together when the transaction commits.

The last rule ensures transaction atomicity; if this rule is not enforced, other transactions would be able to "see" uncommitted results. However, upgrading and downgrading of locks is allowed under 2PL, with the restriction that downgrading is only permitted during the shrinking phase.

The main problem with 2PL in a distributed environment is the enormous message overhead incurred. Consider, for example, a global transaction that processes at N sites. The successful execution of this transaction would generate at least 4N messages:

N "begin transaction" messages from coordinator to agents (for 5 sites, there are 5 agents and 5 messages)
N "ready to commit" subtransaction messages to the coordinator (for 5 sites, there are 5 subtransactions and 5 messages)
N "global commit" transaction messages to agents (for 5 sites, there are 5 messages)

N local subtransaction commit successful messages to the coordinator (for 5 sites, there are 5 messages)

Actually, there will probably be more than 4N messages because most messages require an acknowledgment of receipt (doubling the number of messages). When there are many global transactions involving numerous sites, the overhead becomes unacceptable. Fortunately, this does not happen often. One of the primary reasons for using a distributed system is to store the most frequently accessed data "locally," so the majority of transactions can be processed at their place of origin. This makes implementing distributed 2PL a realistic proposition. Also, the messages can be sent from the controller to the remote sites in "parallel," highlighting the importance of careful data distribution.

This brings up another aspect of data distribution—data replication across the nodes of a distributed system. If a data item is updated, then it is highly desirable that all copies of it be updated simultaneously. One way to accomplish this is to have the update of a replicated item spawn a global transaction that updates all duplicate copies. When using a locking protocol such as 2PL, each local transaction manager at a replicant site must acquire a write lock on the copy of the data item and hold it until all copies have been updated. This method ensures data consistency across the distributed environment.

Another, simpler approach to this problem is to designate one copy of the data as the primary copy and all duplicates as slave copies. Updating transactions must access the primary copy and make their changes there, locking only that copy of the data for the duration of the update. Once the transaction commits and the lock is released, the update can be propagated to the slave copies. This should occur as soon as possible to keep other transactions from reading out-of-date data, but it need not be a global transaction. With this approach, only the primary copy is guaranteed to be accurate, and transactions requiring current data must read it rather than one of the slave copies.

There are times when more than one transaction needs to lock the same data item. A transaction (T_1) can be viewed as a series of read and write operations as it progresses through its processing, and it acquires various locks along the way. If it obeys two-phase locking protocols, it will hold all write locks until it commits. However, if another transaction (T_2) requests a write lock on one of the same data items, one of two possibilities can occur:

T_2 is placed on a queue, waiting for T_1 to release its lock.
T_2 is aborted and rolled back.

With the first option, T_2 retains any other locks it might hold and enters a wait state. In the case of the second option, T_2 must release all of its locks and restart. For a complex transaction, especially a global one in a distributed system, the overhead of having to restart would be very high (the rollback of the agent at one site would trigger the rollback of all agents at all sites). This approach is called a deadlock prevention protocol.

By allowing T_2 to retain its locks in the first approach, a potentially dangerous situation that could lead to deadlock is created. Deadlock occurs when multiple transactions are queued up waiting for a lock to be released. Where there is a possibility of this happening, a deadlock detection protocol is required that will be invoked periodically to check for deadlocks.

It is also possible, using locking protocols, for a transaction to be either repeatedly rolled back or left in a wait state indefinitely, unable to acquire locks, even though the system in not deadlocked. This situation is called, appropriately enough, a livelock, since the transaction is blocked while the rest of the transactions are "live" and continue normal operations. For example, consider a transaction processing in a brokerage data warehouse, whose purpose is to determine how many shares of IBM common stock are owned by the firm's clients. At the same time this transaction is counting shares, the normal trading operations of the company are proceeding, with shares of stock, some of it IBM's, being bought and sold all the time. The "counting" transaction will need to acquire locks on all client stock holdings in order to achieve a consistent view of the table, but may have trouble doing so in light of all the other processing. If it is unable to acquire a full lockset in a reasonable period of time, it is considered to be livelocked. To avoid this, most schedulers employ a priority system where the longer a transaction has to wait the higher its priority becomes. Eventually, the "counting" transaction has the highest priority in the system and can take the necessary locks.

A deadlock condition in a centralized DBMS is normally detected by means of a wait-for graph. In a wait-for graph, transactions (or their agents) are represented by nodes and blocked requests for locks are represented by edges. Figure 4-6 shows a wait-for graph in which there is a deadlock between T_1 and T_2. T_1 is waiting for a lock on data item X_A, which is currently held by T_2. The wait-for graph (G) can also be represented symbolically as follows:

$$G = T_1 \rightarrow T_2 \rightarrow T_1$$

It is possible for a deadlock to occur between two transactions indirectly through a chain of intermediate transactions. For example:

$$G = T_1 \rightarrow T_2 \rightarrow T_3 \rightarrow T_4 \rightarrow T_1$$

Using wait-for graphs, detection of deadlocks in a centralized system is straightforward; if the graph forms a circular shape, there is a deadlock. Deadlock must be resolved by preempting or aborting one of the transactions (aborting any transaction will break the circle). However, the transaction making the request that creates the deadlock is the one normally chosen for rollback.

Figure 4-6. Deadlock situation on a wait-for graph.

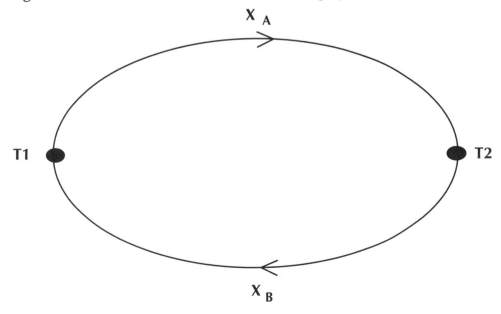

Deadlock detection in a distributed system is more complex since the chain of transactions can involve a number of different sites (Figure 4-7). Additional arcs are inserted into the wait-for graph to account for the agent of a global transaction waiting for the completion of another agent of the same global transaction at a different site. A symbolic representation of Figure 4-7 would be as follows:

$$G = T_{1A} \rightarrow T_{1B} \rightarrow T_{2A} \rightarrow T_{2B} \rightarrow T_{1A}$$

Global deadlocks cannot be detected using only local wait-for graphs.

There are three approaches to detecting a global deadlock situation in a DDBMS:

- Centralized
- Hierarchical
- Distributed

Figure 4-7. Deadlock situation in a distributed system.

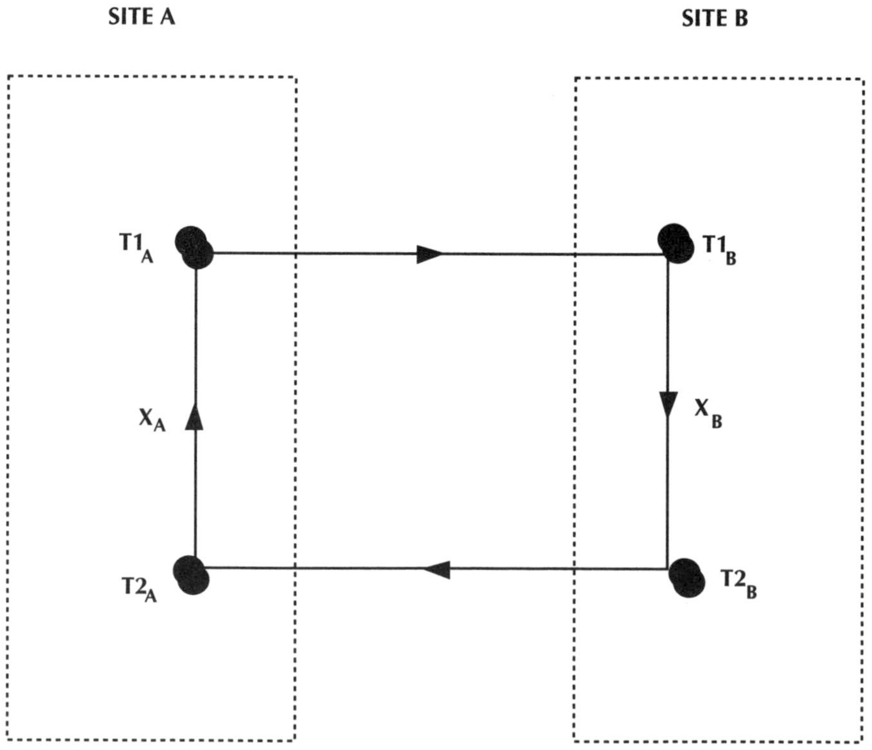

With centralized deadlock detection, all the local wait-for graphs are merged into one, called the deadlock detection site, and examined for cyclic structures. The communications overhead for constructing a global wait-for graph is potentially very high if there are many sites and many agents involved. As with any centralized solution to a distributed problem, the deadlock detection site can become a bottleneck and, if it should go offline for any reason, there needs to be a backup site to ensure continued processing.

When hierarchical deadlock detection is employed, the sites in the network must be organized into a hierarchy so that a blocked site sends its local wait-for graph to the site above it in the hierarchy. Figure 4-8 shows a proposed hierarchy for an eight-site, A through H, network. The bottom of the figure shows the sites themselves, where local wait-for graphs are created. The next level up shows where deadlock detection is accomplished for each pair of sites (it is located at one of the two named nodes). The third level performs deadlock detection for half of the network at each site and the final, or root level, is essentially a global deadlock detection site. Hierarchical deadlock detection reduces communications costs compared with centralized detection, but it is difficult to implement, especially in the face of site or communications failures.

One of the most well known distributed deadlock detection methods was developed by Obermarck and was popularized by IBM Corp. in its much-discussed but never released product R*. This method highlights one of the problems associated with global dead-

Figure 4-8. Hierarchical deadlock detection.

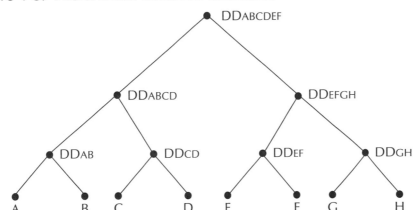

lock detection—how to prove that all actual deadlocks will be detected and that no false deadlocks are accidentally included. Ron Obermarck's method may include some false deadlocks because it assumes that a snapshot of the system's state is captured in the wait-for graphs. However, if transactions are allowed to abort spontaneously (for reasons other than concurrency control), then false deadlocks are inevitable.

With Obermarck's method of distributed deadlock detection, an additional node, labeled EXT, is added to a local wait-for graph to indicate an agent at a remote site. When a transaction spawns an agent at a remote site, an EXT is added to both the local and remote site graphs. The global wait-for graph in Figure 4-7 would be built on the local wait-for graphs shown in Figure 4-9. These graphs, respectively, can be depicted symbolically as follows:

$$G^A = EXT_A \rightarrow T_{A2} \rightarrow T_{A1} \rightarrow EXT_A$$

$$G^B = EXT_B \rightarrow T_{B1} \rightarrow T_{B2} \rightarrow EXT_B$$

This does not necessarily imply that there is a deadlock since the EXT nodes could represent completely disjoint agents, but cyclic forms must appear in the graph if there is a genuine deadlock. To decide if there is a real deadlock, the local graphs must be merged and evaluated. The result will be the same graph as in Figure 4-7, and the cycle indicating a genuine deadlock will emerge:

$$G^{AB} = T_{1A} \rightarrow T_{1B} \rightarrow T_{2A} \rightarrow T_{2B} \rightarrow T_{1A}$$

In general, when the EXT extension appears in the local wait-for graph of site X, that graph should be sent to site Y, the node it is waiting for, where the two local graphs can be combined and evaluated. If no cyclic form is detected, processing can continue. The process stops when a cycle is found, and one of the transactions is rolled back and restarted. Obermarck's method has become one of the most popular approaches to concurrency control for distributed database systems.

However, even with the use of the external agent, deadlock detection in a distributed system is potentially very costly. In a distributed system, it would be far too expensive to take the standard

Figure 4-9. Obermarck's distributed deadlock detection wait-for graph.

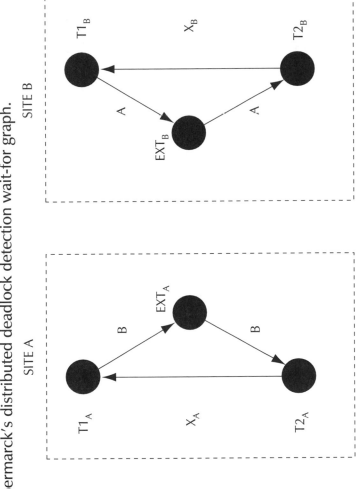

centralized approach of checking for deadlocks every time a transaction has a lock request refused. Yet it is difficult to know just when to check. If it is known that there is a lot of contention in a distributed system, it might be worthwhile checking for deadlock every time an external agent appears in a cycle in a wait-for graph at one of the local systems. Another possible approach is to use a timeout mechanism where deadlock detection is initiated only after a local system has "hung" for a selected period of time. However, distributed systems are prone to all kinds of delays, especially in communications, that have nothing to do with deadlocks, so this method is far from foolproof. Timeouts in a distributed system are just not as reliable an indicator of deadlocks as they are in centralized systems.

Concurrency control algorithms in which the possibility (not necessarily the reality) of deadlocks is detected and avoided are known as deadlock prevention protocols. How, then, does the transaction manager decide to allow a transaction, T_1, which has requested a lock on data item X (currently locked by transaction T_2), to wait and guarantee that this waiting will not give rise to a deadlock? One way is to order the data by forcing locks to be acquired in a certain data-dependent order. This method, however, is almost impossible to define, since users tend to access the database through views that can be defined across any subset of the database. A more realistic approach is to order the transactions and ensure that all conflicting operations are performed in sequence, according to the defined order. Deadlock is thus prevented because transactions are only allowed to wait under circumstances that will maintain the ordering.

The ordering scheme is generally based on timestamps. There are two possible ways to order the transactions using this method:

- Wait-die (where the older transactions wait for the younger ones to either commit or roll back)
- Wound-wait (where the younger transactions wait for the older ones to either commit or roll back)

Using either of these schemes, an aborted and restarted transaction must retain its original timestamp. If it does not, it will be repeatedly rolled back. Effectively, the timestamp mechanism supports a priority system where older transactions have a higher priority than younger transactions, or vice versa. Because this methodology uses locks as its primary concurrency control mechanism, it is classified as lock-based rather than timestamp-based.

Timestamping

Actual timestamp methods of concurrency control are quite different from locking methods. Since there are no locks involved there can be no deadlocking. Locking mechanisms usually involve transactions waiting if they make conflicting requests. With timestamping, there is no waiting; transactions involved in conflict are rolled back and restarted.

The basic goal of the timestamping methodologies is to order transactions globally so that older transactions (those with smaller timestamps) get priority in the event there is a conflict. If a transaction attempts to read or write an item, it will only be allowed to do so if the last update of that data item was performed by an older transaction. Otherwise, the transaction is aborted and restarted, acquiring a new timestamp. Unlike the locking methodology discussed previously, a restarted transaction must be assigned a new timestamp each time it starts. If it is not, a situation could arise where the transaction would never be able to process because the data items it is trying to lock will have been updated by younger transactions. It should be noted that timestamping methods produce serializable schedules.

Timestamps are used to order transactions with respect to each other, so they must have unique timestamps. In a centralized system, this can be accomplished easily using the system clock to stamp the transaction at initiation. Alternatively, a counter can be used, operating like a take-a-number queuing mechanism. When a transaction is launched, it is assigned the next number in sequence by the counter. To avoid very large timestamps, the counter can be periodically reset to zero.

In a distributed system, there is generally no global system clock and no universal counter. Transactions are launched from the individual nodes, each of which has its own clock; there is no guarantee that the clocks are even synchronized. In a centralized system, events do not occur simultaneously, especially with the transaction manager that can launch only one transaction at a time. In contrast, in a distributed system, two or more transactions can start at the same time at different sites in the network. Yet there must be some way to order these simultaneous events with respect to one another.

One possible way is to define "global time" in the network. Most often, this is done with a concatenation of the local time and system identifier:

site clock, site identifier

"Clock" need not mean the system clock; a counter or other time-keeping mechanism can be used in its place. For the purposes of this discussion, all counting/timekeeping devices will be referred to as "clock" and the value of the counter will be called the "timestamp."

Two rules are sufficient to ensure ordering of events both with respect to other local events and to events occurring at other sites:

- The local event clock advances at least one unit for every event occurring at that site (event means a transaction and/or message).
- Intersite messages are timestamped by the sender and the receiver adjusts his clock to an equal to or greater value than that of the sender's upon receipt of the message.

The first rule ensures that if e_1 occurs before e_2 at a given location, then the timestamp of e_1 will be smaller than the timestamp of e_2. The second rule maintains some consistency among system clocks.

Just how does timestamping work to ensure concurrency control? With lock-based protocols, all updates are write-locked until the transaction finishes processing and commits, protecting other transactions from "seeing" partially updated data. With timestamping, there are no locks, so this protection is gone. A different approach must be found in order to hide partially updated data. This can be done by using prewrites (i.e., deferred updates), where updates of uncommitted transactions are not written to the database. Instead, they are written to a buffer and only flushed out to the database when the transaction commits. This has the advantage that when a transaction is aborted and restarted, no physical changes need to be made to the database.

The process of using deferred updates is not quite as straightforward as it seems. It is possible that there could be a number of prewrites pending in the buffer for a given data item, and serializability demands that the corresponding writes take place in timestamp order. Therefore, when a transaction, T_1, attempts a write operation on data item X at commit, it must first check to make sure that no other writes by an older transaction are pending in the buffer. If any such writes are found, then T_1 must wait until the other transaction has committed or restarted. Similarly, in the case of T_1 reading data item X, the system must check not only that the last update of X was by a transaction older than T_1, but also that there are no writes pending in the buffer by an older transaction.

The main problem with basic timestamping is that the absence of "locking delays" is paid for by costly restarts whenever conflicts are detected. A modification to basic timestamping, known as conservative timestamping, substantially reduces the degree of concurrency but eliminates the need for restarts. With this approach, transactions wait until the system knows it cannot receive a conflicting request from an older transaction.

To apply conservative timestamping, each site in the distributed system must maintain several pairs of queues—one read queue and one write queue for every node. Each read queue contains requests originating at remote sites to read local data (with all read requests from the same remote system waiting on the same queue), while each write queue maintains the same information for write requests. Individual read and write requests are labeled with the timestamp of the issuing global transaction and are kept on the queue in timestamp order (the oldest is at the head of the line). For this method to work, the following rules must be observed:

- All sites agree to commit transactions in timestamp order.
- Transactions do not spawn agents, just issue remote read and write requests.
- Read and write requests from a remote site must arrive in timestamp order (transactions must complete all reads before issuing any writes). If necessary, younger transactions at the remote site will wait for an older transaction (at the same site) to finish issuing requests before beginning.
- All queues are nonempty, because if one queue is empty (queue for site N) and an update request is received from a remote system (site M), there is no guarantee that another

request could be received from a different remote system (site N) at a future time, which was issued earlier than the request now processing (from site M).

Conservative timestamping depends on there being a lot of inter-system traffic; otherwise, there could be an empty update queue at a site, which would cause it to "hang." A simple solution to this problem would be for each of the sites in a distributed system to periodically send timestamped null update requests to one another in the absence of genuine requests. These null requests would ensure the other sites that the sender does not intend to issue any requests with an older timestamp than the null request. Conversely, a blocked site could issue a request for a null update to fill its empty queue.

While it does not allow the same high degree of concurrency as the lock-based methods, conservative timestamping does have the advantage of cost-effective function in a distributed systems with high volumes of intersystem traffic. The case can be made that given a very busy, high-contention network, it is by far the more practical choice for maintenance-free operation.

Optimistic Methods

On the other end of the spectrum of distributed systems are those with low-contention or where read-only transactions predominate. For these systems, optimistic concurrency control techniques seem attractive. Optimistic methods are based on the idea that conflict is rare and the best approach is to allow transactions to proceed unimpeded without any waiting. Only when a transaction wants to commit should the system check for conflicts and, if one is detected, force the transaction to restart. To ensure atomicity of the transaction, all updates are made to transaction-local copies of the data and are propagated to the database at commit, after no conflicts are detected. Problem resolution by restart is a very expensive method in a distributed system and is only practical if it occurs infrequently.

With the optimistic method, transactions execute in a three-phase manner:

- *Read Phase.* This is the body of the transaction up to commit (any updates are written to transaction-local copies of the data).

- *Validation Phase.* The results of the transaction are examined for conflicts; if conflicts are detected, then the transaction rolls back.
- *Write Phase.* If the transaction is validated, then the updates are propagated from the local copy of the data to the database.

The read phase is straightforward, except that the "writes" are internal to the transaction. The validation proceeds in two phases. First, in the local phase, all subtransactions are validated locally (the local schedule is serializable). If local validation fails at any site, then the global transaction is aborted. If all local schedules pass inspection, then the second phase, the global phase, continues. The global phase ensures that the same serialization is used at all sites. This can be accomplished by seeing that all agents of global transactions that precede the transaction being validated have completed processing. If any have not, then the transaction must wait until they do (or until it times out and is aborted). A timeout function is necessary because this waiting would otherwise cause deadlocks. After validation, the write phase can proceed using two-phase commit.

As attractive as it seems, no major distributed database product has chosen, as of this writing, to use optimistic concurrency control (IMS Fast Path is one of the very few centralized systems that employs a form of this approach). Studies have shown that unless contention is extremely low other concurrency control strategies outperform optimistic methods by a wide margin. This is largely due to the enormous overhead (especially for distributed systems) of restarting transactions once they have reached commit.

Special Case Concurrency Control

Distributed database management systems differ from their centralized forebears in many ways. One of the most common differences is in data replication. Where centralized systems often house multiple copies of the same data due to poor application/database design, they almost never keep that data under the same name in a duplicate structure. Distributed systems often store several exact copies of the same data for reasons of performance and/or fault tolerance. Performance is improved by locating data at all sites where it is needed, rather than having to access it remotely. Fault tolerance is provided by replicated tables (or databases) since a copy of the data remains available in case of local site or network failure.

Where a DDBMS supports data replication, the system must ensure that all copies of the data are consistent. This can be done by treating the update of replicated data as a global transaction, which can be handled by the scheduler in the normal fashion. Such an approach requires that all sites with duplicates of the data in question be operational and connected to the network. In the event of a network or site failure, it is not possible to update the duplicate data at all. This approach runs somewhat counter to the fault-tolerant purposes of a distributed network. It is therefore common to adopt a consensus approach to updating replicate data. When the global scheduler instructs all sites to commit the update, it takes a poll. If the majority of the sites are available, then the update is committed. Those sites not participating (because of site or network failure) are simply notified of the update when they come back online.

Some particular problems with replicated data can arise due to network partitioning and communications failures. DDBMSs depend on the ability of all sites in the network to be able to communicate reliably with one another. Most networks today are very reliable because the protocols used guarantee correct transmission of messages in the correct order. In the event of line failure, many networks support automatic rerouting of messages. However, communications failures still occur. Such a failure can result in the network being partitioned into two or more subnetworks. When this happens, sites within a partition can still communicate with each other, but not with sites in other partitions (see Figure 4-10).

If replicated data was updated during such an outage, the duplicates in the one partition, subnetwork X, would be altered to match, but not those in the other, subnetwork Y. It would be possible for a second transaction to also process during this time and update the same replicated data items in subnetwork Y. The two network partitions now have different values for replicated data items. These two transactions executed totally independent of one another, and because of the network failure, no communications between sites was possible. The versions of the replicated data have diverged, resulting in a consistency problem.

There are various methods for resolving inconsistencies when

Figure 4-10. Failure-induced subnetworks.

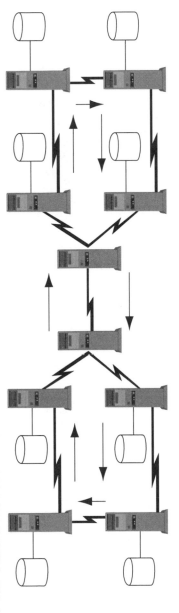

PRIOR TO FAILURE

AFTER FAILURE

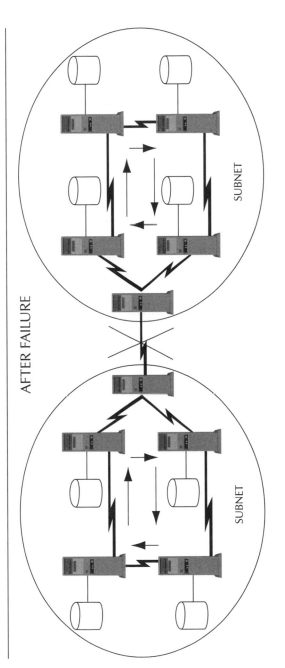

SUBNET

SUBNET

the partitions are reunited. They fall into two groups: those that adopt an optimistic approach and those that take a pessimistic approach.

Optimistic approaches are based on the premise that conflicts are rare. The emphasis is placed on availability over consistency. In the event of a network failure, updates are allowed to proceed independently in the resulting partitions. Very complex strategies are required for detecting and resolving inconsistencies when the partitions are reunited—strategies that can be so complex, in fact, that no one to date has chosen to employ this method in a distributed system.

Pessimistic methods for supporting update of replicated data during network partitioning adopt a very conservative approach. They are based on the premise that data integrity is more important than data availability and therefore conflict should be expected. They sacrifice a degree of availability for the sake of guaranteeing consistency. They avoid the possibility of conflicts when partitions are reunited by confining updates during partition to a single distinguished or majority partition. Updates to the majority partition are simply propagated to the other partitions when the network failure is resolved.

Several options are available that limit update to a single partition. For instance:

1. *Primary/Slave.* Every data item has one copy designated as the primary copy and all other duplicates are slave copies. Updates are directed only to the primary copy, then propagated to the slaves. All reads must first acquire a read lock on the primary copy before reading any copy. If the primary site itself fails, it is possible to promote one of the slave copies to primary, assuming the distributed management product is able to detect that the problem is a site failure and not a communications problem. This promotion is generally accomplished using a voting strategy (see option 2).

2. *Voting.* Using the voting (or quorum consensus) strategy, a transaction is permitted to update a data item only if it has access to and can lock a majority of the copies. This majority is known as a write quorum. When the transaction achieves a majority, all the sites are updated at once, and the change propagated to any other sites. A

similar system, called a read quorum, operates for reads to prevent transactions reading out-of-date versions of a data item. If data integrity is to be assured, a majority of sites must be represented in the read quorum.

3. *Missing Writes.* While the voting strategy provides greater data availability than the primary/slave in the event of failure, this availability is achieved at a high cost. During normal operations, the transaction must acquire read or write quorums for every operation. The missing writes method reverses this situation by involving much less overhead during normal operations at the expense of higher overhead when things go wrong. Using this strategy, transactions operate in one of two modes—normal mode when all copies are available and failure mode when one or more sitcs are unavailable. Timeouts are used to detect failures, so a transaction in normal mode can switch to failure mode when it does not receive an answer from a site in a reasonable period of time. During failure mode execution, a voting strategy is used.

The techniques described thus far apply mainly to homogeneous distributed systems or those with a very limited degree of heterogeneity. In these systems, a global transaction manager (or the local transaction manager temporarily acting in a global capacity) is aware of and can synchronize all transactions in the system. In a truly heterogeneous distributed system, preexisting autonomous databases have been integrated. To ensure concurrency control, there must be a mechanism to synchronize global transactions with local transactions that are under the control of the local DBMS. While the global transactions can be handled by any of the methods discussed thus far in this chapter, it is impossible to synchronize them with the local transactions and retain any degree of local autonomy. Once a global transaction submits an agent to a local system, it loses all control over it. The local DBMS assumes all responsibility and will decide, quite independently of that global transaction's other agents, what should happen in the local system. Therefore, some subtransactions could commit while others abort, destroying the atomicity of the global transaction and compromising the consistency of the distributed database.

The problems associated with providing support for global transactions in the presence of local transactions can be summarized into three points:

- Maintenance of atomicity for both global transactions and their agents
- Serialization of local and global transactions
- Detection and prevention of global deadlocks

Most existing heterogeneous distributed database management products support read operations only; all updates must occur locally. Even with this severe restriction, the problem of dirty (unrepeatable) reads must be addressed. Read-only transactions requiring a consistent view of data have to take into account the possibility that local transactions may be processing against the data they are trying to read.

It might be possible to support global updates in a heterogeneous environment, but only if some of the constraints are relaxed. Any of the following strategies might be employed:

- Reduce local autonomy, yielding some authority to a centralized control mechanism.
- Restrict the types of updates.
- Allow only one global transaction in the system at a time, via centralized control.
- Relax strict serializability rules.
- Use application-specific methods of concurrency control.

Of these strategies, the trade-off most often chosen is between preserving local autonomy and providing full functionality. One way this might be accomplished involves the local transaction manager yielding the local wait-for graphs to the global transaction manager for analysis and action. The alternate would be to restrict the function of global transactions (perhaps to read-only or single-site updates). In fact, this is often the most practical thing to do since the local nodes are managed by proprietary DBMSs whose internal structures (transaction managers and schedulers) cannot be altered.

Another way of preserving local autonomy while still processing global transactions is to adopt a method of concurrency control based on quasi-serializability. Global transactions are essentially hierarchical in nature (i.e., they can be broken down into subtransactions). This fact, taken in conjunction with the desire to preserve local autonomy, makes it very difficult to produce schedules that are globally serializable. However, if global and local transactions could be treated differently, as they are with quasi-serializability, joint processing might be possible. This method of concurrency control requires that all global transactions be submitted serially while local transactions execute in the normal way (i.e., are serializable). Local autonomy is maintained, but no global integrity constraints and no referential integrity between different agents of the same transaction are enforced.

The last method of concurrency control involves using application-specific methods. This method allows transactions to be interleaved with other transactions subject to certain constraints. Rather than having to wait for a transaction to complete, this method exploits advance knowledge of the transaction's operations to allow other transactions to process simultaneously whenever possible. Transaction failure is handled by providing a counterstep for every step in the transaction. Transactions are divided into two or more sets, with the transactions in one group able to process concurrently and those in the other being incompatible, unable to be interleaved together. This method can be taken a step further by dividing the individual transactions into a series of atomic steps divided by breakpoints. The breakpoints represent places where other transactions can safely be interleaved, allowing a greater degree of concurrency control. This method uses a new type of schedule, called a relatively consistent schedule, which is nonserializable but still guarantees consistency.

No matter which method is chosen, concurrency control in a distributed database environment, and especially in one involving heterogeneous systems, comes at a high cost. Because it is simply too important to ignore, concurrency control becomes one of the major obstacles that must be overcome for a distributed system to function successfully.

Data Warehousing and Concurrency Control

One of the most important basic services provided by a DBMS, and one of the most difficult to achieve, is the ability to support multiuser access to the data. Improvements in concurrent "read" and "write" access have been sought since the introduction of the first DBMS, IMS, in the late 1960s. The current interest in data warehousing, combined with the natural desire to exploit the best, most cost-effective methods available, has sparked renewed interest in concurrency control.

The problems of concurrency control are complicated in a distributed warehouse environment by the fact that there are many "local" users accessing data in their departmental data mart at the same time as others are processing "global" queries against the warehouse as a whole. An additional intricacy arises from the fact that most data warehouses constructed today use multiprocessor hardware, either SMP or MPP. This pairing of distributed software with multiprocessor hardware complicates concurrency control beyond being just an issue of proper scheduling that will be handled by the DBMS. A team of architects, designers, system programmers, DBAs, and applications programmers must work in tandem to identify problems and select and implement a successful concurrency control strategy.

Key to devising a concurrency control plan is an understanding of the transaction, the basic unit of work in a DBMS environment, and the classes of problems that can arise when transactions are allowed to process without any attempt at synchronization. But almost all DBMSs try to accommodate simultaneous transactions by means of a schedule and a concurrency control algorithm. A schedule is the entire series, in order, of all the reads and writes of the transactions processing together. The concurrency control algorithm tries to interleave the read and write operations of a transaction with those of other concurrently executing transactions in such a way that they can process together without interference. The concurrency control algorithm is responsible for producing correct schedules where the consistency of both the transactions and the database are guaranteed. Correct schedules are normally those that are serializable, or equivalent to running the transactions sequentially, one after another. While it is possible to have a correct schedule that is nonserializable, serializability is taken as proof of correctness because it is well known and easy to apply.

The three principal methods for concurrency control, described in depth in this chapter, are:

- Locking
- Timestamping
- Optimistic methods

Both locking and timestamping are considered conservative approaches because they cause transactions to be delayed if they might conflict with other transactions at some future time. Optimistic methods are based on the premise that conflict is rare and therefore transactions are allowed to proceed unsynchronized, with checks for conflicts done only when a transaction commits.

Of the three techniques, locking is the most frequently used method for concurrency control. There are several variations, but all are based on the premise that a transaction must claim a read or write lock on a data item prior to performing the operation. While it is permissible for two or more transactions to hold a read lock simultaneously, a write lock gives a transaction exclusive access to an item, and for its duration no other transaction can read or write to that data item. A transaction holds a lock until it explicitly releases it, and it is only then that the results of the write operation are made available to other transactions.

There are times when more than one transaction needs to lock the same data item. When this happens, it can be handled in one of two ways:

- The second transaction is placed on a queue, waiting for the first to release its lock.
- The second transaction is aborted and rolled back.

With the first option, the requesting transaction retains any other locks it might hold and enters a wait state. Allowing the waiting transaction to retain its locks can lead to a potentially dangerous situation known as deadlock. Deadlock occurs when multiple transactions are queued up waiting for a lock to be released and, because of conflicting requests, the waiting transaction is frozen. Where there is a possibility of this happening, a deadlock detection protocol that utilizes wait-for graphs must be invoked periodically to check for and cure any conflicts. With the second option, the requesting transaction must release all of its locks and restart. For a complex transaction, especially a global one in a distributed system, the overhead of having to restart could be very high.

Timestamping methods of concurrency control are very different from locking strategies. The basic goal of the timestamping methodologies is to order transactions globally so that older transactions (those with smaller timestamps) always get priority. A transaction can read or write an item only if the last update of that data item was performed by an older transaction. Because there are no locks, deadlocks cannot occur, but transactions are frequently aborted and restarted to resolve potential conflicts. Timestamping methods produce serializable schedules.

Optimistic methods take the position that conflict in a database system is rare, so it is best to allow transactions to proceed unimpeded without any waiting. Only when a transaction is ready to commit should there be any check for conflicts and, if one is detected, the transaction should abort and restart. To ensure atomicity of the transaction, all updates during processing occur internally, to transaction-local copies of the data, and are propagated to the database after commit, when the system is sure there are no conflicts. Studies have shown that unless contention in the system is extremely low, other concurrency control strategies outperform optimistic methods by a wide margin. This is largely due to the enormous overhead of using restart for problem resolution in distributed systems.

The unique difficulties of distributed database management systems, especially those containing replicated data, must be addressed with their own strategies for concurrency control. When faced with site or network failures, the distributed system can adopt one of several voting methods that allow it to continue process transactions until full function returns. The problems associated with simultaneously processing global and local transactions in a distributed environment can be summarized as follows:

- Maintenance of atomicity for both global transactions and their agents
- Serialization of local and global transactions
- Detection and prevention of global deadlocks

While it is possible to support global updates in a distributed environment, it can only be accomplished with the loss of some autonomy by the local DBMSs or by placing restrictions on the transactions themselves (e.g., read-only, single-system update). The more heterogeneous the distributed system, the more difficult it is to control global transactions and, as a result, concurrency rates diminish.

No matter which method is chosen, concurrency control in a distributed database environment comes at a high cost; but regardless of the time, effort, and system compromises involved, it is worth the effort. To provide acceptable levels of service to the users, all distributed warehouses must be able to process transactions simultaneously—in the same processor (i.e., the same "box") and across the nodes of the network. Effective concurrency control makes this possible.

5

The Web and the Data Warehouse

Information in the hands of decision makers is a powerful tool. Corporate America recognizes this fact and, to meet the almost insatiable appetite for more and better data, businesses are extracting information from operational systems and placing it into data warehouses at a phenomenal rate. The result is that users receive the informational equivalent of a "fast-food meal" that costs the company five-star restaurant prices.

First in the list of expenses is the warehouse itself. Most data warehouses are still centralized, depending on costly mainframe computers to house the core of the warehouse. To populate the warehouse, the data must be extracted from production systems and other sources and cleansed, formatted, organized for user access, and loaded. From there, it is extracted again and formatted a second time for download into the local data marts. But the warehouse and data marts do not operate alone; analytic software has to be loaded onto every user's PC to facilitate data access and handling. Since user requirements, and even the users themselves, change constantly, the result is a significant support burden. Networks must be constructed and dial-up capabilities added to provide support for those whose work takes them away from the base system. The price tag for all this can run into the millions of dollars, far more than many businesses are able to comfortably afford.

The World Wide Web can hold the key to more affordable warehousing for those willing to look and learn. It is the model of a successful distributed environment, and the use of web browsers has taught everyone a better way to deploy software and access data across an organization. The Internet, and especially intranets, can introduce a new level of collaborative analysis and information sharing among decision makers when it replaces older, more costly, conventional networks.

The Web can also change the way data is accessed and analyzed in support of mission-critical decisions. Data published on the Web is easily accessible and, once obtained, ideally suited for query, reporting, and analysis by nontechnical users. For corporations, this could be an alternative, low-cost mechanism for making data available to those individuals who need it. For users, the switch to a web-based environment means a much friendlier and richer pool of accessible information.

The World Wide Web represents a paradigm shift in technology that is gradually changing everyone's life. But where did all this new technology come from? Driving the transformation is the Internet, which is really just a chaotic collection of computers, network connections, and telecommunications lines (it loses its ability to impress when viewed from the perspective of a badly organized heterogeneous system). The Internet was initially designed in the 1960s to meet the needs of the United States Department of Defense (DOD) for secure communications. As a result, certain aspects of the Internet, such as the packet-oriented communications protocol used (see Chapter 8), were intended to prevent interruption of service during a military confrontation. Although it never really fulfilled its original purpose, the Internet's "second life" has revolutionized communications around the world.

For its first twenty years of existence, only a privileged few at military installations and universities had access to the Internet. During that time, various technologies emerged, one at a time, which gradually increased the number of people with access. The development of powerful personal computers with graphical interfaces (e.g., Microsoft Windows and Motif), the rise of service providers (such as the pioneering CompuServe), and improved bandwidth with cheaper transmission rates all contributed to the popularization of the Internet. However, it has only been recently that the number of users "on the Net" has exploded.

This growth is due in large part to the development of some relatively simple software that makes navigating the Internet easy. The first of these developments is the hyperlink, which turned the Internet into the host of the World Wide Web. Hyperlinks freed users from knowing the exact location of each document and the network path that leads to the site where it is stored. Users can simply click on highlighted text or an icon (with an attached hyperlink) to navigate to another set of information located literally anywhere.

But what really sparked the incredible growth in Internet usage in the mid-1990s was the design and commercial success of a friendly user interface to the Internet known as Mosaic. While the infrastructure had been in place for some time and users could theoretically access the vast store of information that is the Internet with arcane operating system commands, very few did so because it was just too difficult. Mosaic changed all that. Originally developed at the University of Illinois, Mosaic was quickly refined and commercialized as a browser by Netscape. Within a matter of months it gained widespread public acceptance and a host of imitators. The ease of use resulting from the pairing of hyperlinks with browsers has caused phenomenal growth in Internet usage.

Emerging Trends

There are millions of users on the Internet every day, all clamoring for enhanced services. They want improvements in usability, manageability, performance, and security. As new products are developed and proven better than existing ones, they are quickly adopted by the web subculture.

For example, the HyperText Markup Language (HTML), still the standard way to access the Web, is rapidly giving way to newer enhancements. Although HTML and the protocol used for HTML communication, HyperText Transfer Protocol (HTTP), are easy to use, HTML places limits on the interaction between user and application. Users may only send and receive information as document forms, with no ability to drag-and-drop or to manipulate objects on the screen. New extensions and enhancements to HTML are making the user interface come alive with reusable application components that run on the local PC. Among the most well known of these are Java (Sun Microsystems), Virtual Reality Modeling Language or VRML (Silicon Graphics), ActiveX (Microsoft), and many others. Within a matter of months, these will have superseded HTML as the preferred method of access.

So, too, are database technologies and access tools making revolutionary advances under pressure from newer technologies. The relational database management system (RDBMS), which appeared in the early 1970s, simplified access to data for programmers with its structured query language (SQL). RDBMSs allowed developers to build data access tools independent of the structure of the database. Before the emergence of the mathematically elegant relational model, all data access mechanisms were database specific and, in many cases, application dependent. Data was almost never shared between applications.

This functional separation of the data access mechanism from the database itself, along with the availability of low-cost desktop processing power, led to another commercially successful trend, client/server technology. Popularized in the mid-1980s, client/server decoupled the access tool processing from the processing of the database engine. Communications were established across corporate networks using vendor-specific middleware and network protocols such as Token Ring, TCP/IP, SPX/IPX, and others. Client/server was so successful that, by the end of the 1980s, all the major relational vendors had ported their products to the new environment.

Along with the proliferation of client/server platforms and RDBMSs came the concept of the open system, where customers were free to mix-and-match multivendor (i.e., heterogeneous) components such as hardware, network protocols, operating systems, databases, access tools and other elements. Industry standards quickly evolved to bring some order to the resulting chaos, ensuring a degree of interoperability between components.

By 1990, most corporations had in place an infrastructure for bringing users and data together. However, access to data was still limited in the following ways:

- Canned forms and reports were still used at the workstation to access data. These static windows gave users a limited view of the available information with no flexibility to adapt the forms. From the users' perspective, this was not much of an improvement over the old printed reports they used to get delivered on schedule to their desk.

• Because of the rapidly changing business environment and frequent business reorganizations, there was a need to drastically shorten the applications development cycle. Companies' IT departments had trouble keeping pace. In some cases, applications development time was estimated to be longer than the application's useful life, or the period during which it would have been relevant.

• Custom tools appeared that were designed to appeal to specialized user groups, but these tools had limited scope or capacity, and most required extensive IT involvement to set up and maintain.

As time goes on and the business-tool industry matures, new technologies are emerging to replace the old. The first tools available performed only one function (e.g., query or analysis or reporting). If users wanted to access the warehouse, they had a tool on their PC designed to do just that. But if they also wanted to analyze the data and report on the results, they needed two additional programs to accomplish this task (provided the user could import the data from one application into another, which itself was often a very difficult task). In spite of these difficulties, the numbers of users involved in decision-support functions continued to increase as data warehouses proliferated. In response to increased demand, tool manufacturers finally have begun integrating query, analysis, and reporting into one product. State-of-the-art products today are the OLAP (online analytical processing) and ROLAP (relational online analytical processing) tools.

Not only are the tools changing, the entire infrastructure is shifting again at the start of the new millennium. In an effort to keep pace with technological and business pressures, corporations have to rethink their approach to data processing. What was "state of the art" in 1990 now seems old and hopelessly outdated. A new architecture is called for to meet the new demands that will be placed on it. This does not mean that all the old hardware will have to be junked; quite the contrary. With careful planning, current equipment can be incorporated and repositioned to better serve the organization's needs.

To develop a new architecture, some decisions must be made. One is how best to distribute and maintain the software that runs on the desktop computers. There are three basic approaches to this issue:

- *Fat Clients.* Fat-client configurations are designed to take advantage of the low-cost processing power of the desktop PC. They are essentially client/server applications that can be enhanced to take advantage of the Web. All decision-support software resides on the desktop and is maintained there. These machines can be easily converted from wide area networks to using the Internet/intranet for communications.

- *Thin Clients.* For environments where it is difficult or costly to manage applications distributed across a large number of user sites, there is the thin-client approach. Using this model, the software on the users' desktop is limited to those components that relate to presentation only. All other activity takes place on the back-end system as directed by the user, with only the result-set shipped down line to the desktop PC. There are many that argue that application processing should be separate from presentation activities, and they point to the thin-client approach as the ideal.

- *Multitiered Approach.* In addition to the question of software installation and maintenance, another important issue is the speed at which a user's request is processed. Performance concerns in the Internet/intranet environment are driving companies toward modularization of the current two-tier (front-end browser and back-end HTML server) environment. Using a multitiered approach, HTTP server activity is separated from application-related processing (which occurs on an intermediate server). While other factors such as bandwidth and equipment used can affect performance, the architecture selected remains the most important issue.

The three models just described are not mutually exclusive. A company might choose a combination of fat and thin clients, as well as taking a multitiered approach to systems development. Regardless of the architecture chosen, the company will need to select an array of applications designed to facilitate data access and analysis. To better keep pace with today's rapidly changing business environment, these tools should also be Internet/intranet compatible. This first generation of Internet decision-support aids must meet certain criteria. They must:

- Support interactive analysis.
- Be able to keep pace with the infrastructure.

- Ensure security.
- Give users flexibility.

Decision support is not just a single function; it is an iterative process consisting of query, analysis, and reporting. The process begins with the user submitting a request for data to the warehouse/data mart. When the query set is returned to the user's PC, it is in the form of a "report." The user analyzes the data by viewing it from different perspectives and varying levels of detail. During the course of this analysis, the user may decide that additional information is needed and request more data from the source. When finished, the user formats a report before distributing his study. Any decision-support tool must allow the user to carry out these activities efficiently.

While the World Wide Web promises to change the way people access data, analyze information, and share their conclusions with others, it has for the moment some limits, as does the intranet-enabled corporate infrastructure. But it is also necessary to keep in mind while designing a data warehouse and choosing decision-support tools that those limits will change during the life of a system built today. It is best to choose hardware and software that play to the strengths of the Internet/intranet, remembering that even more capability will be offered in the near future. Above all, the decision-support tools chosen should not be hardware dependent; as the Web evolves, so will the corporate infrastructure and existing equipment will be replaced with the newer, faster, and better models. To protect its investment, a company must select tools that will work anywhere.

The Web is best suited currently for the publication of HTML pages, navigation across documents (i.e., surfing), and the downloading of these documents across the network. For the moment, network delays limit certain decision-support activities, such as drilling down on a cell in a spreadsheet. Users may not be willing to wait twenty to sixty seconds (typical response time on the Internet/intranet) for detailed data to be returned. Improvements in network speeds and modems will soon eliminate this concern, so it would be prudent to include this capability (if desired) and others in decision-support tools purchased today.

A corporate decision-support environment, like a warehouse, must maintain security for sensitive business-related and personal data. Security requirements include the ability to control:

- Publication rights for users who want to post data on the Web
- Access rights to information published on the Web

A third point—not as critical as the two listed, but still a consideration—is that existing security be reusable. The technology department should not have to redo the entire scheme of an application when it becomes web-enabled, so the decision-support tools must play their part in keeping the network safe. The role of security in an Internet environment cannot be ignored (see Chapter 8). To do so is foolish beyond belief.

A last consideration in choosing decision-support tools must be their adaptability in a changing environment. The Internet is a dynamic, ever-changing, evolving environment. Organizations that deploy web-enabled applications need to ensure that the choices they make now do not trap them in a technological dead end in the near future.

A corporation needs to take a broad view of its intranet—it is not just a place to store and distribute text files and e-mail; it can also be the infrastructure for a comprehensive decision-support environment. Technology has allowed users to become knowledge sharers, and it can be deployed to yield the powerful advantage of shared problem resolution to those prepared to exploit it. Knowledge sharing requires the free flow of all types of information among users, not only text files but also interactive analysis capability that encourages the exchange of ideas and experiences.

By putting a centralized data warehouse on an intranet (Figure 5-1) and deploying a series of data marts that also function as web servers, an organization gains immediate economic and rapid application deployment benefits. Of longer-term interest, users are able to collaborate more freely on business issues, which can lead to a better and more rapid response on critical decisions.

For the business without a prior investment in a centralized warehouse or that already has data marts in place, now is the time to begin constructing a distributed data warehouse (Figure 5-2). Based on an intranet infrastructure, a distributed system can be developed quickly and economically and will confer on its corporate owner all the benefits associated with its more traditional cousin. Because it is extremely flexible, a distributed warehouse conforms readily to meet almost any business need, even the more unusual special-situation

Figure 5-1. Centralized data warehouse in an intranet environment.

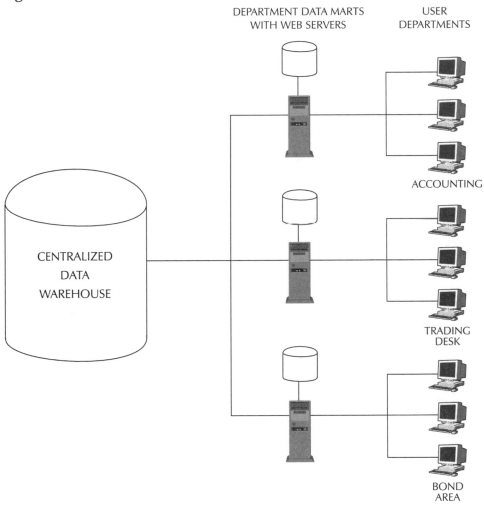

requirements ignored by the centralized warehouse. Regardless of whether it is used to support a distributed warehouse or to enhance the capabilities of a centralized one, the advent of the intranet could be the basis for rethinking the enterprise information infrastructure.

Intranet Basics

To understand the attraction of an intranet, it is first useful to look at the logic of why a data warehouse or almost any business computer

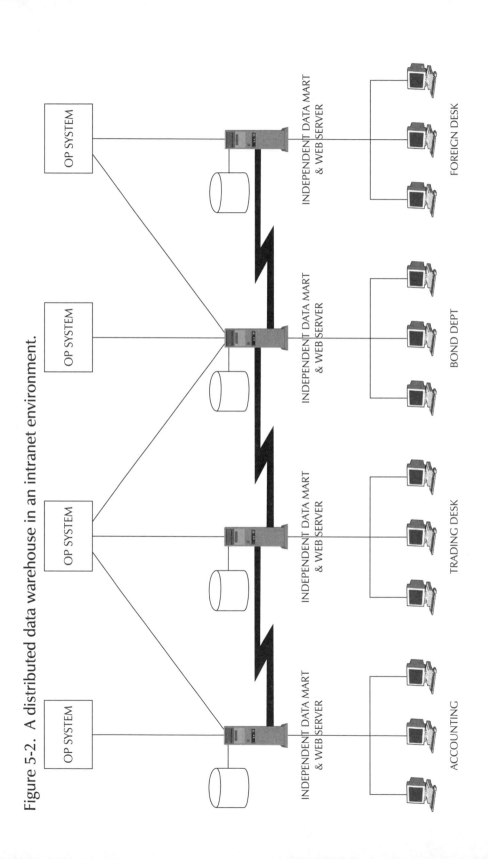

Figure 5-2. A distributed data warehouse in an intranet environment.

system is built. Data warehouses are essentially all about reports. All the information that is put into the warehouse is only there to be taken out again, albeit in a different form. The people who need that data are usually business users. Their job is to make decisions for the corporation, not to manage the business's data or write application programs. They frequently lack technical training, and there really should be no need for them to acquire it.

Communication between the user and the intranet is handled by a web browser, which makes for a simple, single point of contact. The point-and-click paradigm of a browser is such that anyone who can operate a mouse can use it easily. With proper web page design and appropriate security, business users can point-and-click their way to the exact data they need regardless of its location in the network. The user does not need to write a program, learn a new tool, or even know a "transport language"; with minimal (or no) training the user is productive.

By using client workstations with windowing systems, the interface can be simplified even more. A web page link can be placed on the desktop as a shortcut; by double-clicking on this link, the user signals the browser to automatically load the web page. In this way a intranet simplifies data access for users so they can spend more time acting on the information and less time looking for it.

Intranets can be viewed as next-generation client/server systems with a number of standardized characteristics. Like traditional client/server, intranets have three basic elements:

- The client
- The communications protocol
- The server

Each of these elements makes its own contribution to information delivery in a data warehouse environment (Figure 5-3).

The client side of a client/server intranet environment is the browser. It receives HTML web pages from the web server and formats them at the client site for presentation. The presentation characteristics of a web page are controlled completely by the browser; most settings can be altered to suit the user, such as a change of background color or font type. This feature is part of the client/server intranet architecture. The web server delivers the basic page informa-

Figure 5-3. Web-enabled data warehouse.

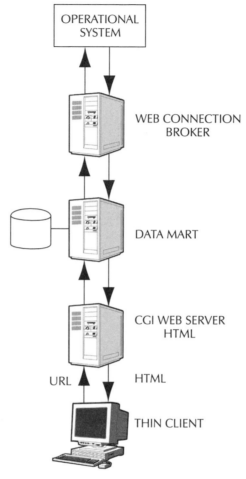

tion while the browser determines how that information will be presented, based on the client hardware/software settings characteristics.

The server component of an intranet is called the web server. It acts much like a file server, responding to requests from its clients. The web server differs from the conventional file server in that it is responsible for passing requests on to other application servers when necessary.

The method of communication, or communication protocol, is often the most challenging part of client/server technology. The Internet uses TCP/IP communications, and it is the protocol provided with most platforms (e.g., Windows NT or Windows 2000) purchased today. In its current form, TCP/IP is easy to deploy and use. Working on top of the communications protocol is the transport language used by the client and server to communicate. In traditional client/server systems, transport languages can cause problems for users because most of them are difficult to use or at least require some training. With TCP/IP as the communications protocol for a client/server intranet, the transport language is HTTP, which requires no special user training.

As shown, an intranet architecture can greatly enhance user access to data, but this alone cannot account for the sudden popularity of corporate intranets. Why are corporations rushing to imitate this particular feature of the World Wide Web? There are many reasons: Intranets are cost-effective, easy to implement, easy to use, and a particularly efficient way to make all kinds of information available to the people who need it. Many corporations have already installed web browsers on the desktop, and the change to an intranet allows them to leverage that investment. Using nothing more than that standard browser, a user on an intranet can access any information in the environment.

Most intranets currently manage unstructured content such as text pages, images, and even audio files as static HTML documents. A data warehouse stores structured content and raw alphanumeric data, but with the right tools and correct architecture, a data warehouse can be accessed through the corporate intranet. This "web-enabled" warehouse forms the foundation of a comprehensive enterprise information infrastructure that can confer three advantages to its corporate owner:

- Improved cost/benefit ratio of an intranet architecture
- Enhanced decision support due to information integration
- Improved user collaboration on projects and key business decisions

The cost of traditional client/server computing is high when all factors are considered. There is not just the price of the client PC and the file server to be tallied; there are also communications, support, and other hidden costs that must be added to the total. In fact, numerous studies conducted within the last twenty-four months suggest that client/server computing is just as costly or even more expensive than mainframe computing. Certainly, the personal computer has "bulked up" with faster clock speeds, extra memory, giant disk drives, DVD readers, software and user-managed files, and databases of considerable size. The result is a fat-client architecture.

An intranet can change the economics of supporting a large community of users. An intranet can certainly reduce communications costs, and many speculate that it may also reduce costs on the client side by utilizing an inexpensive "intranet device" in place of a personal computer. This is possible because intranets are usually based on an architecture that calls for a thin client, which can be a very simple personal computer or even a dumb terminal. Whether corporations ever adopt intranet devices remains to be seen; at a minimum, the intranet will prolong the life of the current round of personal computers because it eliminates the need to upgrade constantly.

The thin-client model (Figure 5-4) calls for server distribution of application software. Java permits software to be served to an intranet browser in code fragments or applets. The only portion of the software that must be installed on the client is the browser. Any application software is acquired only as needed for a specific purpose. Since the application software resides on the server and nowhere else, it is much easier to maintain, upgrade, and administer. The economics of an intranet are such that a corporation has reduced communications costs, less expensive thin-client hardware, and in most cases, reduced application software costs.

Perhaps the most valuable asset of any business is its data. The operational data is acquired and used in the production systems during the course of the enterprise's day-to-day activities. When a business builds a data warehouse, it is organizing that data in a way that is useful to decision makers. By making that data warehouse a part of the enterprise information infrastructure running on an intranet, the business is providing its key decision makers with the access and tools they need to evaluate the data in new ways (Figure 5-5). Users can toggle between different views of data or between structured and unstructured data adding a new dimension to their analysis.

But a web-enabled data warehouse is not just about providing access to data; it is also about communication at an interactive level. No one would dispute that decision making improves with accurate, timely, and complete information. Decision making is also influenced by how the ideas and experiences of a workgroup are exchanged in

Figure 5-4. Thin client.

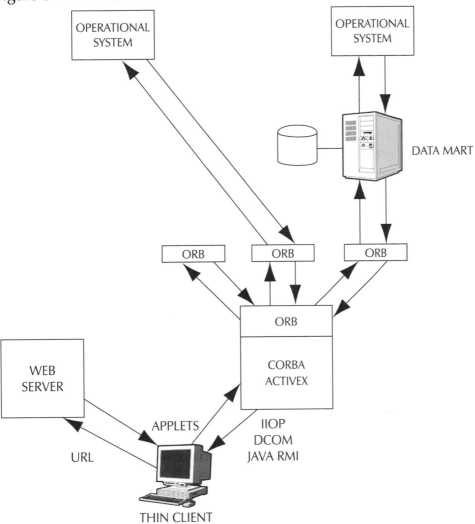

the analysis and problem-resolution process. A regular LAN-based application has many communications restraints that prevent the free flow of ideas within a group. An intranet has no such restrictions and encourages information-enriched communications and collaborative problem solving.

Today, most users can communicate using the corporate e-mail system. While it permits text files to be exchanged, e-mail does not facilitate true collaboration. Sending an EXCEL spreadsheet on Lotus Notes is a step closer, but the emphasis is still on textual file sharing.

Figure 5-5. Enterprise information structure.

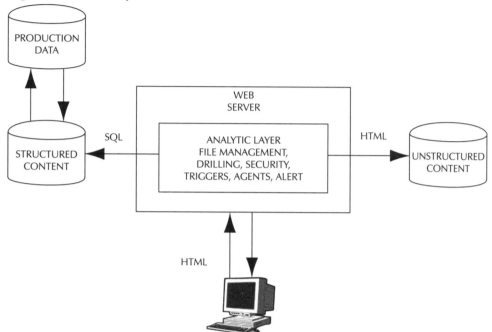

What is needed is a means of communication that allows the recipient to continue the analysis started by someone else, or to branch off in a new direction if he desired. For example, if a user receives a report from a coworker, she should immediately be able to drill down or up on any report dimension, or add additional calculations, and then pass the altered report on to others. This requires dynamic report creation based on the data stored in the web-enabled warehouse. While this example is beyond the capabilities of most text-oriented groupware products available today, it is not fantasy. An enterprise information infrastructure has the capacity to provide truly interactive collaboration and much more.

The Advantages of Intranets and Data Warehousing

Computers have been a valuable business tool for more than forty years. In their earliest form, computers used flat files, similar to lists, for data storage. The next generation of computing brought the concept of databases with it, simplifying information storage and access for the programmer. Out of the database idea grew relational technologies, which changed forever the role of data processing in a corporate environment. Suddenly, corporate data became a valuable asset, a source of information that decision makers consulted to guide the company.

Without relational technologies, data warehousing would not be possible. But it is the next generation in computing, the Internet/intranet, that will make data warehousing cost-effective and available to all those who can benefit from access to its contents. An intranet can deliver vital information and reports to each desktop in an organization at the click of a mouse, regardless of the user's location or the location of the data. Even remote users, traveling or just temporarily away from their desks, can access data through dial-up connections or the World Wide Web, provided correct security procedures are observed.

An intranet offers other, subtler advantages, too. An intranet disseminates a uniform view of information to all users, producing a high degree of coherence for the entire organization. The communications, reports formats, and interfaces are consistent, making the information they contain easy to read and understand. Everyone has access to the same data (regardless of whether it is stored in a data mart or a distributed or centralized warehouse), presented in an identical fashion, thus avoiding misunderstandings and confusion.

Because each desktop has the ability to design, extract, and mine corporate data and is equipped with the tools to generate reports and other time-critical information, an intranet architecture improves the decision-making process. Users are empowered with the knowledge necessary for faster and better-informed business decisions.

As one of its most important advantages, an intranet provides a flexible and scalable nonproprietary solution for a distributed data warehouse implementation. It enables the integration of a diverse computing environment into a cohesive information network. An intranet makes data stored at any node equally available to all authorized users regardless of their location in the company and can be easily extended to serve remote corporate locations and business partners through a wide area network (WAN), an extranet, or even a virtual private network (VPN). In this fashion, external users can access data and drill down or print reports through proxy servers located outside the corporate firewall. Even customers can have limited access through the World Wide Web, visiting the company's home page for information about products and services.

All of this accessibility makes an intranet seem terribly insecure. That, however, is not the case. A web-enabled distributed warehouse can actually be more secure than other warehouse implementations. An intranet both strengthens security and simplifies its administration by permitting a "second line of defense." In addition to overall intranet security, each data mart can employ its own security measures in keeping with the sensitivity of the data stored there. Whereas a business partner might be entitled to access the corporate shipping records housed in Data Mart 1, he could be prevented from seeing the personnel records and financial documents residing in Data Mart 2 by limiting his access to that location. With a little preplanning on the designer's part, all sensitive corporate data is grouped together at a limited number of sites, safe behind a double wall of defense.

As a key component of any intranet, the browser offers at least two sizable advantages. The browser can act as a universal applications delivery platform, making it possible for the business to create and integrate new, more robust applications quickly and economically, without most of the usual postdeployment maintenance costs. Because all users have access to the same applications, training and support costs are also reduced. The second advantage to browsers is their ease of use. The intuitive nature of their interface virtually eliminates the need for user training and drastically lowers the number of help desk calls.

In summary, an intranet is flexible, scalable, cost-effective, and easy to implement, maintain, and use—the best architecture to maximize the benefits of a corporate data warehouse.

The Challenges of Intranets and Data Warehousing

Almost all data warehouses employ relational database management systems for data storage. Structured query language (SQL) is used to retrieve the highly structured data organized in rows and columns in tables. To date, intranets have been used primarily to access unstructured data managed as HTML documents. The challenge in putting a data warehouse on an intranet is in properly enabling SQL access to the warehouse from HTML browsers. For this implementation to succeed, at least three application layers are needed (Figure 5-6). They are:

- Analytic layer
- File management layer
- Security layer

Analytic Layer

Putting structured data on an intranet requires a server-resident analytic layer whose job it is to generate SQL as needed, perform computations, and format reports based on user requests. In fact, a specialized web server is required to support data warehouse access by a user employing an HTML browser. Because the analytic layer typically makes heavy demands on both the relational database management product and the web server, there should be a high-speed network connection between the analytic and database layers, or they

Figure 5-6. The three application layers enabling SQL in an intranet environment.

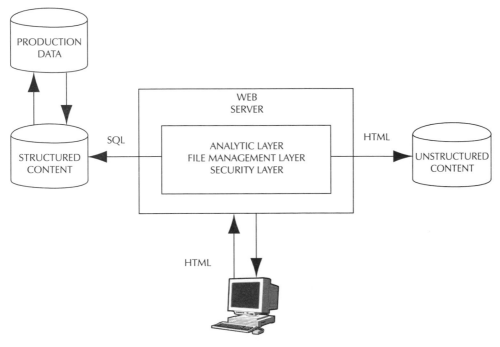

may reside on the same machine if the hardware is sufficiently robust. In either case, the web server must be configured to support the higher processing loads associated with an analytic layer.

The analytic layer shares some capabilities with standard spreadsheet software. Using a spreadsheet, the user has the ability to create custom calculations based on data stored in the cells. For example, similar information is stored in rows numbered 1, 2, 3, and so on, and individual examples of data elements are kept in columns named A, B, and C. By combining the two dimensions, a unique address is created that can be used in a mathematical formula—A1 + B1. The number of calculated rows and columns in a spreadsheet application can exceed the number of the original stored elements.

A data warehouse has more than two dimensions—for example, it stores multiple information such as product, market, time period, customer, vendor, and so on. The combination of values for each of the dimensions again provides a unique address. The analytic layer of the structured content web server allows users to apply calculations based on warehouse dimensions to create useful reports. Additionally, once complete, calculations can be shared with other users, just as calculations in a spreadsheet can be stored and passed on. And, like a spreadsheet, the calculation logic is maintained no matter how often the data warehouse is updated. The resulting reports often contain more calculated elements than raw data. For that reason, a robust analytic layer is needed in front of the data warehouse; without it, the user's reporting capabilities are limited to a simple list of stored data elements. The analytic layer is key to addressing the business questions the users must answer.

File Management Layer

This type of decision support requires both interactive analysis and knowledge sharing that is only possible with an active file management layer. A report created by one user becomes more valuable when shared with others to gain their insights and ideas. The recipients should be able to continue the analysis begun by the report's author, making the process an interactive exchange. When necessary, many users can pursue different analysis paths from the same starting point. A file management layer allows users to continue work on the same copy of a report, or to make their own copy for individual analysis.

To meet the challenge of providing interactive analysis of warehouse data, users must be able to access "public files" and manage their own personal files over an intranet connection. A sophisticated server-based file management layer is required to support user collaboration and maintain security at this level.

Security Layer

While corporations welcome the opportunity to open their information repositories to in-depth analysis by their employees and even some business partners and customers, they fear such access will leave them vulnerable to security breaches. Accessibility is, after all, the web's greatest benefit and its greatest liability. The challenge for anyone building an intranet-enabled distributed warehouse and web site is to achieve a reasonable level of security without impeding opportunity.

The sharing of information and collaboration among employees immediately raises data security issues. The data warehouse contains all kinds of information about the business, some of it proprietary and highly sensitive. Only a very few users should have access to everything; most users should be provided with access to only those portions of the warehouse relevant to their position. The data must be secure, but not so highly controlled that the value of the warehouse goes unrealized. This delicate balance is sometimes difficult to achieve.

Another security measure, encryption, can provide a higher level of protection than is generally available to business applications. Data passing between the client and server can be encrypted by using any one of a number of vendor products. This enables a business to run its applications over unsecured communication lines without worrying about someone tapping into the network and viewing the transmission.

A multitiered architecture, with the gateway server behind a firewall, can ensure that security needs are met. As additional precautions, a server can monitor the identity of users and their usage habits, and the relational product used for data storage has its own security that can be brought into play to limit access to the data itself.

As an example of the need for a robust analytic layer, a file management layer, and a security layer, consider the following: A department head in the brokerage firm (introduced as an example in Chapter 3), who is also a full partner, decides to create a budget analysis. Covered in this report is a breakdown of the expenses of each area by manager, including staffing costs. When the partner chooses to share her analysis with the managers, it is acceptable for them to view the summary numbers for all areas but not to drill down on areas other than their own and view the individual salaries of employees working for other managers. It is contrary to company policy for managers to know the salaries of anyone not working directly for them. This presents an interesting dilemma: Users not authorized to access certain data must still be able to view the report but not to drill down to the forbidden details

For this reason, reports created from data stored in the warehouse cannot be simply shared as HTML text files. All reports must contain the underlying logic, giving the recipient the ability to analyze and modify the report if they are authorized to do so. Before the user can even view the report, much less modify it, the authorization level for that user needs to be verified. For effective decision support, reports need to be shared throughout a group and across the company by appropriate individuals. If the recipients of the report are not authorized, then their access to the underlying logic can be denied.

Common Gateway Interfaces

An integral part of any Internet/intranet solution is the Common Gateway Interface (CGI). It should be examined and understood before attempting any web-enabled warehousing solution. CGI is the original standard for creating plug-in enhancements for web servers. CGI is the interface between the web site's HTTP server and the other resources of the server's host computer. CGI is not a language or protocol in the strict sense of the word; it is just a commonly named set of variables and agreed-upon conventions for passing information back and forth from the client to the server.

The Common Gateway Interface is the "magic" that makes the World Wide Web interactive. It enables users to browse, fill out forms, and submit data to the host. CGI works by using the operating system's standard input/output and environmental variables to pass information between a form, the server, and the plug-in. While binary programs can be used as CGI plug-ins, scripting languages such as Perl are commonly used for CGI. Such scripting languages offer the advantages of portability and ease of modification (even remotely), and they require no compilation or interpretation by the server.

There is a downside to using CGI. CGI scripts typically need to be loaded and unloaded from memory each time they are executed. This, along with the use of standard input/output and environmental variables, seriously impacts the performance of the server. CGI also opens a huge hole in a security system that must be plugged or, at least, defended (see Chapter 8).

The Common Gateway Interface facility of web server software (Figure 5-7) provides a method to execute server-resident applications. Constructing programs for an intranet requires a well-thought-out security strategy as well as the appropriate application architecture. Most web applications provide all users with the same access permissions to the reachable files on the server. But business users require a more refined security approach. A system that maps users to their server account by verifying user names and passwords, called Password Authentication Protocol (PAP), can be used to provide granular security. Access to server applications and files are based on user ID, group assignment, and permission level. Of course, for this to work, users must be mapped to the appropriate user or group in the relational database to control the data that the user can access. Because the number of users can be large, the administration of this system must be centralized and rigidly maintained.

Another issue with the CGI is that it does not maintain a continuous connection between client and server, or server and data warehouse. As a result, it is impossible to support an application that requires multiple interactive queries—a data warehousing requirement. One possible approach to this problem is to employ a message-based protocol between the client and the server-resident analytic layer. By mapping the user to a server account and starting a process that executes as the user, a continuous connection is maintained between the analytic layer and the database that can support iterative queries during the lifetime of the process.

For example, an HTML form can be used to request the user's name and password (and database user name and password, if different). This information is passed as parameters or through environmental variables to a CGI program. That application then verifies the

Figure 5-7. The Common Gateway Interface.

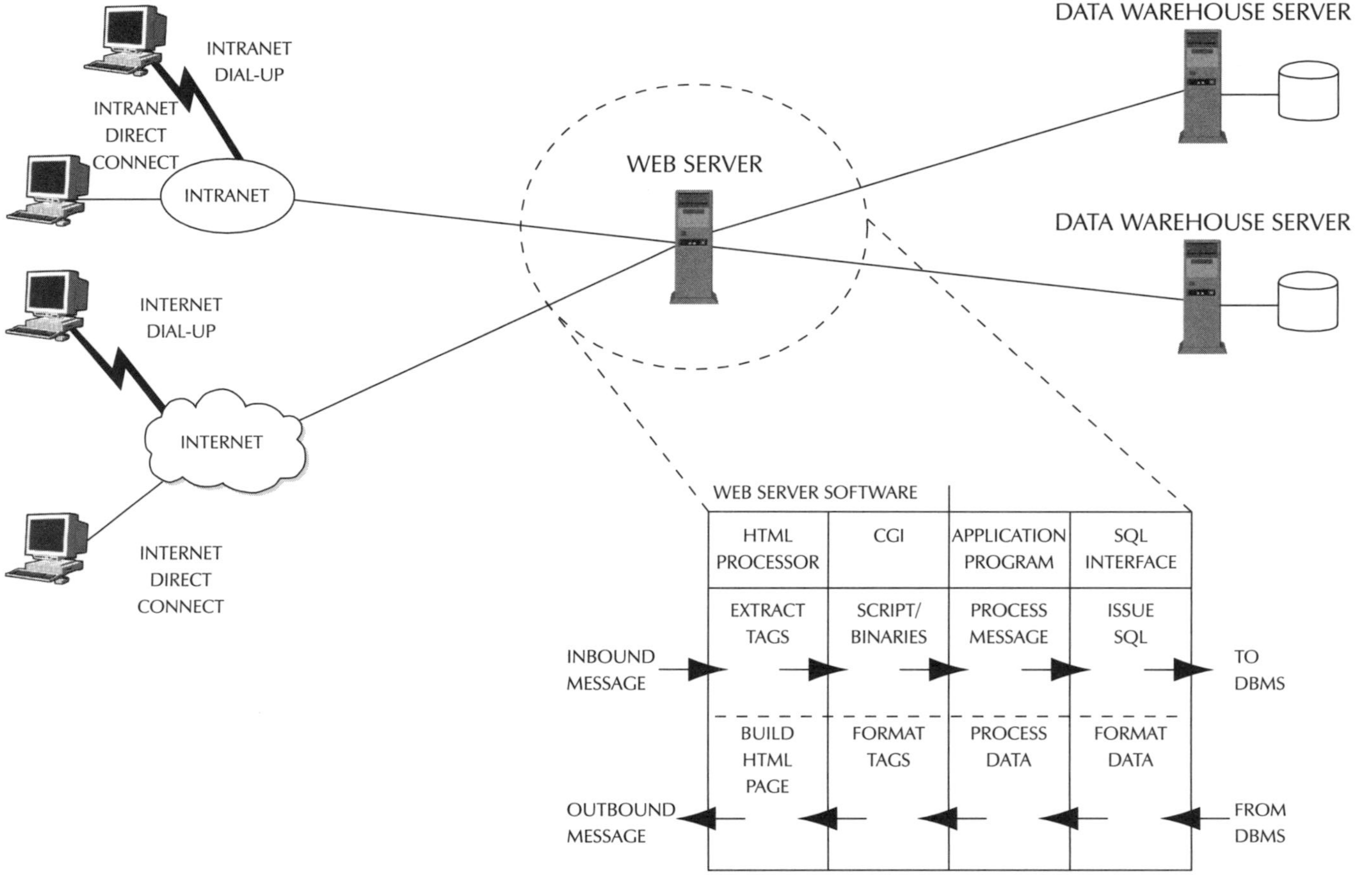

DATA WAREHOUSE SERVER

DATA WAREHOUSE SERVER

WEB SERVER

INTRANET DIAL-UP

INTRANET

INTRANET DIRECT CONNECT

INTERNET DIAL-UP

INTERNET

INTERNET DIRECT CONNECT

WEB SERVER SOFTWARE

HTML PROCESSOR	CGI	APPLICATION PROGRAM	SQL INTERFACE	
EXTRACT TAGS	SCRIPT/ BINARIES	PROCESS MESSAGE	ISSUE SQL	TO DBMS
BUILD HTML PAGE	FORMAT TAGS	PROCESS DATA	FORMAT DATA	FROM DBMS

INBOUND MESSAGE

OUTBOUND MESSAGE

user name and password and starts a process that executes as that user. This process could connect to the warehouse using its Application Program Interface (API) and the supplied user name and password to log into the relational database management system. Once the connection to the RDBMS is established, any number of queries can be processed and the result-sets returned to the analytic layer. A final output report can be generated, converted to an HTML document, and sent back to the client for display to the user.

A set of replacements for CGI is being adopted on some platforms that allow the plug-in to remain in memory and use more direct methods of interfacing. On a whole, these replacements provide better performance on the web server than CGI. Microsoft's Internet Server API and Netscape's API are two of more than a dozen alternatives available now.

Regardless of whether standard CGI or one of the newer replacements is used, an additional component is needed between the web server and the application layer for a successful warehouse implementation. This ingredient is called a web gateway, and it acts as a translator between the HTML language used by web servers and the data warehouse application API/CGI. When users log in to the network, they first view a web page that contains standard HTML and application-specific tags (Figure 5-7). These tags guide the web gateway in what buttons, dialogues, or objects to present to the user. If the user issues a request to update or query the warehouse, that request goes to the web server, which passes it, along with the tags, to the web gateway (Figure 5-8), where the request is translated into data warehouse application commands.

The request results come back from the warehouse server through the web gateway, where it is translated into an HTML table with hidden HTML form controls that contain data for each of the cells. These form controls are important because they can interact with VBScript or JavaScript; these scripts can interrogate and manipulate the controls to perform client-side processing.

Ideally, the web gateway will support both the intranet and the Internet (with access for remote users through the corporate home page) through direct or dial-up links. Since the web gateway generally sends only small amounts of information over the network, performance is excellent even for dial-up users with their slower transmission rates.

Figure 5-8. Web gateway.

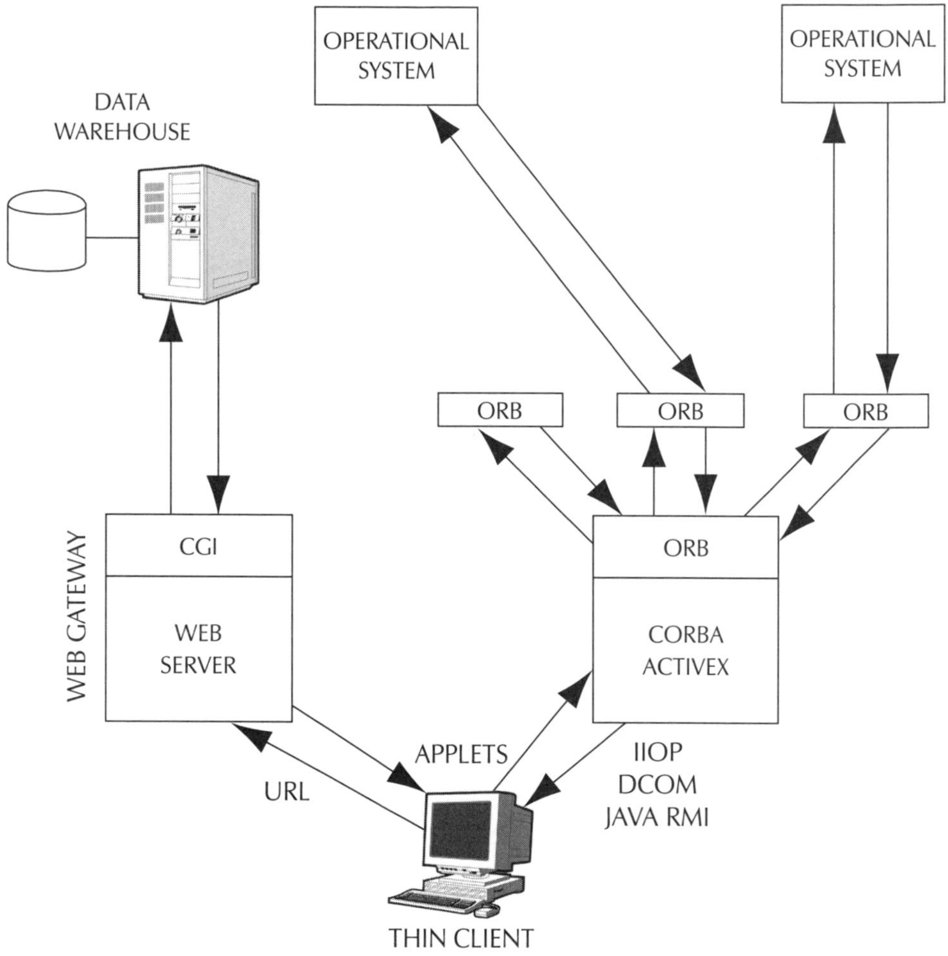

The Future of Web-Enabled Data Warehousing

A data warehouse should not be viewed as just a product or collection of products, or even a standard answer to an end-user data access problem. Rather, a data warehouse is the properly architected solution in which individual requirements, such as browsing capabilities and report creation, are handled in the method best suited to the characteristics of a specific environment. For this reason, no two warehouses will ever be exactly alike; each is an individual creation, designed to service a unique mix of business user needs and corporate structure.

That is not to say, however, that many warehouses cannot share a similar basic architecture. The three-tier or *n*-tiered taxonomy discussed in this chapter can be adapted to suit most of the major classes of data warehousing architecture. It can include the relatively simple centralized reporting system intended primarily for end-user computing and report generation, a moderately complex environment encompassing multiple applications and dependent data marts, and the more sophisticated distributed warehouse with a mix of relational data and text and image documents.

Data warehousing is not new. Almost all large corporations and many midsize ones have at least attempted a data warehouse, but only a small percentage of them succeeded in a meaningful way. Over the next few years, the growth of warehousing is going to be enormous, with new products and technologies becoming available almost daily, most of them web-enabled. To get the maximum benefit during this period, data warehouse planners and developers will need a clear idea what they are looking for. They need to choose strategies and methods that will yield performance today and flexibility tomorrow.

Because of the growing need for warehousing solutions and the relatively low success rate of their implementation, the data warehousing concept has received a lot of attention from the database community. Everyone knows that data warehousing will provide the means for querying the vast amounts of information that has been accumulating but has never been put to any practical use. Until fairly recently, it was impossible to provide a system that could support efficient use of these mounds of data. Data warehousing can provide corporate users with the means to perform such tasks as data mining to find those valuable tidbits of information hiding in the sea of data. In fact, there are now two viable architectures for large-scale data warehousing—the more traditional, centralized model and the new, distributed paradigm. With either method, decision makers now have the vehicle to process in a meaningful way the terabytes of data that are the by-product of the past twenty years of automation. The primary difference between the two approaches to data warehousing is one of perspective: Centralized warehousing is rooted in the past but able to incorporate many of new, web-based technologies, whereas distributed warehousing is future-oriented, built on the best of the current Internet technologies and positioned to incorporate whatever new advances are forthcoming.

Where will the future of web-enabled data warehousing lead? For the near future, the answer will be more complexity and more third-party vendor solutions—at least until the industry begins to normalize itself and a few architectures and enabling technologies become standards. The whole issue of standards continues to evolve. CGI versus its proposed replacements, two-tier versus *n*-tiered architecture, Java versus ActiveX—these are just a few of the many areas where the marketplace needs to make choices.

This process of choice is one of trade-offs. It's disturbing to see developers move away from the standards that made the Internet the great environment it is today, but they are doing so to get around many of the limitations that traditional web technology places in their way. Once again, the industry seems to be moving toward the quick-fix for applications development, just as it did for client/server, only this time with more complexity. History is once again repeating itself. If the past is any predictor of the future, a consensus will eventually be reached to the benefit of all. Until then, warehouse developers should fasten their seat belts—it's going to be a bumpy and fascinating ride!

6

Data Marts

Regrettably, centralized data warehousing has failed to live up to its promise. Instead of providing instant access to mission-critical data for the company's decision makers, the typical centralized data warehouse is stuck somewhere in the development phase. At best, this process is risky, long to implement, difficult to manage, and very, very costly.

This traditional warehouse implementation is mainframe-centric, enterprisewide in scope, and top-down driven. The entire focus of the warehouse is at the enterprise level. This results in one giant database holding all of the decision-support information for all user requirements—reports, analysis, and ad hoc queries—regardless of area of interest. Separate databases are maintained for the corporation's operational systems.

The enterprisewide nature of these implementations imposes enormously complex issues on the data warehouse. Every decision must go through multiple levels of agreement, getting a sign-off at every level of each division, because the warehouse is intended for everyone's use. Often the most trivial item requires six months or more of meetings and paperwork before all areas of the corporation sign off on it. Then, the impact of that one simple change may be enormous because changing one item can affect everything else. The lifeblood of any warehouse is the ability to change to meet new business needs so it can rapidly deliver valuable information to corporate decision makers. The centralized warehouse, however, tends to become bound by its own architecture and enterprisewide nature and unable to adapt to new situations as needed.

This isn't the only problem with a centralized warehouse. Traditional warehouses are built to accommodate predetermined queries, for which they are tuned in advance. But users seldom know exactly what questions they want to ask, and every answer leads to a new question. This results in poor response times, frustrating developers and users alike. There is an almost constant need for new summary and reporting tables to improve warehouse response, but this can cause an explosion in storage requirements. The additional storage is costly and adds to the management burden.

As a result of these challenges to the centralized data warehouse, a new architectural construct has developed that shares the decision-support goals of its predecessor. This distributed data warehouse focuses its approach on data marts, built rapidly with cost-effective, scalable distributed technology. Data marts can provide dramatic returns on investment without the high cost and risk of a centralized enterprise data warehouse project. Organizations can rapidly develop decision-support applications that are able to change and grow as business needs develop and change.

A data mart is a decision-support application system that focuses on solving the specific business problems of a given department or area within the company. A data mart should be constructed with an enterprise data model in hand (to ensure that the finished product can later be integrated with other marts), contain consistent business information, and have the ability to grow. A centralized data warehouse is not a prerequisite for a data mart; in fact, in many ways, it can be an impediment.

Data marts are characterized by their rapid response to ad hoc queries and their low construction costs. In many cases, the expenses for an enterprisewide distributed warehouse composed of several data marts are less than half that of a comparable centralized data warehouse. Distributed warehouses, especially those that are web-enabled, are also easier and cheaper to maintain, and they can provide substantial bonus savings on the equipment needed for user interface.

Data Mart Solutions

Clearly, stand-alone data marts cannot meet all of a business's needs for enterprisewide decision support. As companies build data marts that satisfy users' localized application needs, they begin to learn what data elements are most valuable, what information needs to be most current, and where additional details or external data would be useful. Over time, the data processing department may even determine that some data should be stored centrally, because it is key to all of the data marts.

By implementing departmental data marts, the enterprise is actually building the corporate warehouse slowly, in steps, in direct response to the needs of its various groups. As demand and requirements grow, the company can construct more data marts until eventually, over time, it will have developed a multitiered, distributed warehouse.

In some organizations, the decision-making process is highly decentralized, perhaps even compartmentalized, and as a result, the company will be slow to develop interest in linking the individual data marts together. In others, where top-down decision making is strong, there will be pressure to network the data marts almost from the start. The key to success is to start with a pragmatic approach, focusing on the needs of a single user group and meeting those needs with a data mart. This will ensure a "quick win" for the new mart and help to build user demand for more data marts and eventually the distributed warehouse.

The concept of data marts derives from the fact that any single user has limited data needs. Even though there is always a need for cross-functional analysis, the scope of the data requirements is still narrow in most cases. By concentrating on the needs of individual departments, one at a time, the scope of the distributed warehouse itself is more sharply defined, and this naturally limits the type and quantity of data stored in the data marts. It is a more targeted approach than the traditional warehouse, which in its unfocused way tries to be everything to everyone. With the more clearly defined approach, the warehouse can be completed quickly and remains flexible enough to respond to changing business needs. Figure 6-1 illustrates this approach, with several targeted data marts networked into a corporate data warehouse.

What Is a Data Mart?

A data mart is an application-focused miniature data warehouse, built rapidly to support a single line of business. Data marts share all

Figure 6-1. Networked data marts.

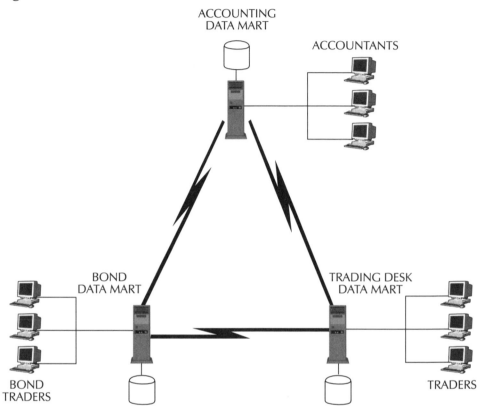

the other characteristics of a data warehouse, such as subject-oriented data that is nonvolatile, time-variant, and integrated. Rather than representing an overview of the complete corporate data, however, the data mart contains a limited subset of data that is specifically of interest to one department or division of that enterprise.

Dependent Data Marts

The typical data warehouse is the center of the decision-support universe for the company it serves, containing integrated historical data that is communal to the entire organization. The warehouse's stores include both summarized data and detailed information, in addition to the metadata that describes the content and source of the data that enters into the warehouse.

From this centralized warehouse, data may flow to various departments for their customized decision-support usage. These departmental decision-support databases are a type of data mart, called a dependent data mart, that has at its architectural foundation the centralized enterprise data warehouse. These data marts exist primarily as a means of improving performance for the users.

While the data is stored at a very granular level in the centralized data warehouse, it is kept at a more refined level in the dependent data marts. In an organization that has several dependent data marts, each contains a different combination and selection of the same data found in the centralized data warehouse. In some cases, the detailed data is handled differently in the data mart than it is in the centralized warehouse to provide a customized look at the information for the user. Each data mart may also structure the same data differently, depending on the requirements of its users.

In every case, the centralized data warehouse provides the detailed foundation for all of the data, both granular and aggregated, found in all of the dependent data marts. Because of the single data warehouse foundation that they share, dependent data marts have a mutual heritage and can always be reconciled at the most basic level.

Several factors have led to the popularity of the centralized warehouse/dependent data mart combination. As long as the centralized data warehouse does not contain a large amount of data, it is able to serve the needs of many different departments as a basis for their decision-support processing. But successful data warehouses never stay "empty" for long and, for various reasons, soon acquire vast amounts of data. As the warehouse grows, the demand for dependent data marts soon mounts up.

The larger and more successful the warehouse is, the fiercer the competition becomes for access to its resources. More and more departmental decision-support processing is done with the aid of the warehouse, to the point where resource consumption becomes a real problem. It quickly becomes nearly impossible to customize and/or summarize the data in the same way it was done when the warehouse was small, placing the burden for dealing with raw data on the user. It is unlikely that the user has the time or resources to deal with the information in its unrefined form. To make matters worse, the software tools available to assist users with access and analysis of large amounts of data are not nearly as elegant or simple as the software designed for smaller quantities of data.

Dependent data marts have become the natural extension of the centralized warehouse. They are attractive because:

- Having its own data mart allows a department to customize the information the way it wants as it flows into the mart from the warehouse. Since there is no need for the data in the data mart to service the entire corporation, the department can summarize, select, sort, and structure its own data with no consideration for the rest of the company.

- The amount of historical data required is a function of the department, not the corporation. In almost every case, the department will choose to store less historical data than is kept in the centralized data warehouse. In those rare instances where more historical data is needed, the department can store it in the exact form it requires to best fulfill its needs.

- The department can do whatever decision-support processing it wants whenever it wants with no impact on resource utilization for the rest of the company.

- The department can select software for the data mart that is tailored to its needs alone, making for a better "fit."

- The cost of processing and storage on a server-class machine, such as is appropriate to departmental needs, is significantly less than the unit cost of processing and storage for the mainframe that supports the entire organization.

For these organizational, technical, economic, and other reasons, dependent data marts are so beguiling that they are becoming a necessary adjunct to the centralized data warehouse.

Multidimensional Data Marts

While the dependent data mart is a powerful and natural extension of the centralized data warehouse, there are other types of data marts. One type is the multidimensional data mart, most often used for slicing and dicing numeric data in a free-form fashion (Figure 6-2). Some of the characteristics of the multidimensional mart are that they:

- Contain sparsely populated matrices.
- Contain numeric data.

Figure 6-2. Multidimensional data mart.

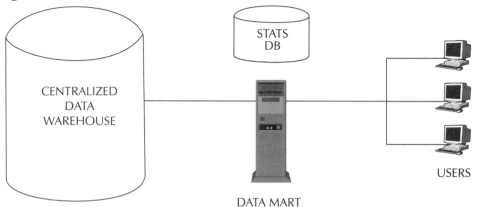

- Maintain rigid structure as the data enters the multidimensional framework.
- Are usually dependent on the centralized data warehouse as their source of data.

ROLAP Data Marts

Another type of data mart is one that can be called for relational OLAP, or ROLAP processing. ROLAP data marts are general-purpose marts that contain both numeric and textual data, and serve a much wider audience than their multidimensional counterparts (Figure 6-3). Some of the characteristics of ROLAP data marts are that they:

- Are supported by relational technology.
- Are used for general-purpose decision-support analysis.
- Maintain structured data.
- Employ numerous indices.
- Support star schema.
- Contain both detailed and summary data.
- Can support both disciplined and ad hoc usage.

While frequently found in conjunction with a centralized data warehouse and dependent on it for its data, ROLAP data marts can also be independent.

Independent Data Marts

Independent data marts stand alone, without the support of a centralized data warehouse. They obtain their data directly from the

Figure 6-3. ROLAP data mart.

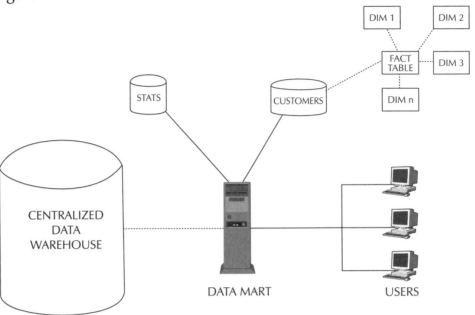

source, either from in-house operational applications or other external systems (Figure 6-4). In most cases, they are general-purpose marts containing both numeric and textual data. Some of the characteristics of independent data marts are that they:

- Are used most frequently for general-purpose decision-support analysis.
- Can be based on almost any technology (e.g., relational, object-oriented, distributed, or hierarchical).
- Contain both detailed and summary data.

The wide-open architecture of the independent data mart makes it the most flexible of all the varying types of data marts. It is often seen in smaller organizations that lack the resources to have constructed a centralized data warehouse, or large corporate environments where they are replacing a failed centralized data warehouse.

Point Solution Data Marts

A variation on the independent data mart, the point solution data mart (Figure 6-5), is built to satisfy the specific needs of a particular

Figure 6-4. Independent data mart.

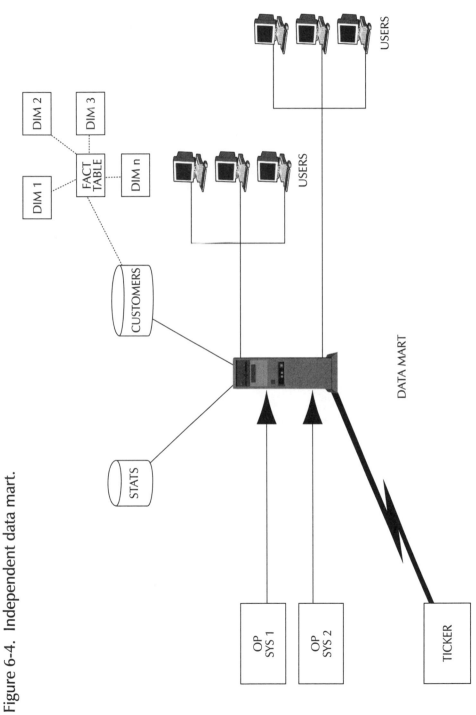

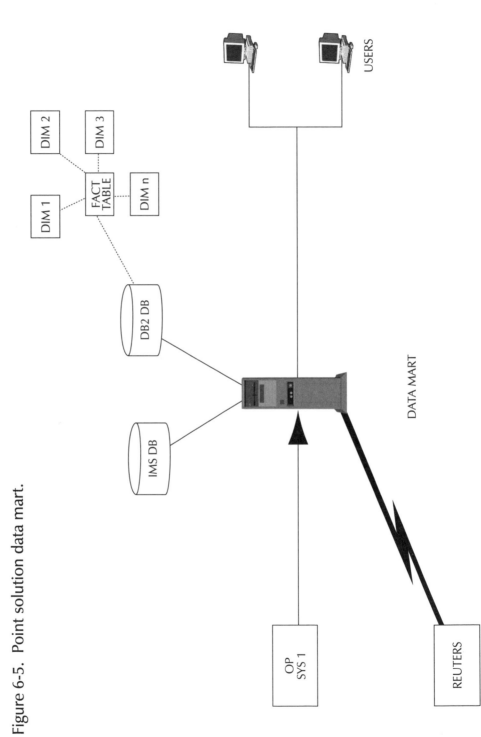

Figure 6-5. Point solution data mart.

group. It is the quickest and easiest kind of data mart to build because no time is spent attempting to integrate the point solution mart with any enterprisewide architecture. Some characteristics of the point solution data marts are that they:

- Are designed for a single purpose in most cases, without regard for compatibility with in-house systems or possible later integration with other data marts.
- Are used most frequently for general-purpose decision-support analysis.
- Can be based on almost any technology (e.g., relational, object-oriented, distributed, or hierarchical).
- Contain both detailed and summary data.

If there is more than one data mart designed this way, all are probably extracting data from the same operational systems and a great deal of redundancy can result. In fact, several point solution data marts can tie up the operational systems to the point that they have no time to perform their primary tasks.

Integrated Data Marts

Integrated data marts are a collection of independent data marts that depend on there being a consistent data architecture that governs the design of each of the independent marts (Figure 6-6). With a standard architecture, the independent data marts can be fashioned into a loosely integrated group, or "data mall." A common example of a data mall is seen in electronic commerce. A group of merchants jointly agree to develop their web sites to a specific set of standards and then link their sites together. End users are given a common user interface (a shopping cart) with which they can browse, shop, and order from any merchant in the group.

Networked Independent Data Marts = Distributed Data Warehouse

Although an independent data mart and its cousins, the point solution and integrated data marts, can certainly stand alone, a new type of warehouse, the distributed data warehouse, can be constructed by networking several independent data marts together (Figure 6-7).

(text continues on page 200)

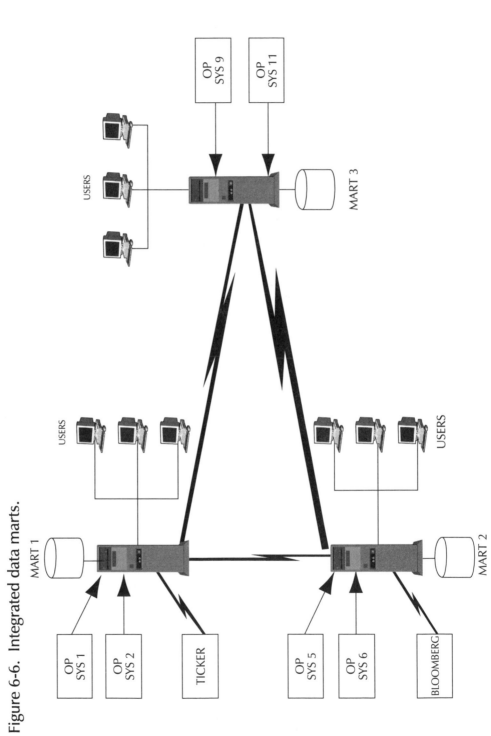

Figure 6-6. Integrated data marts.

Figure 6-7. Distributed data warehouse.

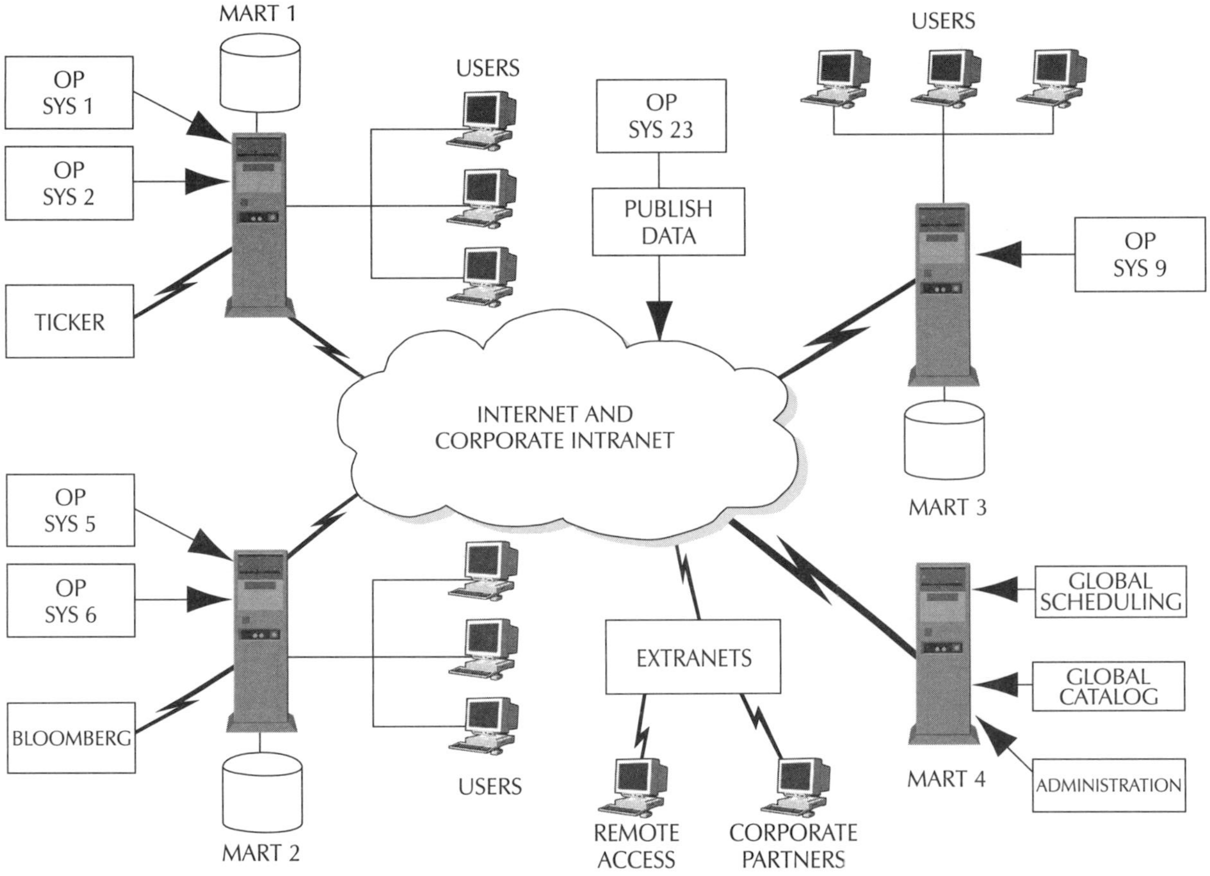

After all, a large corporation may have many subject-area data marts at company headquarters as well as marts servicing divisions located in different geographic areas. Advanced applications, such as a corporate intranet and the World Wide Web, can extend the data mart network throughout the company and even outside the enterprise boundaries.

In a distributed data warehouse, users must be able to look at and work with multiple data marts from a single client workstation, which requires transparency across the network. Similarly, data mart administrators must be able to manage and administer a network of data marts from a single location. Implementation and management of a distributed warehouse not only imposes new requirements on the data marts' DBMSs, it also, and perhaps even more important, requires tools to define, extract, move, and update batches of data as self-contained units on demand. It also needs a whole new generation of data warehouse management software to support each data mart's catalog, schedule, and publish/subscribe functions in a distributed environment.

Sharing data among departmental and divisional data marts brings together information from across the company. To successfully pull information from two or more data marts, the data must still be cleaned up and standardized. Without data cleansing and standardization, data from one department may be meaningless to a user in another division. Users who share data from various data marts throughout the organization will need a standard metadata directory to clarify terms and the business definitions of the departmental data as well as a strong, unified data model. The lack of a shared metadata directory and data model leaves data elements open for misinterpretation, with no road map for definition.

Data marts, on a whole, offer several benefits because of their scalability and incremental approach. For example, an independent data mart can be quickly and inexpensively built to address a pressing business need. This flexibility and simplicity stand in sharp contrast to the complexity inherent in attempting to address the wide range of user needs while building a centralized data warehouse. The past ten years have shown that user needs and business requirements change faster than centralized data warehouses can react to them, or even be built in the first place. The two to three years of development required by the typical centralized data warehouse are far too long for a fast-moving competitive situation.

End users benefit most from data that is customized and focused toward their needs. While this is possible to achieve when a centralized data warehouse is small, the level of customization diminishes as the warehouse increases in size and utilization. Data marts are, by definition, a customized response to the needs of a specific user group and retain their customization throughout their life cycle. Data marts also enable development and administration at a department level and reduce the support burden on the corporate staff.

Independent data marts can be cost-effective and give management the option of starting small. At the same time, this approach gives the business the freedom to expand the concept incrementally to other departments. Over time, this will yield an enterprisewide distributed data warehouse that remains responsive to changing business conditions and is cost-effective and manageable.

Implementing a Data Mart

Once an organization commits to a strategy of developing application-specific data marts, it must define the requirements that need to be met in implementing this strategy. These requirements should pay particular attention to the source data, the type of DBMS used in each data mart, sources of external data, the definition of metadata and creation of a data model, system performance, scalability, flexibility, and security.

Source Data

Virtually the first thing any data mart needs is data. The mart should contain whatever information is necessary for departmental decision-support processing. Contrary to popular opinion, the data mart should contain a diversity of data, with a place for both summary and detailed information. To adequately meet its users needs, it will need both the "prepared" data and "ad hoc" facts. While the data mart might well contain other kinds of data, these two types will comprise the bulk of the information.

DBMS Type

Once the data has been selected, it is necessary to decide how it will be stored. The choice of a DBMS is critically important—it will at least influence, if not dictate, all the other decisions made about the data mart. The three types of DBMSs that are commonly used in data marts are relational, multidimensional, and object. Multidimensional technology is at the heart of slice-and-dice numeric processing, while object technology is often chosen for its speed of development and its good fit with data that is primarily hierarchical in nature. Relational technology forms the basis for all other standard data mart processing and is by far still the most popular of the three techniques.

When using a relational database management system (RDBMS), the types of tables and the number of tables that are found in the data mart vary in accordance with the user requirements. The types of tables most often used include:

- Historical tables
- Summary tables
- Transaction-level tables
- Reference tables
- Analytical (spreadsheet) tables

As time passes and the data mart matures, both the number of tables and the number of types of tables grows. In addition, the amount of data from external sources also tends to increase. The data is generally structured along the line of star joins and seminormalized tables. Star joins and denormalized tables are created where there is a predictable pattern of usage and there is a significant amount of data. Standard relational table design is used as the basis for configuration where there is no predictable pattern. Both forms of structure are able to reside in the same database with no conflict of interest.

External Data Sources

As additional sources of information, external data holds great promise for inclusion into the data mart. There are several important issues related to the use of external data. First, there is redundancy. When the external data needs to be used in more than one data mart, one of two techniques should be employed. If dependent data marts are being used, the data can be imported into the centralized data warehouse and then distributed to the data marts. In the situation where independent data marts are being used, the data can be introduced into one data mart that in turn broadcasts it to the other marts. These techniques ensure that redundancy is controlled and that the data is consistent.

The second issue it that of storage of secondary data along with the external data. When external data is acquired, the history of the data needs to be stored as well as the data. The history of external data includes:

- The source of the data
- The date the data was acquired
- The quantity of data acquired
- The editing criteria applied to the data
- A general description of the data

A reference table can be used to house this information. This table and all other reference tables play an important role in the data mart environment. Data marts allow the end user to relate summary data back to the "expanded" version of that information—an impossible task without the reference tables. Like almost all data, reference table content needs to be managed. Time management of reference data is a complex task that's best managed centrally, either at the centralized data warehouse (for dependent data marts) or by the data processing department or distributed warehouse administrator (for independent data marts).

Metadata and Data Model

Any discussion of reference tables leads directly to consideration of the system's metadata. Metadata in a data mart environment serves the same purpose as metadata in the warehouse environment; it allows the users to find out about the data—its definition, where it came from, and where it is located. Data mart metadata contains the following information:

- A description of the customization that has occurred as the data was imported into the mart

- Identification of the source of the data
- General descriptive information about the data mart itself, including tables, attributes, and relationships

If the source of the data in the mart is the centralized data warehouse, there should be a linkage between the metadata of the data mart and that of the warehouse. This linkage needs to describe how the data at the two locations are related. This description is vital if there is to be drill-down capabilities between the two environments.

Nearly as important as the metadata is a data model of the data mart's contents. This is different from the enterprise data model normally developed as the basis for a warehouse. The data mart data model is much narrower in scope and is specifically designed to give the users a "road map" of the mart or, if the data marts have been networked into a distributed data warehouse, the models are combined into a warehouse map. Users can utilize the combined data model to acquire the information they want, regardless of its location.

Performance

Once the data is stored in the data mart, it is necessary to get it back out again in the form of responses to user queries. Overall performance is an important consideration in data mart implementation and can include some unexpected items, including:

- Load performance (i.e., how smoothly and rapidly data can be loaded)
- Data maintenance and management quality
- Query performance

Effective query applications require near-real-time performance. End users need to be able to seamlessly ask questions, get answers, and ask follow-up questions at a pace matching their own thoughts. They should be able to pursue different lines of inquiry, look at the same information from multiple perspectives, and drill up or down through the different levels of detail available without inconvenient wait-times. For these reasons, query applications require response times measured in fractions of a second or, at worst, seconds. Regardless of the level of detail or size of the database, this level of performance must be maintained in a multiuser environment. Query response time measured in minutes (or hours), as sometimes happens with an overworked centralized warehouse, is completely unacceptable.

These application performance requirements translate directly back to the data mart server and DBMS. The DBMS must include query performance optimizations analogous to those that have consistently yielded online transaction processing (OLTP) performance in the order of thousands of transactions per second. However, the data mart environment is different, and performance optimization must address all aspects of query processing including joins, sorting, and grouping.

Some performance-enhancing techniques for the data mart environment include:

- Limiting the volume of data stored in the data mart
- Making extensive use of indices
- Creating arrays of data
- Using star joins
- Creating prejoined (i.e., denormalized) tables
- Establishing and adhering to a standard maintenance schedule
- Preprocessing raw data before loading into tables
- Limiting the use of foreign keys to improve load times
- Partitioning medium and large tables (to improve both load and query response times)
- Storing data in query sequence (using a clustering key that arranges the data in the order most frequently requested)

Scalability

Another important factor that must be kept in mind during data mart implementation is scalability. While the basic concept of a data mart is to start small, it seldom stays that way for long. The user demand for the data collected, the reports generated, and the relationships established within the data all grow as users become familiar with and proficient in the use of the data mart. As they start to explore the data, users ask for more history, more external data, and more detail in general. Some data marts store only summarized data, expecting the users to drill down to either the centralized data warehouse or the operational system for the detail they want. The problem with this approach is that users naturally want to explore data in different dimensions and if that detailed information is not stored in the data mart, those queries are next to impossible to process.

To support analysis of detailed data, the database engine and platform must support dynamic aggregation and fast, flexible queries against hundreds of gigabytes of detailed data. In addition, the initial single department data mart may eventually be called upon to house even more data so it can support several departments. In this case, the system will need to perform cross-functional analysis for problems that involve more than one department. If it is an independent data mart, it might even join a distributed warehouse, where it will be required to contribute data and processing power to resolve queries that involve several data marts at once.

The subject of scalability is covered further in the section on "Data Mart Architecture" later in this chapter.

Flexibility

Flexibility, another of the implementation issues, refers to the data mart's responsiveness to user queries and its ability to adapt to a changing business environment. Ideally, since many of the requests for data are ad hoc, the database should be capable of functioning efficiently even though it was designed without foreknowledge of what ad hoc queries would be run. Users should be able to drill down and surf through the data to find the information required.

The platform, DBMS, and design of the data mart must support a rapid and iterative implementation. Data marts should deliver results fast—ideally constructed from start to finish in six months or less. The DBMS must support a wide range of queries and not lock the designer into a fixed design (i.e., star schema). This flexible system will be easier to modify to accommodate changing business conditions.

Just like a data warehouse, the data mart requires periodic monitoring. As the data mart grows in size, the monitors take on added importance in relation to the volume of data and the amount of query activity that passes through the mart. When the data mart is new and relatively small, there may be no need for close monitoring of the environment. But as its size increases, the monitoring facilities make more sense.

Security

The data mart and, by extension, the distributed warehouse, needs to be secure just as all components in the decision-support environment require security. When the data mart contains sensitive information there is a need to secure that information, especially if an intranet with connections to the World Wide Web is in use. The typical data mart contains a surprising amount of information that should be secured. For example, it might house:

- Employee records (e.g., payroll, medical histories, credit references, and histories)
- Corporate financial records
- Corporate research and development findings
- Client information

There are many different types of security, and the level and form of security required depends on the data stored. The more sensitive the data, the more draconian the security measures. Typically, data mart (and distributed warehouse) security requires:

- Logon/logoff with user ids and passwords
- Firewalls
- Encryption
- DBMS security measures

The importance of security cannot be overestimated. For a more complete discussion of the whys and hows of data mart/distributed warehouse security, please see Chapters 8 and 9.

In the discussion of data mart implementation so far, it has been assumed that the independent data marts that will form a distributed warehouse all follow the same basic design and therefore use the same DBMS. However, this is frequently not the case. Enterprises today are heterogeneous in terms of their existing databases and are likely to take the same haphazard approach to data mart design, leaving the distributed warehouse designer to deal with several different DBMSs. While this complicates the task, it is still possible to fashion a functional distributed data warehouse from heterogeneous systems.

Regardless of the type of DBMS used, it is a virtual certainty that the data marts/distributed warehouse will be gathering data from multiple sources, representing several different databases. It is very important that the data mart be able to handle receiving feeds or extracts from diverse sources. This is one of the reasons why the publish/subscribe technique of data transfer is so attractive (see Chapter 10)—it eliminates this data mart requirement of being able to process data received in a variety of formats.

Lastly, it must be remembered that data marts, especially multiple data marts, cannot be built in a vacuum. Each data mart must share common data transformation programs and use common data movement tools to ensure corporate data consistency across the data marts. An accounting data mart must share client data with the equities trading data mart, for example, and both need to know that they are analyzing the same information about the customers. Both data marts must be refreshed in a consistent way as new clients are added or old clients leave.

Data Mart Architecture

Data marts can be viewed as miniature data warehouses, but instead of being highly centralized, multiple line-of-business systems, they are single subject (i.e., accounting or equities trading), and are fast and easy to implement. They offer organizations greater flexibility without sacrificing the extremely important requirement of enterprise scalability.

In contrast to the COBOL code-generated approach required by many centralized warehouses, today's data mart technology propagates data from either the centralized data warehouse or operational databases using a real-time extract/transform/load engine or, even better, subscribes to data feeds published by the source systems. By combining one of these newer data acquisition approaches with the latest technologies, such as the highly graphical client/server tools, integrated metadata, and innovative centralized management capabilities, astonishing results can be achieved. Networking the independent data marts together to form a distributed data warehouse will extend the results even farther. This yields a data warehousing system built and managed at a fraction of the cost of centralized implementations, and it is completed in months instead of years.

Many important architectural considerations must be kept in mind when designing a data mart. The first of these, scalability, presents several diffcrent challenges. In one regard, "scalability" is the ability of the DBMS to grow as needed. The choice of technologies, especially the DBMS, can greatly affect the size of the database for a given application. For example, raw data stored in a multidimensional database could easily multiply by 10 to 100 times. On the other hand, the use of compression could shrink the data two or three times.

The history of data warehousing records that no matter where the warehousing application starts, it always grows over time. This is certainly true for data marts too, as more and more data is gathered to satisfy user needs from the business's OLTP systems and is uploaded into the data marts while previous iterations of the same data are preserved as part of history. It is only common sense to assume that techniques that compress data are better data mart choices than those that expand data, to allow for maximum scalability if the situation allows.

Scalability can also refer the number of users a system will need to support. A successful data mart project can attract many users as word spreads of its capabilities. More users mean more simultaneous queries, and this can lead to frustration and disenchantment when the number of users overload the capacity of the system. It is therefore wise to built a system whose response times scale linearly with user demand and whose architecture can support substantial increases in user population.

Shorter response times mean that more users can be serviced simultaneously without saturating the system. Other techniques for handling increasing numbers of users are parallel processing and duplicated data tables. In multidimensional databases, where the size of the database is large, parallel processing is especially useful to churn through the vast quantities of data available in response to ad hoc queries. In distributed data warehouses, entire tables are often duplicated and positioned at various locations in the network. This allows many users to access the same information "in parallel," speeding response times.

Finally, there is the scalability of the number of data marts that compose the enterprise system. In the ideal implementation of the data mart architecture, the individual data marts all fit seamlessly together into an organizationwide distributed warehouse, where cross-functional analysis is not only possible, it is transparent to the end user. This form of scalability is only possible when there has been the development of and adherence to standards and an overall enterprise architecture, under which the data marts are constructed and operated. Without an enterprise architecture to guide data mart development, the resulting distributed data warehouse will have "gaps" and "blind spots" where critical information is missing.

Any warehousing project must be implemented to allow the maximum flexibility for both users and management. Users need flexibility in designing their queries. OLAP tools make possible a discovery process whereby the user's initial query results may well lead to further queries, many of which were not considered when the data mart was designed and built. Management needs flexibility in responding to user requests, managing the expansions of the data mart into new areas, and coordinating the interactions among the data marts.

Organizations want to be in a position to react quickly, so the data mart(s) must be easily and quickly deployable and allow the organization to reap benefits almost immediately. A major factor in the speed to deployment is rapid and simple integration with existing OLTP data sources. The data marts must be able to accept all the various types of input (flat files, relational loads, and others) it could receive from the source systems, or a publish/subscribe system must be in place.

Once in place, data marts must be easily modified to respond to user needs, organizational restructuring, and the myriad other changes that are likely to occur in today's business environment. A critical part of this flexibility is the ability of each data mart to integrate with the other data marts to form a distributed system. This interoperability will not happen without adherence to standards, compliance with an overriding architecture, and the consistent application of the same vendor products, used the same way, throughout the system.

Hardware Architectures

Advances in hardware and software architecture have significantly contributed to the rapid growth and explosion of data warehouses and data marts. The price/performance and acceptance of multiprocessor machines, coupled with the attendant vendor rewrites of existing products and tools to take advantage of the new hardware architecture, have made it possible to work with very large databases, in the gigabyte to multiterabyte range.

The two hardware architectures most commonly used in data warehousing are symmetric multiprocessing (SMP) and massively parallel processing (MPP). In SMP, a number of processors operate cooperatively using a common memory pool. Sometimes the SMP architecture is called a shared memory processing architecture because of this fact. MPP systems have large numbers of processors working in parallel, each with its own system resources. These systems are often referred to as "share nothing" systems. Recent innovations in hardware architecture and database systems have blurred the lines as to where one architecture outperforms the other in terms of cost and speed.

Traditionally, SMP machines do not scale as well as MPP, and at some point, the overhead associated with coordinating the processors becomes so high that adding another processor produces no noticeable increase in processing power. However, new hardware techniques have obviated the problem, and now SMP machines can scale linearly well beyond the 64-processor mark. Advocates of SMP technology say this demonstrates SMP's superiority over MPP; they also point to the fact that with a shared memory architecture, it is far easier to add memory effectively to the common pool. It is undoubtedly true that SMP systems are cheaper, and if the initial system requirements are small but will eventually need to scale up, SMP will be there, ready to perform, when the time comes.

MPP advocates are equally impassioned about their choice. They take the position that once the applications are in an MPP environment, the upside potential of the system far exceeds the capability of SMP. The inherent latency is still far lower for MPP systems, the advances in SMP notwithstanding. In addition, a recent architectural development known as NUMA (Non Uniform Memory Access) allows MPP to share common memory and take advantage of the flexibility of this feature while still maintaining low latency. The use of shared memory also helps to eliminate the greatest downside of MPP technology—the "hot spot."

A hot spot occurs when a processor is dedicated to a certain portion of a query and that portion requires much more processing than the others. That processor may run out of memory or other system resources while the other processors involved in the query sit idle waiting for it to complete. For example, a broker issues a query to ascertain how many shares of IBM stock his firm has traded on behalf of its clients during the last week. The system divides the query into five subqueries, one for each day of the week. All five subqueries begin processing, but the one responsible for Friday takes much longer than the others because Friday was a "triple-witch" day and trading was unusually heavy due to the expiring options. Using NUMA architecture, additional resources would be made available to the "Friday subquery," balancing the processing load more equitably.

All the major relational database vendors have rewritten their products, attempting to keep current with these new architectures and improve performance by adding parallel query capabilities that spread the work of a single query over a number of processors. Parallel query processing can improve response times for large bulk-type processing operations that scan a great deal of data, such as update and refresh maintenance and report generation, among others. Adding processors enables a data mart or warehouse to scale up to maintain performance as the amount of data and the number of users grows. When used in combination with compression and table partitioning, this technique can extend the longevity, utility, and return on investment for the data warehouse.

DBMS Schema and Indices

There is one last architectural consideration to be examined—that is the internal design of the DBMS chosen for the data mart. Today, almost all data warehousing applications are based on one or another of the major relational systems, although a few are cautiously experimenting with object databases. Important factors in choosing an RDBMS are the type of schema and indexing methods they support.

Star schema is a technique frequently used to improve the decision-support performance of RDBMS products. A star schema produces a large "fact" table and many smaller "dimension" tables that extend the different aspects of the facts. During the query process, the dimension tables are processed first, narrowing the range of detailed records in the fact table that need to be read to complete the query.

Because all the tables are prebuilt, this design is most effective when the nature of the queries is well understood before construction of the data mart/warehouse begins. This approach has major limitations when it comes to delivering performance with ad hoc queries. Additionally, star schemas can lose some detail under certain conditions. The technique does not handle multiple many-to-many relationships in the same detail record. For example, if a transaction has several line items and multiple methods of payment in effect at the same time, then one of these details must be collapsed to avoid an explosion (or at least multiple records for the same transaction) in the size of the fact table. Combining these elements is impractical, because of the many-to-many relationships.

Star schema fact tables are, by their very nature, expensive to query if the query does not include a highly selective dimension table. When it does not, a large portion of the table must be read at considerable expense to the system. As a result, effective tuning of a star schema–based system often means limiting the scope of the queries to only those that can be supported with good performance.

Another tempting relational design involves using multidimensional schema. With this approach, data is preaggregated and stored in hypercubes. As the number of dimensions increases or the cardinality of each dimension increases, there is a significant increase in the size of the hypercubes generated. In one example the author witnessed, the raw database was a modest 5 gigabytes, but the supporting multidimensional tables topped 20 gigabytes. The preaggregation required by multidimensional database limits the flexibility of the system, and the raw data is not available to the user for drill down.

Since, in an ideal world, users want the option of looking at segments of their data in a multidimensional way without incurring the overhead of having a database administrator (DBA) set up a customized database for each query, a good alternative is purchasing one of the multidimensional tools now commercially available. More and more vendors are adding a multidimensional viewing capability to their relational products. For these tools to work, the underlying database must be tuned to perform fast aggregations on the fly when the user needs it.

Traditionally, RDBMSs have improved retrieval performance by the use of indices. An index is a shortcut to finding a particular piece of data because it keeps track of the values of certain selected fields and can point directly to the data page containing them. To find the record for a particular customer, the system simply reads the customer index (assuming there is one) and goes directly to the data page with information about that customer. Indices eliminate costly table scans by pointing instantly to the relevant data. Indices designed for traditional OLTP systems are not very efficient for warehousing applications. New techniques have been developed that, in combination with conventional techniques, can offer tremendous advantages in a decision-support environment.

The traditional balance tree (B-tree) index is not without merit. It keeps track of the values for specific fields and points to the rows that contain them. The primary feature of a B-tree index structure is that it always maintains a constant depth in terms of levels of access, so all indices are reachable with approximately the same number of disk accesses. B-tree indices are well suited to finding and retrieving a small number of rows. An example of an index with this type of high cardinality would be a customer identification number or an account number. Unfortunately, B-tree indices have three characteristics that make them a poor choice for the complex, interactive type of queries so common in a data warehousing situation:

- First, B-tree indices are of little or no value on data with few unique values, such as cash/credit card or single/married, because using the index eliminates so little of the data.

- The second limitation is the cost of building and maintaining the B-tree indices. B-tree indices contain actual data values and other information, and the indices grow larger and larger as more data is indexed. The warehouse can balloon to many times the size of the raw data. These indices are also sensitive to bulk inserts and updates that can unbalance them and ruin performance. A relatively small percentage of change in the raw data can necessitate an index rebuild.

• Finally, B-tree indices are designed for environments where queries are simple and access paths are known in advance. The database usually evaluates B-tree indices sequentially, which works well when the index is designed to be very selective. In data warehouse conditions, the query conditions are often far less selective than desired. As a B-tree index becomes less selective, the amount of data that needs to be scanned increases in an almost inverse relationship to the selectivity.

All in all, B-tree indices have limited applicability for data warehousing, but are of value to data marts if the table sizes are kept relatively small. They are most useful in speeding predetermined queries and generally do not do much good with generalized ad hoc queries that can make up 30–50 percent of the warehouse's activity. B-tree indices always require intensive tuning, such as constructing clustering indices for known queries, to produce the best results.

There is another type of index, called a bit-mapped index, which is far older than the B-tree index. It has been resurrected in response to demand for complex queries in decision-support systems. The basic concept of this technique is to save space and time by using a single bit to indicate a specific value of data. Bit-mapped indices are generally used against low cardinality data with very few possible values.

Bit-mapped indices address some of the limitations of B-tree indices. Bit-mapped indices are extremely efficient for low cardinality data, are much smaller and easier to maintain, and can be processed simultaneously. But they are unsuited to high cardinality data because, as they are implemented in most products, they require a separate array of true/false bits to be implemented for every unique value. This clearly is impractical for data that can have many possible values.

Regardless of the type of index used, the system will, in most cases, have to process the detailed records, and often the entire table, for queries that combine low and high cardinality data, eliminating any savings realized from using bit-mapped indices. Bit-mapped indices are also limited in their ability to aggregate data, implement relational joins, and retrieve the actual raw data. The best solution for most warehouse implementations is a combination of the two types of indices.

The Future of Data Marts

A data mart is more focused than the traditional centralized data warehouse. Because it is targeted at a single business problem, a far narrower scope of data needs to be collected and rationalized compared with the larger enterprise model. This in turn makes the underlying data model, and the data mart itself, simpler, more stable, and easier to identify, design, implement, and maintain. In addition, the cost of building enough data marts to form a distributed enterprise data warehouse is only one-third the expense of a comparable centralized data warehouse.

Data marts derive their power to satisfy business needs from one very simple fact—they are always targeted at a known business problem, making it easier to align the system. When building an enterprisewide centralized warehouse, compromises are always necessary to enable the warehouse to address the larger expanse of business issues, which makes the fit between the individual departments' requirements and the technology less than perfect. Even in the case of a distributed data warehouse, the component parts started life as stand-alone data marts that provided solutions to some critical business issues. It was only after the individual data marts were networked together that any "holes" were filled to fashion them into an enterprise data warehouse. Distributed systems are not riddled with compromises like their centralized peers are.

Once a data warehouse or data mart has satisfied a user need, it cannot remain static—it must continue to satisfy the demands of the users throughout its lifecycle. Business goals and user needs do not remain constant over time, and neither should the warehouse. Through changing market conditions, altered financial circumstances, reorganizations, mergers, and takeovers, the warehouse must continue to deliver its benefits to the user community. The smaller, simpler data marts tend to be easier to modify to meet changing business circumstances.

Often, the need for change comes not from business pressures but from the users themselves as they gain experience. As users become more familiar with the capabilities of the technology, they begin to demand new reporting formats, enhanced features (e.g., drill-down capabilities), and new relationships that were not a part of the original data model. In a smaller data mart environment, the impact of enhancing functionality is not as severe as in a centralized data warehouse environment.

The compartmentalized structure of the distributed data warehouse provides another advantage to the users. Each data mart within the distributed warehouse has its own data model, and these simpler data models tend to be more user-friendly than the gigantic enterprise model generated for a centralized data warehouse. Since users tend to be relatively unsophisticated about modeling technology, they find navigation of the smaller models more straightforward.

Users who have trouble understanding the schema of a large data warehouse are prone to making errors in structuring queries and even in interpreting their results. Since mission-critical decisions may be made on interpreted results, the case can be readily made that simpler schema, which are easier for users to understand and make for better interpretation of the resultant queries, lead to better business decisions.

Finally, today's leaner organizations have little place for a centralized warehouse costing millions of dollars and hundreds of thousands of worker-hours. More and more management direction is toward decentralization and user empowerment. Decision making is moving down the corporate ladder, to the users whose departments are directly involved in specific issues. Application-specific data marts facilitate this management model by making access to decision-support systems available to those users most directly involved in the decision-making process.

And it cannot be forgotten that data marts are much faster to implement than their centralized counterparts. A standard data mart can be assembled from beginning design through implementation in an average of six months; many data marts are functional, at least in part, in as little as twelve weeks. This rapid development cycle endears the data mart to its users, who have little patience for waiting years to see results. Best of all from the user perspective, the department does not surrender control of its data. While this means that users must carry the burden of ensuring data accuracy and timeliness, it also means that the data remains under their direct control. This resolves one of the nastier political issues that plague the centralized warehouse.

All in all, data marts are better suited to the fast-paced corporate environment of the twenty-first century. They are quickly and easily installed, less expensive to maintain, and directly address critical business issues providing for a fast payback on investment. When they can be networked into a distributed data warehouse, the entire enterprise benefits from the enhanced view of corporate data the distributed system provides. Data marts provide decision makers with the information they need now, with better response times and more customized features, at a reduced cost. It is little wonder that data marts are rapidly replacing centralized warehouses as the decision-support tool of choice.

7

Object Technologies

Corporations today are under assault on all sides—from a rapidly shifting business environment, global competition, an increasingly fragmented marketplace, and technological advances. A company must be constantly reengineering itself to keep pace. When it needs to implement a data warehouse or any large system, it must cope with these business issues while still effectively managing the application—not an easy task. In particular, the current business climate puts pressure on an organization to speed up the development cycle to keep pace with constantly changing requirements. The data warehouse that meets these business challenges head-on and provides timely decision support will thrive in the new millennium; if it takes too long to produce results or cannot adapt quickly enough, a data warehouse will fail.

As with most major endeavors, the task of "business reengineering" to meet today's challenges is increasing in complexity. The objective of any redesign is to bring order out of chaos while taming the complexity of the situation. This requires different approaches to problem solving and new ways of thinking about business processes and their relationship to the corporate information infrastructure.

Business processes must be designed to accommodate constant change, and as the processes change, the underlying information systems must adapt, too. Rapid response to shifting business needs requires that both business processes and their related IT systems be modeled together and evolve together. This is true of all applications to some degree, and data warehouses are more sensitive to change than most. One of the best approaches currently available for dealing with business process/data process evolution is a collection of methodologies and software products jointly referred to as object-oriented technology.

Object-Oriented Technologies

Object-oriented technology is based on simulation and modeling. Instead of deploying the traditional applications development life cycle to resolve a problem, models of the business (or business area) are constructed. These models are in turn shared by many individual applications. The model itself must be designed to change so it can always reflect any alterations in the business it represents. In fact, the business model is often used to simulate proposed process changes.

The term *object orientation*—meaning a way of thinking and problem solving—applies to a broad spectrum of disciplines and technology tools. Areas as diverse as operating systems and design methodologies, programming languages and databases, and development tools and code-libraries all have a place in the object-oriented world. But the object world is inhabited by more than just technological tools; there is a place in it for business concepts and processes also. The business community thinks in terms of people, places, things, and events, all of which are object-oriented. Examples of business objects include:

- People and the roles they play (e.g., salesperson, stockbroker)
- Places (e.g., office, NY Stock Exchange)
- Things (e.g., securities, municipal bonds)
- Events (e.g., stock trade, bond placement)

An object contains both data and logic in a single package, consisting of its own private information (data), its own procedures (private methods) that manipulate the object's private data, and a public interface (public methods) for communicating with other objects. Objects provide properties representing a coherent concept and a set of operations to manage these properties. This fusion of process logic with data is the distinguishing characteristic of an object.

Each object is capable of acting in much the same way as the real object it represents behaves in the real world. Objects are assigned roles and responsibilities, and they contain all of the information they need to carry out their activities. However, the only way to use an object is to send it a message requesting that a service be performed. The receiving object acts on the message and sends the results back as a message to the requesting object.

While it seems simple, this "action by messaging" has profound data processing implications. Sending a message to an object resembles a traditional function call. However, the difference lies in the fact that the rest of the system does not see how the object is implemented; if the object's internal implementation (i.e., code) is changed for some reason, there can be no integration problems with the rest of the system. This forces the programmers to program without assumptions. Functionality is well defined, and programmers cannot assume they know how potentially shared routines or systems work on an internal level, which has often led to needlessly complex code or, worse, incorrect code that is almost impossible to debug.

In addition, object orientation is inherently modular. The practice of building larger components from smaller ones is known as chunking. This approach to modularity results in object-based systems being very granular, formed of many simple components that can be reused in other systems. This reusability is the key to many of the benefits of object technology—productivity, quality and consistency. Another important benefit is that modifications tend to be local to a single object, making maintenance simpler and less costly.

While the business definition of objects is useful for a general understanding, a more complete definition is required to make them technologically useful. The foundation of objects encompasses three general principles:

- Polymorphism
- Inheritance
- Encapsulation

Polymorphism is the concept that two or more objects can respond to the same request in different ways. This allows developers to use the same name for similar kinds of functions. Rather than create unique names such as tradeMuni, tradeFannie, tradeFreddie, or tradeFarmer, a single method named "trade" may be used. The polymorphism mechanism of the receiving class, depending on the kind of object sending the message, will implement the appropriate method such as "trade a municipal bond."

The concept of class brings order to the world of objects. Classes function like templates and are used to define the data and methods of similar types of objects. An object created as a part of a class is referred to as an instance, to distinguish it from the mold (i.e., the class). Object-oriented programming languages and design methods both use classes as a means of sharing common characteristics among objects.

Inheritance is the process of creating a definition by the incremental modification of other definitions. For example, a new class of objects can be defined using the rule of inheritance by naming another similar class of objects and only describing the difference. For example: Class A Stock is defined as representing 1/1,000,000 share of corporate assets, being purchasable directly from a corporation in lots of any size using a dividend reinvestment plan, being listed on the AMEX and London Exchange, declaring dividends on the tenth business day of each physical quarter, and entitling owner to one vote per share; and Class B Stock is the same as Class A except it entitles owner to ten votes per share. This not only saves a lot of time but also provides the developer with two other advantages: First, inheritance introduces support for code reuse at a language level. If the developer needs to change the way several classes of objects perform a certain task, she makes the change in only one place. The modified behavior is applied to each of the related classes via inheritance. Second, inheritance reduces redundancy. By making it very easy to reuse existing code, inheritance discourages writing unnecessary duplicate code.

Most of the data and many of the descriptions of operations reside within the objects themselves in an object-oriented system. This hiding of internal information within objects is called encapsulation. To use an object, the developer needs only to be aware of what services or operations it offers (i.e., which messages the object will respond to).

Object-oriented systems are always constructed in a modular fashion. Each object (module) is engaged only through its defined interface (messages). Objects are never interdependent at the level of their internal code or structure. The advantage of encapsulation is that the internal structure of an object can change, being improved or extended, without having to change the way the object is used by the rest of the system. The overall result is that changes tend to be local to an object, making maintenance simpler.

As additional object-oriented systems are implemented, more reusable components become available so that finally, programming becomes more a matter of assembly rather than one of coding. Once the object-oriented infrastructure matures, programming is confined to exception programming based on modifications of existing objects. These assembly and exception concepts are supported by graphical programming environments where objects are just wired together to create applications.

As discussed previously, objects can be thought of as individuals, each having specialized knowledge (attributes) and special skills (methods), some of which they get from their ancestors (inheritance). Much like a society, the individuals are able to work together to perform complex tasks by communicating with each other (messages). Different individuals may react differently to the same request, but their response is always in keeping with the intent of the request (polymorphism).

In brief, objects encapsulate their knowledge and behavior, inherit common functionality, communicate entirely by messages, and respond appropriately based on their individual capabilities when messaged by other objects. Although the various object-oriented languages support these features to varying degrees, the essentials of the technology are always the same.

Object technology can bring four advantages to computing:

- The quantity of "new code" required to develop an application is limited, and the total amount of code needed to support the business is significantly reduced.
- The time needed to develop code is reduced, and the quality of the code improves.
- The applications behave in a consistent fashion since they reuse the same objects.
- The overall quality of the information systems improves.

However, to achieve the best results, object-oriented technology must include more than just a programming methodology. Objects in the real world involve all kinds of arrangements of data, many of which are hierarchical in nature. Object-oriented systems accommodate and, many people believe, simplify the management and manipulation of such hierarchical data objects. When these complex structures are stored using a two-dimensional system, such as a relational database, the programmer is forced to recompose the data when he retrieves it and to decompose it to store the data.

Object databases (ODB) are emerging as a means of storage for hierarchical arrangements of data. These databases store and manage data in the same basic way a program does—as objects. In contrast, relational systems store data in two-dimensional tables where each item exists as a row within the table. Complex data items are achieved by joining rows from different tables based on a construct such as a foreign key that facilitates reconstruction.

Proponents of ODBs stress the three advantages of the methodology:

- There is no difference between the data in memory and the data stored in the database. Composition and decomposition programming are not required, and an object database management system (ODBMS) needs no data manipulation language as a result.

- Because the data is stored maintaining hierarchical relationships, data retrieval is often much faster in an ODBMS than in a more conventional system.

- The encapsulated models produced in the design phase are the same as the database models. During the life cycle of a traditional system, the design model is different from the programming model, which in turn is different from the database model. The use of an ODB can eliminate these redesign steps.

The strategic reason for implementing an ODBMS is the ability to create an information management system that more closely mimics real life. The most advanced of the object databases now have the capacity to query the processes of objects as well as the data. This means a business user, say, a stockbroker, could query the database for her clients' expiring stock options without knowing the business rules for "expiring options" or having to structure those rules in the query language.

By supporting this sort of object process query capability, an ODB opens the door to even more "detail hiding" within objects. In this environment, business methods and rule changes need not disrupt existing applications or queries. This extended capability helps ensure the consistency and integrity of information presented by all queries, programs, and reports across the system.

If properly implemented, object-oriented technologies can be of great benefit. However, improper or incongruous usage can result in a disaster. Incorrectly defined objects behave in an erratic fashion and their inconsistencies can be passed along through inheritance to a class, or even several classes of objects, complicating the debugging process. Poorly trained and/or careless programmers seem to regard the principles of reuse as a joke as they create new, duplicate objects at every turn. They, however, seem to be often tempted to try to reuse "objects" that should never have existed. Rather than simplifying programming, objects proliferate at an astounding rate, with every programmer owning his own "set" of personal objects that are incomprehensible to everyone else.

The area of object databases opens a whole new realm of potential misuse where the inexperienced and confused can create data structures that yield wrong answers. In most object-oriented environments, there are no data specialists, and the databases are designed and created by the programming staff. When a programmer needs a certain bit of data he creates the appropriate object, often without checking to see if that information is already available as an object and usually without much thought for reuse. At best, this system results in programmers having individual data stores, which they reuse; at worse, everything is re-created from scratch each time it is needed. The lack of a data manipulation language sometimes encourages programmers to create objects to encompass data that is already available in the system as two or more objects. All of this can lead to such multiplication of objects that no one is able to find and reuse anything.

Still, object databases are the best candidate available for the next generation of database management products. However, relational technologies also offer continuing advantages, especially to corporations with a heavy investment in them, or for the storage of certain types of data, and the technology continues to evolve (see the section on "Extended Relational Database Management Systems" later in this chapter). These two models will coexist for years to come, hopefully blending the best of both into a better system. Relational data structures can be used now within object databases, and bridges to existing relational databases, called wrappers, can play an important role in preserving existing assets while incrementally migrating to objects.

Distributed Object Computing

The data warehouse of the future will need to be spread across multiple, and sometimes specialized, hardware that will cooperate within the distributed system and with outside sources, such as legacy systems and Internet correspondents. To meet the demands of business, the warehouses built today and tomorrow must be constructed to take advantage of the available distributed technologies and paradigms, including distributed object computing.

Ideally, these new warehouses will place the focus on the computer system correctly conveying information in a form that humans can process naturally. The information should reflect reality as perceived by people and not the artificial constructs of transactions, tables, and spreadsheets. Long relegated to the sidelines, cognitive science can finally step onto the playing field and assume a central role in a new era of information processing. Systems rooted in human cognition can enable instant use (no training required), correct assimilation, confirmation of user intentions, and relatively error-free communication between man and machine. Such systems are demanded within the business community and can, with proper planning, be delivered by the new warehouse.

Most of today's development tools and techniques suffer from a number of problems—application scalability, modularity, granularity, and maintainability. They have brought technology to its current position, but are unlikely to advance things much beyond this point because they add no new value in terms of timely and cost-effective development. But the issues limiting systems development today are not just technical. In the rush to develop faster and better technology, business concepts have been pushed aside, struggling along as the indentured servants of a high-performance infrastructure. Client/server technology is a case in point; it continues to evolve technically but by itself does not supply a uniform cognitive model for sharing information among systems and people.

There are other limitations of current client/server implementations that promise to make them tomorrow's legacy systems. Even as tiers are added to decouple business logic, user presentations, network operations, and database processing, the fundamental design method remains centered on user screens and forms. Screen-based designs do not promote reuse, nor do they support workflow processes or other applications that grow out of business reengineering. Conspicuously missing from most client/server systems are the key abstractions of the business and any real concern for the data system/ people interface. This is where object-oriented technologies can add significant value to current client/server models. The blending of the cognitive and semantic integrity of objects with the distribution potential of client/server architecture holds great promise for meeting the challenge of enterprise computing.

Distributed object computing (DOC) is a breakthrough framework for computing in tomorrow's business environment. It is the natural product of the synthesis of object-oriented and client/server technologies. When radio and motion picture technologies converged, something completely new happened—television pervaded and fundamentally changed society. TV combined the distributed advantages of radio with the richness of the real-world view of motion pictures. The result was far more than the sum of the two technologies.

Distributed object computing blends the distribution of client/ server with the richness of real-world information contained in object-oriented models. Distributed object computing has the potential to fundamentally change the information landscape—in fact, new things have already begun to happen. Case in point: The way business software is developed has already changed forever.

DOC is a computing paradigm that allows the objects to be distributed across a heterogeneous network with each of the components interoperable to form a unified whole. To a distributed data warehouse constructed in a distributed object environment, the network is the computer. There are still the familiar problems of data placement and concurrency control to manage, but the issues of data location and message routing disappear. Objects interact by passing messages to each other representing requests for information or services. During any given interaction, objects can dynamically assume the roles of clients and server as needed.

The physical glue that binds the distributed objects together is an object request broker (ORB). It provides the means for objects to locate and activate other objects in a network, regardless of the processor or programming language used to develop either the client or server objects. The ORB makes these things happen transparently.

It is the middleware of distributed object computing that facilitates interoperability in heterogeneous networks of objects, freeing the developer to concentrate on the business objects themselves and the services they provide.

Although universal clients and servers live in their own dynamic world outside the application, the objects appear as if they were local to the application because the network functions as the computer. The whole concept of distributed object computing can be viewed as a global network of heterogeneous clients and servers or, more precisely, cooperative business objects. Even legacy systems can participate in a distributed object network. They can be wrapped so that they appear to the developer as just another set of objects to be used as needed.

Most corporations have a significant investment in computer systems that were developed prior to the advent of object-oriented technology, so a solid business case probably cannot be made for converting these legacy assets to the new technology in the near future. However, a strong business case can be made for a staged approach to change, with all new development based on object-oriented technology that leverages the existing systems. Wrappers will allow a business to enjoy the benefits of the new technology while extending the life of expensive legacy systems for several years.

Several different approaches can be taken to wrapping the legacy systems, from simple screen scraping to direct function calls to existing code. The approach used depends on what kind of legacy application is to be wrapped: A mainframe COBOL application, an EXCEL spreadsheet, or a relational database in an existing client/server application all require different approaches. Regardless of the means used, the result is that the existing assets can become full participants in the newly developed distributed object applications.

In brief, distributed object computing is an enhancement of client/server technology, but there is a difference in its working process and its implementation. With client/server, there is normally an application running on the server while another runs on the client. These two applications communicate across a network and relay data to one another, usually by way of some middleware in the form of an Application Program Interface (API) or function call library.

A distributed application is made up of objects, just like any other object-oriented application. However, the objects in a distributed object application may reside scattered throughout the network. Distributed object computing is not magic; it is a very complex computing environment and requires a highly sophisticated and robust technology infrastructure with well-trained developers and programmers to make it work.

The change to distributed object-oriented technology can have a profound impact on both the computing environment and on the business that it supports. Object orientation can radically simplify applications development, and distributed object models and tools extend the benefits across multiple systems. With this type of distributed computing, the objects may be physically located on different computers throughout a network and yet appear as though they are local within an application. But this is not the only computing advantage derived from a distributed object environment. There are several others:

• *Legacy assets can be leveraged.* Object wrappers can be applied to various computing resources throughout the network to simplify communications with these resources. All communications between objects, including distributed objects, occur as messages. This eliminates the need for applying different middleware and network interfaces for each legacy system. In this way, today's legacy systems are able to become full partners with tomorrow's new development, preserving the massive investment and the associated intellectual capital invested in these systems.

• *Objects can reside on the networked computer best suited to their function and usage pattern.* As discussed in Chapter 3, data placement is one of the primary challenges all distributed systems must face. A distributed object environment gives the architect more freedom to choose where an object should reside. This environment does not negate the rules for data placement, but it reduces the penalty for incorrect choices.

• *The addition of new hardware, and even its complete replacement, is transparent to the user.* Because objects appear to be local to their clients, a client does not know what machine, or even what kind of machine, an object resides on. As a result, migration of implemented objects from platform to platform is made much easier. The migration can be accomplished in steps without affecting the clients.

- *Systems integration can be performed to a higher degree.* The goal of creating a single system image can be achieved as applications are assembled from objects resident on disparate platforms.

The overall technical goal of distributed object computing is simple: to advance client/server technology so that it is easier to use, more efficient, and more flexible. The benefits listed previously are the solutions to many of the problems with the existing client/server paradigm.

The effects of a distributed object environment are not limited to changes in the computing environment alone—when combined with the use of business objects, it may represent the next generation of business computing. Although the ultimate next-generation methods and tools are still in development in the laboratory, sufficient standards and resources are already in place for those with the foresight and risk-taking spirit to begin developing systems now.

Distributed object technology will create a new generation of client/server systems. Objects encapsulate data and business logic into one neat package that can be located anywhere within a distributed network. Users do not need to know where the objects are stored or in what language they are written to utilize them. This makes distributed object technology a perfect fit with Internet/intranet technology—an object may reside on the user's own desktop computer, on the corporate intranet host, or on a web server located halfway around the world.

ORB Architecture

The object request broker (ORB) manages interaction between clients and servers. This includes the distributed computing responsibilities of location, referencing of parameters, and results. An ORB functions within a common object request broker architecture (CORBA) where its interfaces and services are rigidly defined but, as with all architectures, no implementation details are specified. ORBs are modular components, so different implementations can be used to satisfy the needs of different platforms.

CORBA specifies a system that provides interoperability between objects in a heterogeneous distributed environment, and it does so in a way transparent to the programmer. The object-oriented vendors are currently offering quite a variety of products that, taken together, provide excellent capabilities yet have somewhat differing goals. By choosing carefully, it is possible to assemble the best infrastructure and tools that comply with published standards and offer maximum performance and manageability.

The client-side architecture mandated by CORBA provides clients with an interface to the ORB and objects. It consists of the following elements:

- The *dynamic invocation interface* that allows for the specification of requests at runtime. This is necessary when the object interface is not known at runtime. Dynamic invocation works in conjunction with the interface repository.

- The *interface definition language (IDL)* stub of functions generated by the IDL interface definitions and linked into the program(s). The functions are actually a mapping between the client and the ORB implementation. In this manner, ORB capabilities are made available to any client for which there is a language mapping.

- The *ORB interface* may be called by either the client or the object implementation. It makes available the functions of the ORB that may be directly accessed. All ORBs must support the ORB interface.

- The *ORB core* is the underlying mechanism used as the transport level. It provides basic communication of requests to other subcomponents.

- The *object definition language (ODL) skeleton interface* is called by the ORB to invoke the methods requested from clients.

- The *object adapter (OA)* provides the means by which object implementations access most ORB services. This includes the generation and interpretation of object references, method invocation, security, and activation. The object adapter actually exports three different interfaces: a private interface to the skeletons, an interface to the ORB core, and a public interface used by implementations.

In summary, ORB manages the interactions between clients and object implementations, where clients issue requests and invoke methods of object implementations.

Standards

Along with the increasing number of distributed computing environments has come a wider variety of tools and technologies especially designed to assist developers in that area. Many developers are competing to provide the infrastructure for distributing large-scale applications, the foundation of the emerging network economy. Some of these technologies come from standards activities and others from hardware and software vendors.

Each technology, including Java, ActiveX, HTTP/HTML, CORBA, and DCOM (Distributed Component Object Model), offers its own unique possibilities for enhancing development productivity or providing an enhanced capability to the user. But as an applications developer commits to using a specific tool or technology, that commitment may limit the developer's ability to retarget or adapt the core capabilities of the system, which limits the ability to respond to change.

Every tool, API, and even distribution technology chosen represents a significant investment in software, hardware, training, and operation infrastructure. Ideally, the developer wants to leverage the best of each with relatively little compromise. For example, a developer might want to write a web-based data warehouse application that is to perform in a three-tier environment with a PC running Microsoft Windows for the client, an NT or UNIX middle-tier containing the organization's business logic, and a mainframe using DB2 with a CICS front-end on the third tier (see Figure 7-1).

Internet Inter-Orb Protocol (IIOP), sanctioned by the Object Management Group (OMG) standards organization, could be used as the infrastructure. These specifications are used worldwide to develop and deploy applications for many different types of businesses. By choosing IIOP, the developer has opted for excellent products and positioned the organization to be responsive to future changes.

ORBs are another OMG-approved approach that, when selected as the middleware, allow companies to build scalable, reusable software that can change as the business changes. The features and benefits of object technology in general have attracted the attention of business leaders as well as corporate technologists, who have long searched for a technology that allows a business to write software once and use all or part of it over again in a different application.

Figure 7-1. Example of three-tier architecture.

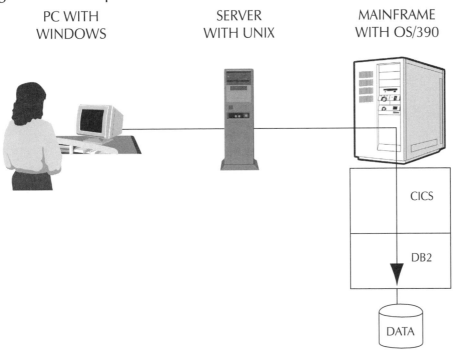

Object request broker technology is used to build three-tier applications, update enterprise code, and create web-based information systems. It provides a means for interoperability between various types of object-oriented software. As middleware in a distributed computing environment, ORBs enable objects to locate and activate other objects across a network, regardless of processor type or programming language used to develop and implement the objects. Like other kinds of middleware, ORBs are part of the "plumbing" in a distributed client/server environment. They work behind the scenes, facilitating communications between distributed objects.

IIOP and ORBs are both standards-activities-driven technologies. An example of a vendor-driven technology is the Distributed Component Object Model. DCOM has evolved over the last decade from the following Microsoft technologies:

- Dynamic Data Exchange (DDE), a form of messaging between Windows programs
- Object Linking and Embedding (OLE), a way of embedding visual links between programs within the same application

- Component Object Model (COM), used as the basis of all object binding
- ActiveX, COM-enabled technology for the Internet

In a distributed environment, DCOM extends COM to support communications between objects regardless of their physical location. Microsoft's starting premise is that communication between objects located on different physical machines is virtually the same as interprocess communications between objects that reside on the same computer.

DCOM is competitive to CORBA. Even though CORBA has a significant head start, Microsoft has an extremely large installed base and considerable marketing muscle, and so the two technologies will probably both thrive and eventually interoperate. However, the two distributed object models are quite different and may never be fully compatible. Those writing component software will likely have to choose between the two models, at least for now, unless the enterprise can afford to support both.

Data Warehouses and Object Technologies

Data warehouses, regardless of their physical implementation, involve extracting data from operational systems and transforming, integrating, and summarizing it into one or more database systems residing on one or more dedicated servers, often web-enabled. Typically part of a client/server architecture, the data warehouse server(s) may be connected to application servers that improve the performance of query and analysis tools running on desktop systems (see Figure 7-2).

Successful implementation of a web-enabled data warehouse, and especially a distributed data warehouse, requires high performance and a scalable combination of hardware and software that can integrate easily with existing systems. Object technologies fit nicely into this architecture, benefiting both developer and user.

The combination of the Internet/intranet with CORBA and DCOM offers great promise and flexibility to developers, as well as a clear path to widespread deployment for distributed object vendors. As with any combination of technologies, there are some rough edges

Figure 7-2. Client/server architecture with application and data warehouse servers.

PC WITH   APPLICATION SERVER   DATA WAREHOUSE
WINDOWS   ON UNIX   SERVER
                                          ON UNIX

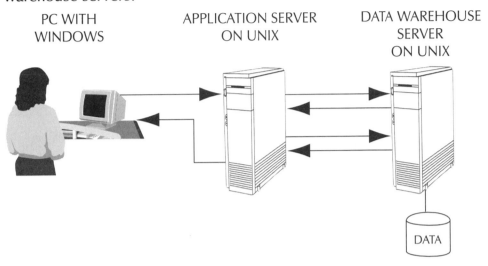

that still need work. One of the most important is how best to retrieve both an object's state and its methods in a seamless fashion. For the present, it is up to the developer to standardize the underlying framework offered by CORBA or DCOM. Despite its shortcomings, this technology deserves serious consideration for any organization embarking on a distributed data warehouse.

Extended Relational Database Management Systems

It seems very unlikely that object-oriented database management systems will replace relational technology in all application areas. RDBMS and SQL are now an accepted industry database standard, and many organizations have invested a lot in the technology through its use in complex applications, especially data warehouses. Moreover, for many organizations, the relational approach is perfectly satisfactory. They have no need of complex objects, long-lived transactions, or abstract data types, so they have no incentive to change. The most likely course for the foreseeable future is for object-oriented and relational to coexist in the marketplace.

Relational technology will not stand still, either—it will continue to evolve and improve over time. Improvements in the technology will extend the relational model to overcome some of its present shortcomings. In particular, there are three areas that extended RDBMSs must address:

- It must support complex objects (including text, graphics, and images) and rules (not just relational integrity), in addition to the standard data management functions.
- It must provide all the capabilities of regular RDBMSs, including data independence and nonprocedural access through query languages such as SQL.
- It must be open to other subsystems (this is especially important for relational use as part of a distributed heterogeneous system).

There is an agreement between the proponents of object-oriented databases and the Committee for Advanced DBMS Function that extended relational databases will include support for object-oriented concepts such as objects, functions (i.e., database procedures and methods), inheritance, and encapsulation. There is also a good deal of work being done with SQL to enable it to support objects. The first of the extended RDBMSs with improved SQL should be available in mid year 2001.

It is obvious that relational technology has taken the first step toward accommodating the rival object-oriented systems. It is up to object technology to take the next step toward improved intersystem communications.

In Brief

Client/server technology, distributed systems, and the Internet/intranet have greatly improved companies' abilities to organize and access historical data. Data warehouses that take advantage of these newer technologies provide many improvements over traditional decision-support systems, including easier and faster data access and analysis.

One of the benefits of object orientation in distributed data warehousing is to provide interoperability among the various CORBA-based distributed object systems forming the warehouse, and between the warehouse and the World Wide Web. The key elements of the design are the representation of HTTP in IDL and the gateways that translate between HTTP and the IIOP encoding of the interfaces. The gateways allow HTTP to be carried over IIOP and provide full interoperability between the Web and CORBA clients and servers.

Object technology can be used to provide interoperability between diverse systems, such as legacy systems or web-based databases and the data warehouse. IIOP can be seamlessly integrated into the web by means of servers and proxies. Even the traditional centralized data warehouse can enjoy some of the benefits of distributed object technology and the WWW, such as ease of programming, extensibility, manageability, encapsulation, and systems integration. Distributed object technology will help the data warehouse to evolve into the information environment demanded by its users.

The biggest distributed system ever built, the World Wide Web, is now testing distributed object technology. The results are frankly mixed, more because of a lack of adherence to standards than any flaw in the object paradigm. Object technologies can be a very powerful and useful tool, especially in a distributed environment, when used properly. A sloppy or careless implementation will only lead to disaster.

8

Security Issues for the Distributed Data Warehouse

Everyone knows at least a little something about security on the World Wide Web. Every day, thousands of people buy goods on the Internet using their credit cards, without making a phone call to the vendor or faxing instructions. Millions more use the Web for electronic banking and the buying and selling of stocks. Why do all these people trust the Web?

The Internet operates much like a postal service, only at lightning speed, sorting and routing mail through various "post offices" in seconds. As good as the Web is at message handling, it is inherently terrible at security because of the way it is designed and implemented. These web security issues can be broken into three areas. First, anyone and everyone can be a "postmaster" on the Web, and there is no built-in security to keep the postmaster from reading, copying, and even altering the mail as it passes through that post office. Another drawback is that unlike the post office, there are no such things as registered letters requiring signatures and return receipts. As a result, correct delivery cannot be confirmed.

The third, and most daunting security problem for the Internet, is the architecture of the Internet itself; it was conceived and built to be an open system. Any computer can read a message that is just "passing through" (Figure 8-1). When a user surfs to a URL or submits a message to a server, that information passes through anywhere from one to hundreds of computers on its way to its destination.

However, a secure business environment using the Web can be achieved. There are four features required for security:

Figure 8-1. "Just passing through."

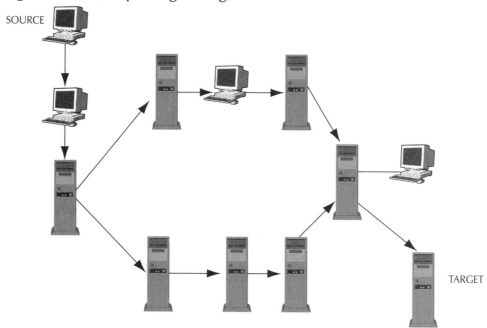

SOURCE

TARGET

- Authenticity
- Confidentiality
- Integrity
- Accountability

All four of these features are possible in today's web environment through the use of data cryptography and the implementation of special data handling protocols in both web client and web server programs. This is why millions of people feel secure enough to transact personal business over the Internet.

The most familiar example of such an environment would be using a browser to send a credit card number to some cryptographically enabled web server, say, at a fictional company such as BUYABOOK.com. When the browser sets up "secure" communication with the web server, it opens an SSL (Secure Sockets Layer) connection to the server using public key cryptography. As part of the process of making the connection, the browser and the server can exchange digital certificates that have been digitally signed with each computer's public key. This exchange authenticates the two computers to each other. The server has a good idea exactly who is initiating the order, and the person placing the order can be relatively confident that she is going to give her credit card number to BUYABOOK, not some nefarious individual like the reincarnation of Edward Teach at blackbeard.com.

After the browser and server have authenticated each other, they negotiate an encryption methodology for use during the rest of their secure interaction. This encryption provides confidentiality, preventing some snooper from casually eavesdropping on the exchange of credit card numbers.

As an added level of security, both programs (browser and server) include a separately encrypted hash count with each message sent between them. This hash count is generated by a special algorithm applied by the sending program to the entire message. The receiving program can then use this count to ensure message integrity. That is, upon receipt, the receiver can verify both that it received the entire message and that the message it received was not altered during transmission. Finally, the browser and the server can exchange "digitally signed" electronic receipts in order to provide accountability (or nonrepudiation) for the completed transaction.

This method works well for the World Wide Web, but just how does security, especially web security, apply to a data warehousing project? A web-enabled distributed data warehouse implementation requires security over the connecting networks, either the Internet or an intranet, as well as the normal data security and authorization. However, many people dispute whether this is possible—in fact, they argue that it is impossible to make any network completely secure. This distrust arises from the origins of network construction. Networks were created to cure data isolation in the early days of computing—the antithesis of a security environment. Data "owned" by one computer could not be accessed by anyone outside its immediate environment until networks were established as communications bridges. No thought was given to security; if a company did not want to share its data, it just remained isolated. Intersystem communications have changed a great deal in the past forty years, as has the need for network security.

This in no way implies that network security is unnecessary or that management should ignore it and adopt an "isolationist" policy—quite the contrary. The explosion of information access across networks, intranets, and the Internet has raised both the enterprise's need for information and the specter of corporate espionage to new levels. Businesses today know that information truly is power, and those companies that control their information appropriately gain a competitive advantage.

Key Concepts of Security Planning

Any security plan for a distributed data warehouse must first identify vulnerabilities and threats, then anticipate attacks and assess the chance of their succeeding and the amount of damage they might cause, and finally implement countermeasures against those attacks considered serious enough to counter. In detail, the key concepts in warehouse security are:

- *Vulnerability.* Defined as a susceptibility to risk, vulnerability is a potential weakness. A vulnerability in and of itself may not pose a serious threat, depending on what tools are available to exploit that weakness.

- *Threat.* An action or tool that can expose or exploit a vulnerability is a threat that compromises the integrity of a system. Not all threats are equal in terms of the damage they might do. For example, some viruses can do a lot of damage while others are merely annoying.

- *Attack.* An attack defines the details of how a threat can exploit a vulnerability. An example is a Trojan horse attack, where a virus is packaged within a desirable object, such as free downloadable software. The vulnerability is the user's desire to have the free software; the threat is the embedded virus; and the attack is, of course, the activated virus.

- *Countermeasures.* These are the actions taken to protect systems from attacks. Countermeasures might include a program for virus detection and cleansing, packet filtering, password authentication, and encryption. Countermeasures are essential ingredients of a data warehouse.

These four concepts are all about risk; security itself is all about the identification and management of risk. Security is a very relative term and must be tailored to meet the needs of the individual data warehouse.

For example, a Trojan horse attack could succeed at a company, destroying very valuable data. The same attack on a different business, although activated in precisely the same way, would only cause minimal damage because no sensitive data was stored on the infected system. Each of these organizations should employ their own unique security strategies with different countermeasures tailored to their specific situations.

Management must consider all four factors in shaping a security strategy and should also understand the costs of defending against all possible attacks. Security measures always cost money and/or system performance. Each business must determine for itself the costs of specific countermeasures and balance that against what it is willing to spend to protect its data. Only then can an organization determine which of the spectrum of possible attacks it will defend against and which should be ignored; this decision is the starting point in formulating a security strategy.

Malicious Programs

The major threats facing companies today can be divided roughly into three categories: the introduction of a malicious program into the system, snooping, and physical theft of data. For the first—introduction of a malevolent program into one or more components of the network—the term *virus* is widely used to cover a host of harmful attacks. Some specific attacks are the following:

• *Trojan Horse.* As mentioned earlier, a Trojan horse is a program that conceals harmful code. It is usually hidden in an attractive or useful program, luring the unwary user to execute it, thus giving the program a chance to damage the system. Many Trojan horse programs lay waste to the operating system or data files, but there are others whose chief mission is espionage on behalf of the sender. For example, stealing the password file from the computer it has invaded and e-mailing it to another location is a fairly common strategy.

• *Logic Bomb.* This is a program that checks for certain conditions and then, when those criteria are fulfilled, it starts to do its damage. Like the Trojan horse, these programs are often paired with an attractive host, which the user downloads to his system. An intruder or even a disgruntled employee can implant a naked logic bomb in a system. Once in place, the logic bomb "hides," waiting its chance. Sometimes the trigger is a date, but it can be almost any event or parameter, such as a name or account number, or a combination of parameters.

- *Worm.* A worm is a self-contained program that replicates itself across the network, thus multiplying its damage by infecting many different nodes. It usually enters a network by piggybacking on another program or file and spreads across the network in the same fashion.

- *Virus.* A virus is a bit of code, not an entire program, that plants versions of itself in any program it can modify. A good example from a few years ago was the rampant Microsoft Concept virus. Once a system using Microsoft WORD was infected, all documents opened by the user became infected too and could only be saved as "template" files. In all other regards, WORD continued to function normally. Though it was not an especially destructive virus, it was certainly very annoying.

These threats are not mutually exclusive. A Trojan horse might also deliver a worm, or a logic bomb could plant a virus. Additionally, each of the threats could have different or multiple missions, such as theft of data, the compromising of data integrity, or the disruption of computer service to the organization.

Snooping

The second major threat, snooping, involves the theft or compromise of data while in transit between endpoints of a network. In most cases, the attacker simply eavesdrops on the electronic communications, copying all or part of the network traffic. Because of the passive nature of the attack, it is nearly impossible to detect. Two variations of the snooping threat are:

- *Replay Attacks.* In a replay attack, the copy of a specific transmission is played back later, either in its original form or in an edited state, to serve the purposes of the snooper. Using this method, it would be possible to alter an individual's stock holdings (i.e., sell

1,000 shares of IBM instead of 100 shares), tamper with a bank account (i.e., send an electronic transfer to the snooper's account), discredit a user in the eyes of a service provider (thereby leading to the termination of service), or even flood a service provider with thousands of seemingly "legitimate" messages.

• *Man in the Middle.* Even worse is a variant known as the "man in the middle," where a transmission is intercepted in transit by the snooper and altered in real time. After passing on the changed message, the snooper waits for the response from the server and, in due course, captures, alters, and sends it along to the client. Both client and server believe they have successfully completed a transaction until later, when one or the other discovers the discrepancies.

Physical Theft of Data

The third and final major threat is decidedly low tech, but many of the methods used to accomplish it are very sophisticated. The physical theft of data is the oldest form of corporate espionage and is more prevalent today than ever. The difference is that thieves nowadays have the marvels of technology and miniaturization to help accomplish their goals. Client lists, corporate plans, product designs— almost anything of value—can be copied from the corporate data store to a diskette, portable ZIP drive, or backup tape and removed from the relative safety of corporate headquarters. There are no bulky blueprints, heavy computer printouts, or large reports to sneak past security, and there's no need for James Bond–style tiny cameras with which to photograph documents. Literally anyone, from the company CEO to the janitorial service, has the opportunity to try to breach the data store. Taken together, these three categories—malicious programs, snooping, and physical theft of data—represent the major threats to data warehouses today. Network managers must deal with these issues, and senior management needs to be aware of them, since they are the determining parameters for the types and costs of data warehouse security.

Given the variety and severity of the threats facing the distributed data warehouse, a reasonable question might be: What tools are available to help mitigate these security threats? The good news is that many technologies can be brought to bear that are impressively effective (Chapter 9 covers specific security technologies).

The bad news is that no amount of technology can compensate for a poorly planned, badly implemented, or nonexistent security policy. A good example of this is something that happened to the author recently. While she was waiting on line in the bank, a customer approached the Special Services window. He asked the teller to assist him in transferring funds from his money market account to his checking account. The teller, trying to be helpful but not knowing the password for the money market system, queried his co-worker, positioned three windows away. The second teller responded, in a loud and clear voice, with the appropriate information. Now the teller, the customer, the author, and everyone else on premises knew the password to the bank's money market system. This breach of security resulted from poor policy, not any technological failure.

The security of data in any business is primarily dependent on the quality of the security policy and the way in which the company imposes that policy internally. If the security policy is lax or not uniformly enforced, or has gaping holes in it, no amount of technology will help. Organizations concerned about security should consider the following points well before they install encryption, proxy servers, packet filters, and other expensive technological solutions:

- What kind of passwords are allowed? Do the users choose "obvious" passwords based on proper names, initials, or the application name (i.e., "moneymkt")?

- Are passwords changed frequently?

- Do employees keep their passwords written on a piece of paper and hidden under the mousepad or keyboard?

- Are the employees aware of the need for security? Is there a program in place to disseminate security procedures? Are the employees reminded periodically of the importance of security?

- Are there guidelines in place to help identify different levels of security for corporate data? Is there someone responsible for assigning a security level to important documents?

- Do employees understand that there are different levels of security, and what level applies to what data?

- Who is ultimately responsible for security? Is it someone in upper management, and are they really held responsible when something goes wrong?

- Is any action taken when there is a violation of security policy, or do the employees consider it a joke?

It is evident that any organization concerned about security must first get its own house in order. It needs to identify its security needs based on the type of information it handles and develop an appropriate security plan. Only then can a business begin to research what type of technological assistance it may need. Some steps in a good security plan are as follows:

1. Develop physical and procedural security, because they are just as important as technology to the overall plan.

2. Develop security requirements based on an understanding of the corporate mission, the type of data at risk, the threats to that data, and the implications of a successful attack.

3. Define different levels of security and develop appropriate security plans for each level.

4. Identify users who should access each level and grant them authorization based on those levels.

5. Define the mechanisms for security and appoint staff (usually the IT department) to administer those mechanisms.

A key tool in securing a distributed data warehouse is the ability to recognize and verify authorized users. This security feature is called authentication. Traditionally, Password Authentication Protocol (PAP) has been used, employing special names and passwords to authenticate the users, but this method is only as good as the users' ability to keep the name/password secret and protect it from use by unauthorized users. There are three newer, generally accepted techniques for improving the authentication process:

- *Authentication by Physical Device.* In this technique, the user is given a token, such as a card key or smart card, by the company for use during the authentication process.
- *Authentication by User Information.* This is a variation on PAP. Challenge Handshake Authentication Protocol (CHAP) takes the concept one step further by asking the user to answer a question (usually something personal that only the user would know). CHAP is fre-

quently used in combination with a smart card, which uses an encryption key to encode the response. Only if both code and response are correct is the user granted access.

- *Authentication by Physical Characteristic.* Here, there is a mechanism that recognizes some physical characteristic of the user that hopefully cannot be duplicated or faked. Biometrics technology identifies fingerprints, retinal scans, manual signatures, or voices to validate the potential user.

It is not just users who must be authenticated in a distributed data warehouse. Authentication is also necessary when two computers initiate communication. For example, what should the host computer do when another system, say, a desktop computer, sends a message asking for the company's "three-year plan"? How does it know that the computer requesting the data (forget about the user for a moment) has a legitimate reason to access that information and is not some external hacker trying to steal corporate data?

As seen, those managing distributed data warehouses must recognize the vulnerabilities and the threats facing them, and make plans to defend themselves from attacks with the appropriate countermeasures. Good security planning and implementation, taking care to emphasize the physical and procedural threats as well as the technological ones, are necessary to preserve warehouse integrity.

Network Security Issues

All of the security issues surrounding a modern data warehouse also apply to any network. There is no substitute for skillful security planning, implementation, and vigorous enforcement of the corporate security policies. There are, however, some security challenges peculiar to networks that must be addressed by any successful distributed data warehouse security team.

Repudiation

Networks commonly have a problem with repudiation, where the sender or receiver denies their involvement in a certain communication. For example, when a person sends a certified letter through the U.S. Postal Service, the recipient must sign a form to verify that she has the letter. That receipt is returned to the sender as proof of the transaction. This prevents the recipient from later claiming that she never received the correspondence and using that as an excuse. This issue relates to accountability, as mentioned at the start of this chapter.

In computer networks, this kind of service must also be available and is becoming increasingly important as commerce on the Internet becomes more common. There are two types of nonrepudiation services available in network messaging:

- Nonrepudiation of delivery service
- Nonrepudiation of submission service

Nonrepudiation of delivery service is very similar to the post office's certified letter. It provides the sender with proof that the computer message was successfully delivered to the intended recipient. Many e-mail packages offer senders the option to request a return receipt. This return receipt provides the sender with a nonrepudiation of delivery service—the recipients cannot legitimately claim they did not receive the message.

Nonrepudiation of submission service is similar to the delivery service. This service offers proof that a certain message did in fact originate with a specific user at a noted time. To go back to the postal example, when mailing legal documents or other important papers there are many times when it is considered prudent to send the package by registered mail. When doing so, the sender is given a time/date-stamped receipt with a unique number attached to both it and the parcel. In this way, if the recipient does not receive the package or contends that it was not sent in time, the sender has proof that it was mailed on a given date. Again, many e-mail packages offer a receipt service, providing verification of sender and time.

Nonrepudiation services are especially popular in conjunction with auction bidding on the World Wide Web. At various sites on the Internet, one-of-a-kind items are offered for sale without a fixed price, and offers-to-buy are restricted to a set timeframe. An antique pocket watch might be available from 7 a.m. to 7 p.m. on a certain day, with several hundred bids received during that period. The watch will be sold to the highest bidder and, in case of a duplicate high bid, it will go to the first person offering the accepted bid. The advantages of a nonrepudiation service to this application are obvious; proof of bid is extremely important to the successful bidder.

Integrity

Another important service is integrity. Integrity refers to the completeness and fidelity of the message as it travels through the network. The key is making sure that the data passes from source to destination without tampering. It might be impossible to stop someone from "tapping" or snooping (i.e., inspecting or copying) the message, but it is possible to detect attempts to alter a message and to reject it if any such modification attempt is perceived.

If the order of transmitted data is also ensured, the service is termed connection-oriented integrity. Anti-replay refers to a minimalist form of connection-oriented integrity whereby duplicate or very old data units are detected and rejected. TCP/IP, the communications protocol of the Internet, is a connection-oriented protocol, ensuring that the receiving application sees messages in the same order and format in which they were originally sent. SMTP, which is an e-mail transfer protocol, is an example of an IP service that does not make such guarantees to receiving applications. Proxy servers and application gateways can encase messages in wrappers to ensure that they are received unaltered. As noted previously, the Secure Sockets Layer protocol can send encrypted hash counts along with messages that act as trip wires to alert receiving systems of alterations.

Confidentiality

Confidentiality can be equated to privacy. It is a security property that ensures that data is disclosed only to those authorized to use it, and that it remains hidden from those not privy to it. The key point here for enabling confidentiality on a network is to deny information access to anyone not specifically authorized to see it. Encryption is a technological tool frequently used to guarantee confidentiality. With encryption, only those who have the encryption key are able to decode and use a message.

Access Control

The final security principle is that of access control. This relates to the acceptance or rejection of a user requesting access to some service or data in a given system. The service could be a particular application or a device such as a scanner, and the data could be a text file, an image, a library (a collection of files), or any combination of these data types. The real question is: What are the risks of allowing access to the system's devices, services, and data to individuals requesting it?

In some cases, such as the company's home page on the corporate intranet, the answer is very little, if any, damage could occur. The objective of such a page is to give general information about the organization, so access control is not an issue. On the other hand, access control is the issue if someone requests access to the payroll database, which lists all employees' salaries. In almost all companies, this information is limited to a very few individuals.

It is necessary to define a set of access rights, privileges, and authorizations, then assign these to the appropriate users within the system. It is equally important to appoint responsible individuals to administer any such security regime, for without proper oversight, the scheme will fall into disuse.

Additionally, access considerations might need to be extended to include machines in addition to user access. When identifying various computers and other physical devices on a TCP/IP network, IP addresses are the most common form of credentials. However, since IP addresses are not inherently secure and are subject to reassignment or duplication, they are not really suitable as identifiers for a sensitive application such as a data warehouse. Public key infrastructure (PKI) environments or DCE (distributed computing environment) authorization servers can provide more reliable identification than simple IP addresses, albeit at greater expenditure of money and effort.

Once the security principles applying to networks and distributed data warehouses are identified and understood, they can be used to form the basis of a solid security plan. However, one more key ingredient is necessary to a successful security scheme—an understanding of network architecture and how the specific Internet architecture fits the model.

Overview of Network Architecture

The International Standards Organization (ISO) published a network architecture in the early 1980s known as the Open System Interconnection (OSI) reference model for communications protocols. This seven-layer ISO model (Figure 8-2) defines how different telecommunications functions are handled by different standard "open" layers of the architecture.

The lowest layer in this architecture is the physical layer, which is responsible for the physical transmission of the data from the computer to the network. The physical layer entails network cards, electronic circuits, cables, and mechanical connectors that define and limit how transmissions occur across modems, coax Ethernet, twisted-pair Token Ring, or any other medium for data transmission.

The next layer is the data link layer, which ensures the integrity of the bit stream between any two points. Here, there are standards for parity, redundancy checks, and retransmission protocols to establish that the same sequence of bits sent from point A is received at point B.

The network layer extends the concepts of the data link layer

Figure 8-2. ISO protocol stack.

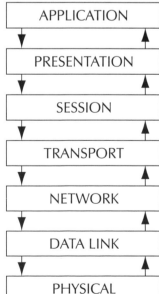

into multiple networks, which may or may not be compatible. Internetworking implies that this layer must also be aware of the multiple routes available to connect a sender with the recipient (if more than one transmission route exists).

The fourth layer, the transport layer, works with the network layer to ensure that different transmissions, which are part of a sequence (message) but may have transversed the network by different routes, are appropriately resequenced at the receiver's site.

The session layer manages the connecting and disconnecting of interactions between two computers. It controls how the data is to be exchanged (e.g., duplex or simplex). The presentation layer goes one step further and determines what code-set (e.g., ASCII or EBCDIC) will be used for the data exchange. Finally, there is the application layer, where specific applications (e.g., e-mail, X.400, VTAM) reside.

The architecture of the ISO model provides for each layer using the services of those layers "below" it, and each layer providing services to those "above" it, giving the appearance of a "stack." In fact, the model is known as a protocol stack, and almost all of the other instances of communications architectures, such as TCP/IP, follow the same stack model.

TCP/IP "Stacks"

Almost everyone is familiar with the abbreviation TCP/IP (Transmission Control Protocol/Internet Protocol). It is the foundation of communications on the World Wide Web and is in wide use in corporations everywhere. As a relative of the ISO model, it implements the protocol stack architecture in its own unique fashion. By using the concept of data packets and packet switching, it is able to support simultaneous access by literally millions of users. Transmissions between any two points are broken up into smaller pieces, called packets, which are sent interleaved with all the other packets in the network, granting nearly the same performance to all users.

Each connection to a TCP/IP network is assigned a unique address, usually written as four numbers that, in turn, indicate a network number and a host number. These IP addresses are usually assigned to a given machine by a network administrator. Packets are shipped to a destination through routers that use IP. This scheme forms the backbone of data transmission on the Internet

(Figure 8-3), allowing information to be shipped from point to point with integrity. The Internet layers roughly conform to the ISO model, except for the session and presentation layers (Figure 8-4). Internet applications must handle the tasks normally managed by these layers.

While getting a message from point A to point B is essential, it is not enough. It is like having a phone number of someone in a foreign country and using the phone book to obtain direct-dialing instructions. It is possible to establish a telephone connection between the United States and the foreign country, but the parties may still not be able to communicate—they may lack a common language and not have an interpreter on call. Once a packet arrives at the proper destination, the IP component on the receiver passes it to the TCP (Transmission Control Protocol) software. TCP assembles all the packets belonging to a single message and passes it to the appropriate service in the application layer. Similarly, there are protocols and tools specific to the application layer that correspond well to the telephone analogy.

The oldest commonly used method of file transfer on the Internet is FTP (file transfer protocol). With FTP, users can browse the files on the host, select certain ones, and transfer them to their own system. A slight improvement over FTP, Telnet is an application and set of protocols that allows a user's connected terminal to act as if it were directly attached to the host computer. SMTP (Simple Mail Transfer Protocol) and POP (Post Office Protocol) provide basic electronic mail services.

Today's browsers, notably Netscape Navigator and Microsoft Internet Explorer, have vastly improved how a user interacts with these various application protocols. They reside on the user's computer in the application layer above these other protocols and take most of the pain out of using TCP/IP communications (Figure 8-5).

The Internet community is constantly seeking new ways to improve function. One concept that is rapidly gaining acceptance is named the Level 2 Tunneling Protocol (L2TP). This protocol would ensure that even though a given communication is being transmitted over the Internet, it can travel by means of a private session limited to those members allowed to work within that channel by using data encryption. The technology is known as "tunneling" because the correspondents are establishing a tunnel of sorts through the public

Figure 8-3. TCP/IP message flow.

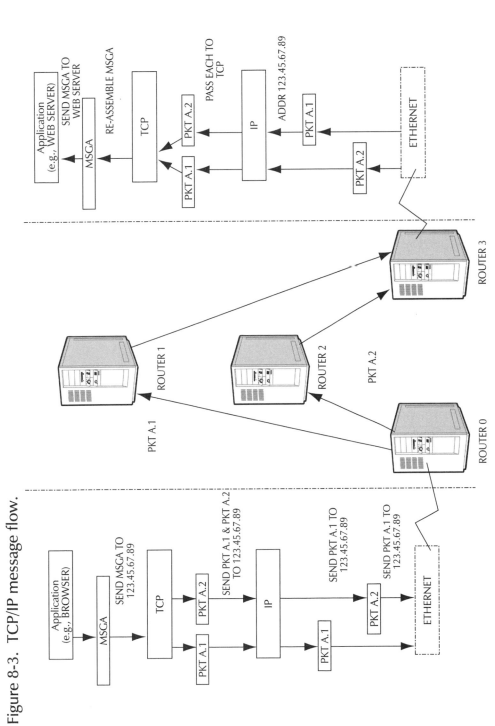

Figure 8-4. Comparing ISO and TCP/IP "stacks."

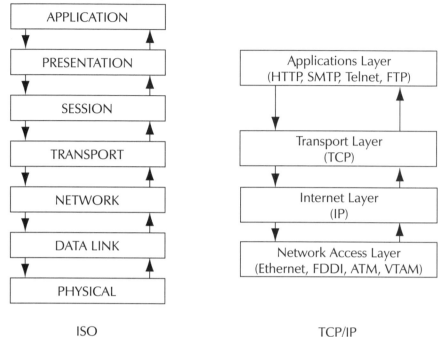

packet traffic that exists on the Internet and exchanging private communications within it. Curiously, the concept traces its origins to the Middle Ages, when tunnels were dug between fortified towns and castles to allow their inhabitants to travel in comparative safety, hidden away from the potential dangers of roving outlaws and besieging enemy armies camped outside their gates.

The use of tunneling allows the implementation of another good idea, the virtual private network (VPN). Companies needing a less expensive alternative to a wide area network can use a VPN on the Internet and develop their own private network, safe from unwanted intrusions yet riding on the cost benefits of the Internet mass volumes.

TCP/IP Network Security Architecture

Given the general architecture of the ISO model, and the more concrete example of the Internet implementation of TCP/IP, what are the vulnerabilities of this architecture to attack, and what countermeasures can be taken to thwart a potential security breach? The answers

Figure 8-5. The browser in the TCP/IP stack.

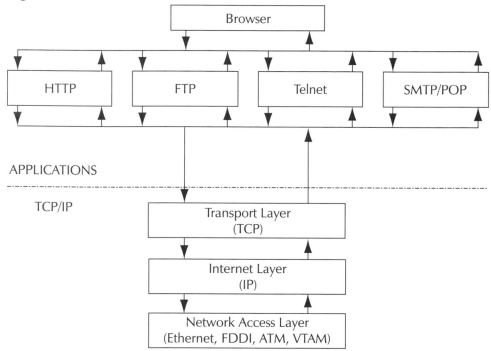

to these questions form the basic components of a security architecture for an Internet/intranet–style network. Like all architectures, the individual pieces of the security architecture are designed with a great deal of flexibility and, depending on the particular needs of an organization, the selection of components and their interrelationships may vary greatly.

Over time, two distinct approaches to designing a network security architecture have arisen:

- Network-coupled security
- Application-coupled security

As their names imply, network-coupled security favors concentrating security measures on the network infrastructure while the application-coupled approach builds security into the applications themselves. With network-coupled security, the focus is on ensuring that the network is a trusted and secure subsystem. The applications assume that the data being transmitted is safe, comes from authorized users, and is being delivered to the correct recipient. When the network is secure, the applications do not participate in the first-line security scheme—they simply assume that the network is performing all of those security functions (the applications may still perform other security functions, such as database security, for example).

Applications running in the traditional ISO environment, or even on the Internet, do not concern themselves with the details of communications, such as the sequencing of packets or validation of IP addresses. The applications assume that the layers below them in the protocol stack have done their jobs and therefore the applications can concentrate on data content. Similarly, in a secure network environment, applications can assume that the lower levels are handling the security.

This is the greatest advantage to network-coupled security; applications do not have to be security aware. Existing applications, which are not network security conscious, can be moved unaltered to the network environment. Less obvious but nearly as important is the use of a consistent security scheme. The applications can "interoperate" from a security standpoint, with all applications using the same authorization standard and key management scheme. With the network-coupled approach, the entire system is secured at the same time, rather than in a piecemeal approach.

There are, however, proponents of the application-coupled approach. They argue that the application knows best what kind of security it needs. For these proponents, the need to create security-aware applications is not a disadvantage but an obvious result of the need to implement security at an application level. Similarly, the lack of interoperability is not a drawback but a flexible approach to securing the system. They view the "one size fits all" approach of network security as insufficient to secure the broad range of application types.

Whichever approach or combination of methods is chosen, it is critical that the security team not lose sight of what is really important in the maze of design possibilities and technological tools—network security is about managing risks. These risks can be characterized by two criteria:

- The likelihood that a particular attack will succeed
- The consequences if the attack is successful

Security costs money and system resources, and those commodities must be spent where there is a real potential for serious damage.

A risk management strategy can focus on minimizing the possibility of an attack succeeding (by installing countermeasures) or minimizing the consequences of the attack. A good security plan will encompass both, carefully weighing what to defend against and how to best mitigate the damaging effects.

Common Gateway Interface (CGI)

No discussion of the Internet/intranet architecture would be complete without an examination of the CGI, even though it is not strictly a part of TCP/IP. The CGI is the interface between the web site's HTTP server and the other resources of the server's host computer. CGI is not a language or protocol in the strict sense of the word; it is just a commonly named set of variables and agreed-on conventions for passing information back and forth from the client (i.e., the PC with a web browser) to and from the server (i.e., the computer that sends the web pages to the client).

The Common Gateway Interface is the "magic" that makes the World Wide Web interactive. It enables users to browse, fill out forms, submit data to the host, and much more. Throughout the companies, research facilities, universities, and user communities that make up the WWW, CGI scripts are developed, improved, shared, and sometimes compromised. For all of its magic, CGI opens a huge, gaping hole in a security system that must be plugged, or at the very least, defended.

Reduced to its simplest form, there are two basic parts to a CGI script:

- An executable (which may be a system call, shell script, Perl script, or compiled program)
- An HTML page (which drives the executable)

The CGI script can be used without user input and without an HTML page, but its function is severely restricted. If there is to be any user input, the HTML page is necessary. When both the executable and HTML page are properly constructed, the action proceeds in the following manner:

1. The user pulls the HTML page from the server onto his "client" machine.
2. The user "fills out the form" by entering data or clicking on the desired field.
3. The user submits the form.
4. The user's browser interprets the form into an executable request, which it forwards along with the information entered by the user to the server.
5. The server executes the requested program, utilizing the forwarded information.

The strength of CGI is its simplicity. Entering data and any other manipulation is performed on the client side; all the server does is execute a request when one is received. However, CGI's simplicity is also its weakness. Because the bulk of the action happens on the client machine, users have unrestricted access to the downloaded HTML page and can input unexpected data, edit the page, or generally do whatever they want. Sometimes the resulting executable request is very different from what was anticipated.

The most common example of a CGI security breach is persuading the operating system shell into performing something unexpected. Hackers and ill-intentioned users have employed this method to steal password files and other important information, insert a Trojan horse, inject a virus, and install and run their own programs. This isn't the only "hole" in CGI. Other vulnerabilities include the following:

- Some early mail programs allowed any user to execute arbitrary programs.
- The server has been tricked into executing commands embedded in HTML commands hidden in the input.
- C programs have been used to execute other programs resident on the server through very long input (caused by the C program having ill-defined array boundaries).

These are only the most common breaches. Many others have been identified, and more are invented all the time. Obviously, CGI must be used with caution.

As with any other area of security, the basic idea behind securing

CGI is to understand the threats (both demonstrated and potential), to install countermeasures against those threats, and to monitor system activity for unusual occurrences. A good place to start is with a secure server that is protected by:

- Doing appropriate screening at the router
- Creating a nonprivileged WWW user and group
- Restricting the server's file system
- Turning off all unused daemons

Other restrictions may be necessary depending on the intended audience and the importance of the data on the server. Critical corporate data should never be stored on a CGI-using server, or if it must be stored there, additional security measures are vital.

Beyond these basic security measures, there are other simple methods for improving CGI security. For example:

- Before opening the shell, always check for special characters by either restricting input or "escaping" any dangerous characters.
- For server "includes," check for "<" and ">" characters to identify and validate embedded HTML tags.
- Check for any occurrence of "/../" to guard against user attempts to access higher levels of the directory structure.
- For selection lists, validate the indicated choice.

It is also a sound idea to use compiled programs instead of interpreted scripts. A compiled program is much more difficult for the average user to understand and modify than is a script. For example, the binary executable from a compiled C program is almost impossible for the programmer who wrote the program to alter and is completely incomprehensible to the average user. This is another simple security measure.

Keep in mind, however, that whenever a program is called directly it is a trade-off between the known vulnerability of the shell and the unknown risk of the program. While users certainly need to be able to execute CGI scripts, they do not need "read" or "write" permissions to them. In the same vein, users need to read the HTML driver files and to read and execute their directory, but do not need "write" or "execute" permission to the driver files or "write" permission to the directory.

There are many CGI scripts freely available on the Internet. They may make a good starting point, but as with any freely downloadable software, they should be examined carefully with an eye to security. Most scripts obtained in this way need to be modified to suit the borrower's needs and security concerns. Above all, never run anything that is not thoroughly understood.

CGIs are so common and useful that they are nearly impossible to avoid even if a company wanted to. This, however, does not mean that they should be adopted "as is" into a company's distributed data warehouse. All of the reasonable security measures discussed previously must be adopted to avoid creating an opening in security that will endanger the entire distributed data warehouse and the network that supports it.

Managing Security

Technological tools alone cannot provide adequate security for a distributed data warehouse. Before implementing any tools, these fundamental issues of network security must be addressed:

- The type of data housed at each location must be identified and assigned a security level.
- The possible threats to the network should be identified and categorized as to severity.
- A security policy must be drawn up and agreed upon by all concerned.
- Everyone, from the CEO to the lowliest user, must be made aware of the company's security policies.
- Someone must be "in charge" of security, and the position of head of security should be treated seriously.

Most medium-size and large corporations already have a well-established security department, but these employees alone are not enough to handle security concerns for a distributed data warehouse. Their efforts will need to be augmented with support from at least two other areas. The telecommunications department, especially those concerned with the distributed network's configuration and routers, must play a key role in securing the data warehouse. The warehouse management team should also contribute to the overall security effort; in fact, this management team should take the lead in formulating and implementing all aspects of warehouse security.

Although a company will want to purchase and implement different packaged security solutions (some of which are covered in the next chapter), it cannot be emphasized enough that the security of the data warehouse is dependent primarily on the quality of the company's security policy and the way in which it imposes that policy on itself. If the security policy is inadequate, not uniformly enforced, or has huge holes in it, no amount of technology will cure the problem. It is only with a well-thought-out policy and strict enforcement that any organization can hope to protect itself from damaging security breaches.

Tools for Distributed Warehouse and Web Security

No one, not the federal government, not even the U.S. military, can afford "security at any cost." Even if the measures necessary did not outstrip the corporate budget (and that is a very big "if"), they would certainly exhaust the system's resources. Security for the web-enabled distributed data warehouse is, of necessity, something of a compromise. The warehouse security team must involve itself with two main areas of concern:

- Managing the risk during the design and development stage
- Managing the risk during the operational stage

Risk assessment for a security architecture is technically complicated in a distributed environment where many protocols and products might be used. That is why it is so important to build a security team that possesses the appropriate knowledge and skill set. In most companies, it is necessary to tap several different areas to assemble the team, including:

- Data security for overall knowledge of security procedures, especially implementation, maintenance, and enforcement
- Telecommunications for knowledge of networking and protocols
- Warehouse management for information concerning the internals of the distributed warehouse
- Architecture for knowledge of corporate infrastructure
- New technology (i.e., the "tools" group that tests new releases of software) for the ability to evaluate software packages

Shifting through all the possible hardware, software, and protocol packages is a daunting task, even for this highly skilled team. Making the wrong choice can mean disaster—both in terms of inadequate security and excessive costs.

The job is, in part, so complex because there is no shortage of technological tools available to help secure the Internet/intranet–based distributed data warehouse. It is not so much a question of whether to use these tools, but more one of deciding what tools at which layer will best suit a company's needs. Chosen carefully, technological tools form an important component in the comprehensive security plan for the distributed data warehouse.

Firewalls

Whenever the issue of Internet or TCP/IP security is raised, the traditional reflex has been to think of a firewall. This name derives from the practice of building a stone wall around a medieval town or castle to discourage enemy attempts at burning the buildings (in fact, most were constructed of mud or timber, with thatched roofs, and burned really well). A modern firewall keeps the "fire" of unsecured communications outside of a protective "wall."

The main goal of a firewall is to prevent undesirable messages from entering the secured network and, conversely, to prevent unauthorized messages from leaving. Should a damaging message enter the network, a secondary goal is to minimize its effect on the environment.

Firewalls are compound environments usually composed of the following elements:

- Special network configurations
- Special host configurations
- Screening routers
- Proxy servers

Special network configurations limit the number of computing and network resources directly exposed to Internet/intranet traffic. These configurations typically take the form of subnets—separately addressable segments of the network, uniquely and easily identifiable solely by the IP addresses of the components. It is common practice to assemble all the components necessary for a given application, like a web site, into their own subnet and limit Internet access to only that subnet. This protects the rest of the distributed environment from exposure to unnecessary risks such as hackers and logic bombs, among other threats.

Special host configurations limit the resources available to an intruder if he is able to get past the other barriers placed in his way. Only the minimal services necessary to perform the host's intended task are installed when a special host configuration strategy is in place. For example, if the host is a web server, just the software necessary to support HTTP protocols is installed; file transfer protocols or e-mail programs are not installed, as would normally be the case, unless they are required. Similarly, if Java is installed, a Perl runtime environment may not be. In most circumstances, a C compiler is not available on hosts employing the special host configuration strategy because it poses too great a risk to the network.

Routers are special-purpose network interface computers designed specifically to send IP messages to remote destinations and receive messages on behalf of their local servers. Screening routers have the added functionality of being able to examine and discriminate among the network traffic based on certain criteria. Should a particular message violate one of the router's rules, it can reject the message (either inbound or outbound) following IP-specified procedures.

These screening rules can be based on many different criteria, depending on the manufacturer's specifications for the router. However, most operate solely on the limited information contained in the IP header attached to message packets. This information consists of:

- The IP address of the computer sending the packet (i.e., source IP address)
- The IP address of the computer that is to receive the packet (i.e., destination IP address)
- An IP protocol number identifying the transport protocol that is to receive the message from IP at the destination (i.e., a code specifying TCP)
- A port number that is used by TCP to identify the destination application of the packet (i.e., a code specifying the HTTP application)

Note that nowhere in these headers is a field caller USERID. An application can require a user id and password, but that information is passed as part of the IP packet's data field—not as part of the IP header. Most screening decisions are made based only on the four IP addressing criteria listed previously. Thus, screening criteria must be phrased in terms of "reject any HTTP packet that is not destined for host x.y.z.a"; "accept any HTTP packet from host a.b.c.d destined for host m.n.o.p"; or "reject any UDP packet not from a host whose IP address starts with q.r.s."

Because the capabilities of screening routers are obviously limited, many organizations also use proxy servers to reduce the risk of damage from a "dangerous" message from a source the screening router judges to be acceptable. A proxy is a special copy of an application program that has had supplemental enhancements made for web service. For example, an organization may have several e-mail servers on its internal intranet, but only one proxy e-mail server, on a special firewall IP subnet, that is visible to the Internet. The local servers send all e-mail to the Internet through this proxy server and receive incoming Internet e-mail only from the proxy. As far as the outside world is concerned, this organization has only one e-mail server, the proxy. The proxy's e-mail program may have been modified so as to:

- Produce a log file of all routing activity.
- Forward e-mail to only particular Internet sites.
- Not accept any e-mail from certain Internet sites.
- Encapsulate any message from the outside in an HTML "wrapper," to reduce the chance of catching a virus from an e-mail message.
- Screen all incoming e-mails with a virus detection program.
- Inspect every outgoing e-mail for certain keywords or phrases.

For most of the Internet's existence, the standard firewall—a combination of network configuration, host configuration, screening routers, and proxy servers—has provided the best security available at the TCP/IP system level. However, this set of four technologies, based on TCP/IP specifications alone, has its limitations. Authenticating the source and destination computers for each message by checking IP addresses is limited because they are easy to change or fake.

Because TCP/IP was designed to be an open system, the confidentiality of messages was not addressed in its early specifications; all messages were sent "in the clear." Integrity checking is limited to simple byte counts of transmitted data, and accountability is not even considered.

New TCP/IP specifications (see the section on "Internet Protocol Security" later in this chapter) have been proposed that will help resolve some of these issues. They call for implementing message encryption as part of TCP/IP, and some vendors already offer encryption as an option in their TCP/IP implementations. These new specifications are relatively recent, however, and many applications currently available have taken other approaches to reduce their security exposures. Some of these measures involved adding a large amount of code inside application programs. Others have taken a more general approach by adding new layers of software such as Secure Sockets Layer (SSL) and virtual private network (VPN) programs to sit between TCP/IP and the applications.

In addition to these design issues, it must be remembered that firewalls are complex environments, susceptible to problems caused by administrative errors and failure to enforce the corporate security policy. Writing screening rules for routers is an arcane art and subject to the very human error of "fumble-fingers" (i.e., typing 22.36.*123*.872 instead of 22.36.*124*.872). Coordinating router screening policy among several proxy server administrators can pose organizational and managerial challenges. In fact, local security on the organization's hosts may be lax in general because the administrators have the attitude that "the firewall will protect us from Internet problems."

However, even with all of these issues, firewalls can still be a valuable security asset. Separating the Internet functions into their own subnet and minimizing the security exposure of the rest of the distributed environment is a good idea. Limiting the computing facilities available on the network segment exposed to the World Wide Web significantly reduces the chances of a "hack" succeeding. Having log files generated by proxies helps solve many types of problems, not just those related to security issues, and using proxy servers as a "first-line defense" against viruses is a bit like getting a flu shot—it is foolish not to do it. The organization just has to realize that a firewall is only a partial solution to the task of providing a secure distributed environment. Other tools may also have to be brought to bear in order to complete the picture.

Encryption

Throughout both this chapter and Chapter 8, there are numerous references to encryption as the solution to various security problems. Everyone is at least slightly familiar with the process of encryption. As children, virtually everybody played spy games involving "secret codes"—perhaps the substitution of the numbers 1–26 for the letters of the alphabet or a similar, simple key. Many who participated in scouting learned Morse code or semaphore signals, two more forms of encryption. Encryption can be as simple, or complex, as the user wants to make it.

Basically encryption, as used in data processing today, is just the process of applying a mathematical algorithm and some related key to a plaintext (e.g., a word processing document) to create a ciphertext. Decryption is the process of applying the same algorithm and an associated key to the ciphertext to re-create the original document. The obvious benefit is that if the document is in cipher form, its contents are obscured from plain view. While encryption can be put to any number of different uses (even the children's game mentioned), it is especially helpful in an Internet/intranet environment.

There are two major types of encryption algorithms used with TCP/IP: symmetric and public key.

Symmetric Algorithms

Symmetric algorithms use the same key to both encrypt the plaintext and decrypt the ciphertext (Figure 9-1). In a communication setting, this means that both parties must share the same secret key in order to securely transmit data back and forth. This shared key is typically a digital number which is at least 40 bits long to reduce the chance that a "brute force hack" will succeed. One of the big drawbacks to symmetric keys is distribution of the common key among the communicating parties without passing it over an unencrypted, insecure channel. This normally leads to establishing a set of noncomputer

Figure 9-1. Symmetric key encryption.

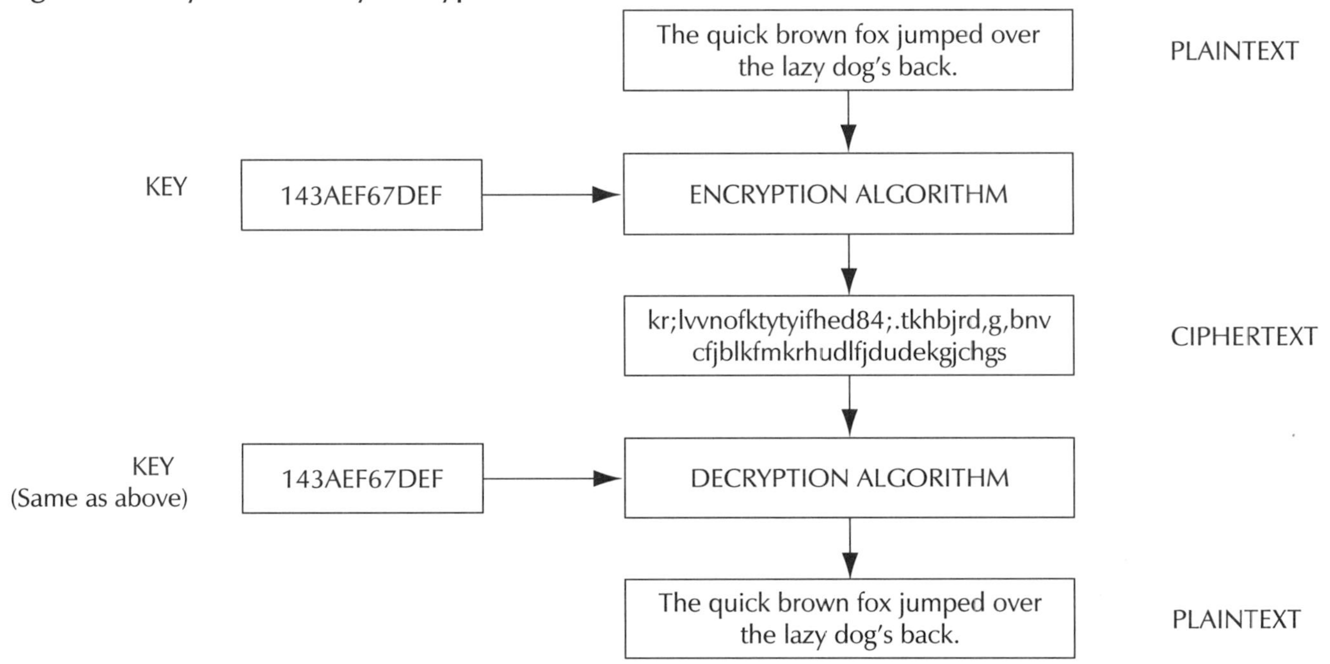

PLAINTEXT

The quick brown fox jumped over the lazy dog's back.

ENCRYPTION ALGORITHM

CIPHERTEXT

kr;lvvnofktytyifhed84:.tkhbjrd,g,bnv cfjblkfmkrhudlfjdudekgjchgs

DECRYPTION ALGORITHM

PLAINTEXT

The quick brown fox jumped over the lazy dog's back.

KEY

143AEF67DEF

KEY
(Same as above)

143AEF67DEF

physical procedures in order to share the secret (e.g., mailing or faxing the key).

Public Key Algorithms

Public key algorithms, on the other hand, use different keys on each end of the transmission; one to encrypt the plaintext and a different one to decrypt the ciphertext (Figure 9-2). For example, to use public key algorithms a corporation, called Company A, runs a security program that simultaneously creates both a private key (secret within the corporation) and a public key for use by anyone who wishes to conduct confidential communication with it. Company A then distributes the public key and a list of the encryption algorithms that it supports to all its business partners who wish to conduct secure communications with it.

To send Company A a private message, the business partner needs only to encrypt their plaintext using one of Company A's supported algorithms and its public key and send it, rendering it useful only to the owner of the private key—in this case, Company A. Similarly, when Company A wants confidentiality with someone else, it encrypts its plaintext message with the recipient's public key and encryption algorithm; the recipient then decrypts the ciphertext with its own private key. In this manner, secure messages can be sent to any public key encryption user without including the decryption key as part of the message. In fact, because the private (decryption) key is never transmitted at all, a company's public key and the list of supported algorithms can safely be distributed by e-mail or even posted on a public site such as the corporate web page

The biggest drawback to public key encryption, however, is the amount of CPU time required to execute these algorithms. In contrast, symmetric algorithms are much faster and better suited to heavy processing loads—in most cases, they are at least 10 times faster than public key encryption. As a result, many of the most popular web-based communication solutions have implemented a hybrid approach to data encryption. Such a hybrid starts by using public key encryption to initialize and authenticate a series of communications. Under the protection of the public key encryption, the two parties exchange appropriate symmetric keys and continue exchanging messages using lower-overhead symmetric algorithms. Examples of such hybrid processing include SSL and most VPN packages.

Figure 9-2. Public key encryption.

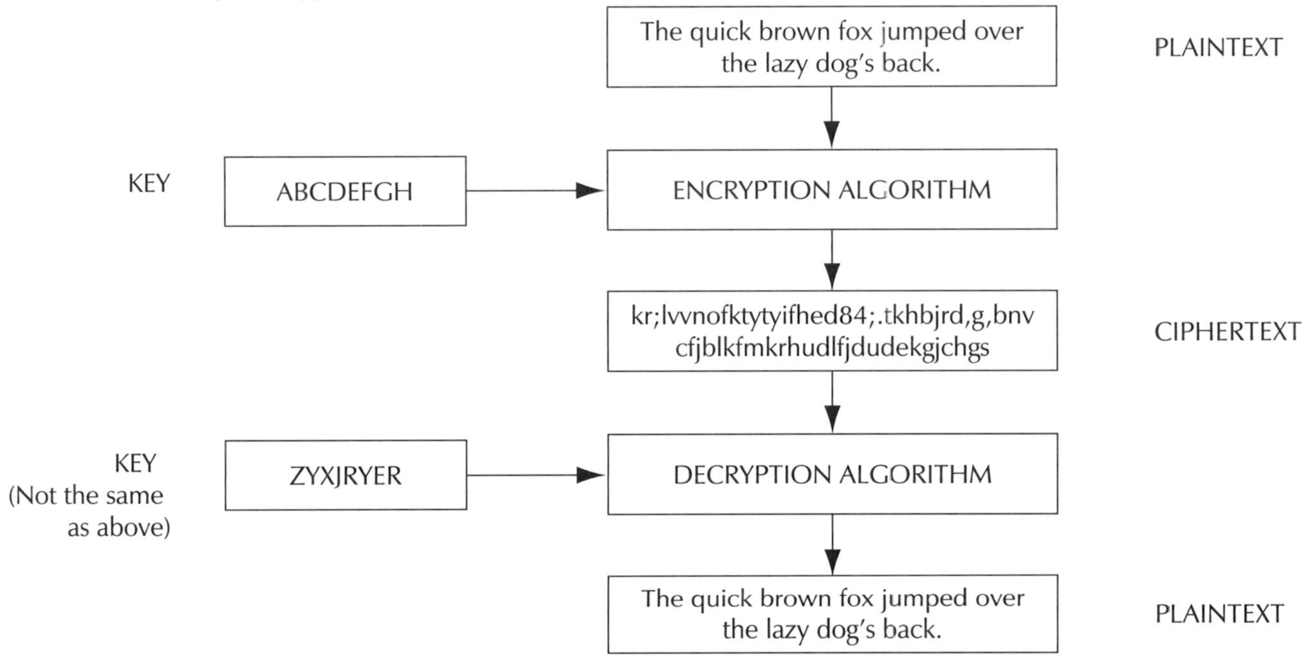

PLAINTEXT

The quick brown fox jumped over the lazy dog's back.

ENCRYPTION ALGORITHM

KEY

ABCDEFGH

CIPHERTEXT

kr;lvvnofktytyifhed84;.tkhbjrd,g,bnv cfjblkfmkrhudlfjdudekgjchgs

DECRYPTION ALGORITHM

KEY
(Not the same as above)

ZYXJRYER

PLAINTEXT

The quick brown fox jumped over the lazy dog's back.

Public key algorithms are also well suited to lightweight encryption tasks such as:

- Digital signatures
- Digital certificates
- Message hash counts

If the public and private keys are out of synchronization (i.e., don't match), decryption of these known structures will produce easily detectable garbage. Digital signature processing is a good example of this technique.

A digital signature is a field appended to a message that enables the recipient to verify both the signer's identity and the fact that the contents of the text have not been changed. The signer creates this field by applying a message digest algorithm to the entire text. The end result of this algorithm is a digital number of some known length (the actual length varies depending upon the particular algorithm used). After generating the digest number, the signer then encrypts it using her private key and appends the resulting "signature" to the text. The validation process (Figure 9-3) consists of the recipient applying the same message digest algorithm to the text (minus the digital signature, of course) to create his own message digest number. He then decrypts the digital signature using the signer's public key and compares the resulting plaintext to the message digest number he just computed. If they match, the reader can safely assume that he knows who signed the document and that is has not been altered since being signed. If the two digest numbers are not equal, the text must be considered suspect. Unfortunately, this procedure does not identify exactly why or how the text has changed, only that it has been altered.

Note that in order to validate such a signature, the recipient must know three things:

- The public key algorithm used to sign the message digest
- The public key used by the algorithm that signed the message digest
- The particular message digest algorithm used to create the digest

Figure 9-3. Validating digitally signed documents.

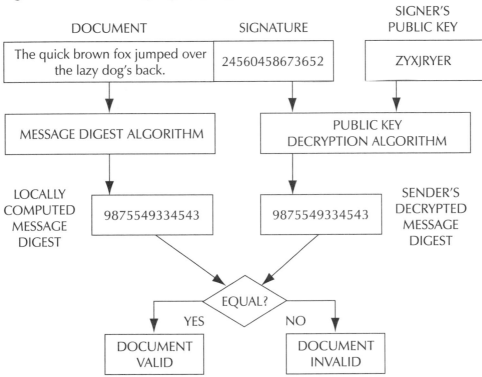

To minimize the potential of exposure to cryptographic attacks, a cautious signer probably has a separate private/public key pair for digital signatures from what she uses for general message encryption. The user is also likely to distribute this key much more discreetly than she does her general public key. If message digest processing looks familiar and seems to resemble the rather nebulous hash-count processes, there is good reason; message digest processing is just a specialized example of hash counts.

Digital signature technology is taken one step further with digital certificates. Digital certificates are data structures that identify a particular entity—be it a machine, an organization, or an individual user. Public key certificates, in particular, identify the entity, its public key and various pieces of information about the entity such as e-mail address, physical location, and its distinguished name. Such certificates, which follow the X.509 v3 standard (Figure 9-4), can be used to both authenticate the entity during message processing and provide the recipient with the appropriate public key for decrypting

Figure 9-4. Data content of an X.509 v3 digital certificate.

Name of Field	Description
Version	Version of X.509 used
Serial Number	Issuer's certificate serial number
Signature Algorithm	Subject's digital signature algorithm (both the message digest and data encryption algorithms)
Issuer	Name and country of organization issuing certificate (e.g., VeriSign or AT&T)
Validity	
Start Date	Earliest valid date
Expiration Date	Last valid date
Subject	Name of subject and type of certificate
Subject Public Key Info	
Public Key Algorithm	Public key algorithm supported by subject
Public Key	Subject's public key in modulus and exponent form
Signature Algorithm	Algorithm used to sign this certificate (both the message digest and data encryption algorithms)
Signature	Digital signature of this certificate

the message. However, these data structures are easily forged and should not create, by themselves, great confidence in the bearer's authenticity.

This deficiency can be remedied by having a third party validate the information on the certificate. The validation typically takes the form of the third party, a Certification Authority (CA), digitally signing the certificate. This digital signature accompanies the certificate whenever it is presented as an identification credential. The validation process for these third-party certificates consists of the following steps:

1. The recipient computes its own message digest of the certificate (excluding the digital signature), using the message digest algorithm identified in the certificate.

2. The recipient then uses the public key algorithm identified in the certificate to decrypt the appended digital signature and uncover

the embedded message digest. The public key used to decrypt the digest, however, is the Certification Authority's, not that of the message's originator.

3. The decrypted message digest is compared to the one just computed. If the two digests match, the recipient can be reasonably certain that this certificate has not been modified since the Certification Authority signed it, and therefore the information it contains is accurate and valid.

Data Encryption Software

One final point should be made about public key algorithms—the most popular algorithms have, at one time or another, been the subjects of software patents. As a result, encryption algorithms have a long and checkered history of patent-infringement lawsuits and corporate infighting. These patents started to expire in 1997 and probably no longer represent a legal risk to commercial users. However, prudence should prompt any new purchaser of data encryption software to confirm the patent and license status with the vendor.

Since this discussion has deteriorated into legal issues, there is the whole nasty little matter of when data encryption can legally be used at all. Within the borders of the United States, there are no limitations on the use of data encryption software. However, the United States does impose export restrictions on software with data encryption facilities. These restrictions are quite technical, including, among others, the 40-bit limit on encryption keys noted at the beginning of this section. The net result of these restrictions is that many software vendors produce two versions of their products: one for use in the United States and another for export. A large multinational company that wants to establish a VPN may need to conduct some additional research into browser specifications at all sites, U.S. government regulations on encryption, and the local regulations in the foreign countries in which they operate. France, for instance, forbids any commercial use of data encryption not related to regulated banking, though encryption can be used to ensure message integrity in hash counts.

Some of the better-known data encryption algorithms include:

Symmetric Algorithms

- *Data Encryption Standard (DES)*. Developed by IBM in the 1970s, DES was expanded to a general ANSI standard in the 1980s.

- *IDEA*. A patented algorithm developed in Zurich, Switzerland in 1994, IDEA is primarily used in Europe.

- *RC2*. A block cipher (i.e., one that operates on a block of data) that was developed by RSA Data Security, Inc. (RSADSI) as a trade secret.

- *RC4*. A stream cipher (i.e., one that operates on a stream of data) also developed by RSADSI as a trade secret.

Public Key Algorithms

- *Diffie-Hellman Key Exchange*. Not an encryption algorithm per se, but rather a secure method for exchanging symmetrical keys.

- *RSA*. A public key algorithm developed by RSADSI; the key may be of any length and is useful for encryption/decryption and digital signatures.

Message Digest Algorithms

- *The Hashed Message Authentication Code (HMAC)*. A technique that uses a secret key and a message digest function to create a secret message identification code; it is used to make other message digest functions more resistant to cryptographic attack.

- *MD2*. Developed by Ronald Rivest, MD2 produces a 128-bit digest and has relatively high CPU consumption.

- *MD5*. Also developed by Ronald Rivest, this technique is less secure than MD-2, but requires less CPU than MD-2.

- *The Revised Secure Hash Algorithm (SHA-1)*. Developed by the National Security Agency for use with DSS.

- *DSS (Digital Signature Standard)*. Developed by the National Security Agency and adopted as a Federal Information Processing Standard (FIPS), DSS is intended only to provide digital signature facilities.

Encryption is yet another valuable piece of the Internet/intranet security puzzle. The organizations that are currently using or will soon be using the World Wide Web as an important part of their corporate strategy need to be well informed about encryption technologies. For that reason, it is important to note that this discussion is merely a brief introduction to the subject. Others have done a much more thorough and rigorous explanation of encryption.

Authentication Services

Traditionally, computer systems have employed user ids and passwords to identify and authenticate users, machines, and processes. However, there is a problem when using TCP/IP. The TCP/IP suite of protocols (IPSec, which will be discussed later in this chapter, notwithstanding) does not even include the concept of a user. Identification and authorization are, as a result, left to the application layer. Anytime users are asked to provide a user id and password on the Web, they can be reasonably certain that they are signing into either a specific application or a layer of software between TCP/IP and the application (Figure 9-5).

Application-level security has some major drawbacks. The first is that unless the user id and password travel in an encrypted packet, they are susceptible to eavesdropping on the communications line. This opens a giant hole in system security, almost begging someone to "hack" the network. The second problem is ensuring consistent behavior across more than one application; unless special attention is

Figure 9-5. Context of "signon" in the TCP/IP stack.

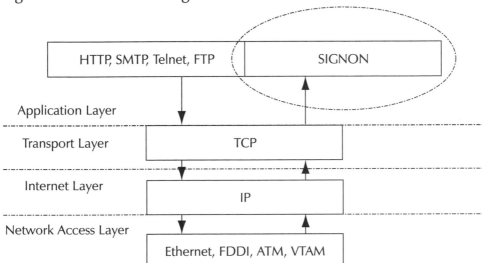

paid to this problem, a user will likely have a different user id and password for each individual application. "Single logon" screens, where a user signs on only once for all applications, tend to be fairly high on user wish lists. The third difficulty is that applications development is complicated when each program has to be concerned with the mechanics of user authentication.

Rather than leaving all authorization issues to be resolved by application programs, the computing community has attempted to establish some standard structures and processes to specifically address these issues. Two general approaches to these issues have emerged over recent years: the OSF/DCE specifications and public key infrastructures.

DCE/Kerberos

Distributed computing environment (DCE) specifications have been developed by the Open Software Foundation (OSF) in order to provide tools and a framework for building secure distributed applications in a multivendor environment. These facilities, critically important to distributed warehouses, cover a number of the disparate issues including timing coordination, RPC (remote procedure call) specifications, and distributed file systems. As might be expected, security issues have attracted a large measure of this group's attention.

DCE security services start by assuming that the network is insecure and that any information on it may be subject to unauthorized examination and modification. No trust is placed in the unauthorized identity of any network member, either client or server. To ameliorate this situation, DCE security provides a number of services. It enables ACL (access control list) services for servers. It provides a single registry of clients and servers, and it can securely authenticate clients and servers using the Kerberos authentication model. It also supports message protection options such as data encryption and message digests (hash counts).

DCE encryption is based entirely on symmetrical algorithms, primarily because of their performance advantages. However, the Massachusetts Institute of Technology (MIT) group that developed the Kerberos authentication model also wanted to avoid the patent and licensing issues surrounding public key encryption at the time.

The Kerberos authentication model is named after the three-headed dog that guarded the gates to Hades in Greek mythology be-cause it is a three-way security process. Using Kerberos, both the client and the application server agree to trust the word of a third computer, the security server, as to the identity and authorization of each other (Figure 9-6). When they boot up, both the client and the application server identify themselves to the security scrver using user ids and passwords. At no time during these exchanges do the user ids or passwords travel over the network without being en-crypted (in fact, in more recent specifications, the actual passwords never traverse the network at all). Then, when the client wishes to establish a session or connection with an application server, it re-quests an application ticket from the security server. The client ap-pends this ticket to its request for a session and sends it to the application server. Upon receipt, the application server examines the presented ticket and forwards it to the security server for verification and validation. If the security server validates the ticket, the applica-tion server establishes the session and returns its own credentials to the client. The client can then choose to either continue the session or, if it finds the server's credentials unsatisfactory, terminate it.

The Kerberos model can be used to authenticate users, ma-chines, and applications. Once identities are established, the connec-

Figure 9-6. Kerberos architecture.

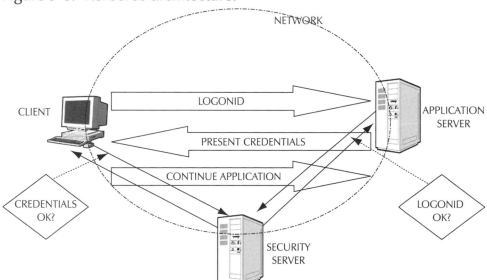

tion process can set up temporary, short-lived session keys to enable message encryption and encrypted hash counts.

The DCE environment is intended to be of general applicability across many types of environments, not just those using TCP/IP. However, regardless of network type, many observers have noted performance problems related to the amount of network traffic generated by the three-way interaction among client, application server, and the security server. In response to this criticism, recent software implementations of DCE offer many options intended to improve performance while still providing good security. In turn, this has increased the complexity of DCE administration. In general, DCE is perceived as slow and hard to administer. Relief for these problems will come with future improvements in network speeds and the development of better administration tools.

PKI

Public key infrastructures (PKI) provide an alternate approach to authentication issues. A PKI provides management services to facilitate widespread use of public key encryption. When a user creates a public/private key pair to enable secure communications with another user, server, or application, the problem arises as to how to securely distribute the resultant public key to these significant others. These keys are very long hexadecimal (or octal) numbers that are difficult for users to work with. Generally, users will install a public key on their hard disk for use by the computer's communication software. Typically, the file containing these keys is separately encrypted as part of the local system's security.

During the early days of public key encryption, two communicants would exchange floppy disks or even e-mails in order to share public keys. More recent approaches to this problem, however, involve exchanging electronic X.509 v3 certificates. These certificates uniquely identify an entity and its public key. Different formats distinguish machines (server certificates), users (personal certificates), and application programs (software publisher certificates). A fourth format identifies a CA (Certification Authority) that issues certificates.

A CA is a third party that vouches for the identity of a certificate owner by issuing the certificate. Each certificate specifies its format (i.e., personal, server, or software), the name of its owner, the owner's public key, the algorithm used to generate the key, the name of the issuing CA, and the CA's digital signature. The authenticity of any given certificate can be verified by decrypting and validating this digital signature on the certificate using the CA's own public key. The certificates of some CAs, such as the VeriSign Corporation, AT&T, and the U.S. Postal Service, usually come built into Internet browsers. These CA certificates are crucial to the SSL protocols implemented in both the Netscape Navigator and Microsoft Internet Explorer browsers. CA certificates are also available when requesting a personal certification from the aforementioned authorities. These CAs are intended to serve the entire Internet, providing worldwide coverage.

Commercial software packages are also available to allow organizations such as corporations to provide their own certification and PKI services. This software provides public/private key generation utilities, certification services, certificate verification routines, and certificate revocation facilities. Additionally, these packages include the programmatic interfaces necessary to successfully integrate the PKI with other services such as SSL and IPSec software.

As with DCE/Kerberos, performance is a major concern with PKI/public key authentication. Public key decryption is relatively expensive in terms of CPU utilization, and verification of digital signatures may often require additional telecommunications in order to obtain the appropriate public keys for validation. Typically, public key encryption is used only until a symmetrical key environment can securely be established.

Comparing PKI authentication to DCE/Kerberos is difficult because it is comparing apples and oranges. DCE/Kerberos is a complete solution to security, part of an extensive distributed architecture. A TCP/IP application may only be just one part of the entire environment covered by a DCE cell. PKI facilities, on the other hand, are more limited in scope, useful only in conjunction with other communications or application software. Within the TCP/IP world of Internet/intranets, however, PKI facilities are included and, indeed, crucial to some of the most important TCP/IP security initiatives (e.g., SSL and IPSec). DCE specifications, in contrast, do not even appear on the radar screen of current TCP/IP initiatives other than being an option in providing application-level security.

Secure Sockets Layer/Transport Layer Security

Secure Sockets Layer (SSL) is a separate layer of communications software that, in TCP/IP terms, sits between the application layer and the TCP transport layer (Figure 9-7).

SSL was initially developed by Netscape Communications Corp. as a way to securely transport sensitive financial data such as credit card and bank account information over the Internet. Netscape's original motivation was entirely driven by competitive concerns. It wanted to increase demand for licenses of its cryptographically secure web server software by bundling the client-side cryptography software in its web browser with minimal copyright and patent protection. In reaction, most of its browser competitors also adopted the methodology and a de facto standard for secure web communication was born. Microsoft Corp. developed the separate but related Private Communications Technology (PCT) protocol, but it also supports SSL. The Internet Engineering Task Force (IETF) has developed the Transport Layer Security (TLS) specification based on SSL 3.0. However, SSL remains the de facto standard.

Figure 9-7. Context of SSL in the TCP/IP stack.

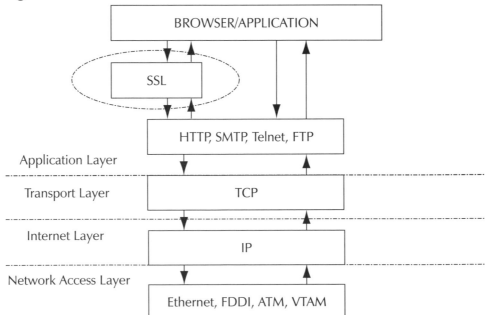

Briefly, SSL functions as follows:

1. When a client browser requests a secure connection to a web server, both the client and server use public key encryption to exchange digital certificates and establish a "secure" connection. As part of this process, they negotiate symmetric key encryption algorithms, message digest algorithms, and a series of four "secret" keys.

2. The four secret keys are then used to encrypt the subsequent exchange of messages, as follows:

- The first encrypts messages from the client to the server.
- The second encrypts messages from the server to the client.
- The third encrypts message digest numbers for messages from the client to the server.
- The fourth encrypts message digest numbers for messages sent from the server to the client.

3. When the connection is terminated, the secret keys are destroyed.

This set of exchanges meets the standards for secure messaging because it guarantees:

- Authentication of both parties, as provided by the exchange of digital certificates
- Confidentiality through the use of message encryption
- Integrity because of the use of message digests to insure the messages
- Nonrepudiation through the exchange of certificates

To reduce network overhead, SLL also compresses each message before encrypting it. This is done first to maximize the benefits of the compression algorithms, which are otherwise generally ineffective on encrypted data. Obviously, on the receiving side, SSL decompresses the message immediately after decryption.

SSL can be invoked directly from a client application program. It can also be invoked from an SSL-enabled browser by changing the URL of the server system from beginning with http: to starting with https: (e.g., http://www.server.com to https://www.server.com). Any further communication with that server will be secure—until or unless the server sends notification to the contrary.

While the concept of certificates is probably not familiar to most browser users, they use them all the time. CA certificates absolutely required for SSL are installed with the browser software but hidden from the casual user. Most browsers also include the facilities required to request personal certificates from the most common Certification Authorities—usually VeriSign (the first CA), the U.S. Postal Service, or AT&T. These requests involve filling out an identity questionnaire and paying a registration fee (using an SSL-based credit card protocol, of course). The browser can also accept certificates from other media. Once a certificate is received, the browser encrypts and stores it in a disk directory.

Most browser users, however, have never requested a digital certificate and are unaware of their existence. These users do, however, still participate in SSL sessions to exchange financial information. This is because a web server can be set up to conduct business with them over a secure link, even if they do not present a valid personal certificate. This is generally a business decision on the part of the merchant, based on a risk-reward tradeoff. The client may not have a valid digital certificate, but is willing to give the server (representing the merchant) a valid credit card or bank account number that is much more negotiable to the merchant than a VeriSign digital certificate. So the merchant is willing to take the small risk of enabling the communication.

SSL is one of the truly proven web technologies. Most of the negatives reported about SSL revolve around arguments that liken it to "using a howitzer to kill a fly." This is primarily because the additional encryption overhead is noticeable when compared to "clear" traffic. However, most of this overhead is incurred during the initial handshake to establish the secure connection. Once started, the overhead is barely visible, due in no small part to the data compression methodology.

Of greater note is the fact that SSL is oriented to application-level security and must be invoked from that level. SSL is not a system-level solution to TCP/IP security. An additional, related limitation is that SSL only secures message text; the routing information contained in the TCP and IP headers (i.e., source and destination headers, services, and ports) is transmitted in the clear and is subject to unauthorized inspection.

Internet Protocol Security

Internet Protocol Security (IPSec) is a series of open standards that address TCP/IP security issues at the system level: that is, within IP itself. These features grew out of IETF specifications for a new release of the Internet Protocol, version 6. Rather than waiting for the new version of IP to be adopted and rolled out, however, the IETF extracted these features from IP and re-specified them to be "added on" to the current version of IP, version 4, as IPSec.

IPSec's primary goal is to provide authentication, confidentiality, and integrity for messages transmitted over an insecure network as part of that network's infrastructure (Figure 9-8). No changes to existing (or future) applications are required to invoke these services. IPSec consists of three major standards: an authentication header, the encapsulated security payload protocol, and the Internet key exchange protocol. They function in the following way:

Figure 9-8. Context of IPSec in the TCP/IP stack.

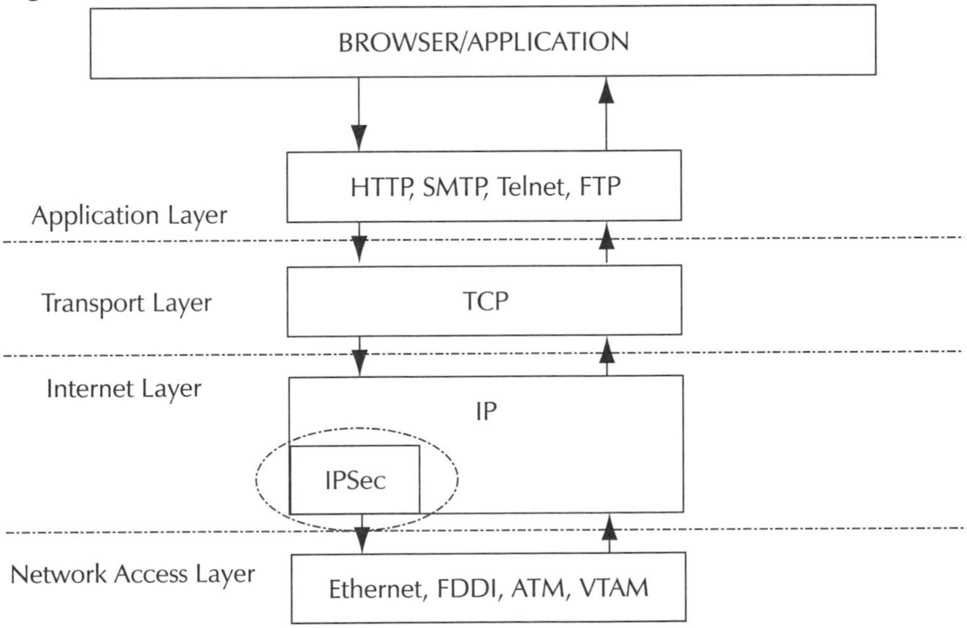

- *The authentication header (AH)* identifies the origin of a message and provides for data integrity through use of various message digest methodologies. AH services can be used with or without the encapsulated security payload protocol (see the following item). If AH is used without encapsulated security payload services, the message is transmitted in the clear, but still with authentication and integrity. Optionally, AH can also provide anti-replay services.

- *The encapsulated security payload (ESP) protocol* provides data confidentiality by encrypting the message's data. The ESP specification calls for the use of secret-key algorithms to encrypt message traffic, although the actual choice of algorithms is left up to the network administrators and vendor. ESP can be used without AH, but forfeits authentication services and anti-replay detection. *The Internet key exchange (IKE) protocol* is used to identify the routers, firewalls, and hosts communicating and to set up the security policies for both authentication headers and encapsulated security payload protocols. Setting up the security policies includes negotiating the ephemeral secret keys required by both AH and ESP (using the Diffie-Hellman Key Exchange protocol) and establishing two data structures for securing the communication. The security association (SA) structure keeps track of the communication, and the security parameter index (SPI) structure accompanies each message in order to point to the appropriate SA record associated with the communication on both ends. SPIs travel; SAs do not. Both AH and ESP require one SA/SPI pair apiece and, in turn, each also requires one SA/SPI pair for each direction of the conversation. Therefore, if a connection used both authentication header and encapsulated security payload protocol and participated in two-way communication, four SA/SPI pairs would have to be set up.

It should be noted that the IKE specification (which was formerly known as the ISAKMP-Oakley protocol) does not specifically address how the routers/firewalls/hosts involved should identify each other. Currently available IPSec-compliant software provides a range of identification options, from sharing predefined keys to verifying CA certificates using PKI software to invoking the "forthcoming" Secure Domain Name System (DNSSec).

Early IPSec implementations have concentrated on virtual private networks and other remote access applications, primarily because of their ease of implementation. However, there appears to be no reason not to extend IPSec to single-logon applications as well as intranets and extranets. With IPSec, TCP/IP networks finally have strong, system-level authentication and security facilities. Like SSL, IPSec's major liability is the CPU overhead of connection setup and encryption. However, most IPSec software vendors provide the means of selectively applying different levels of security, allowing the network to be tailored for different uses and levels of security relatively easily.

Virtual Private Networks

Virtual private networks allow computers existing outside of an organization's firewall to securely connect via TCP/IP to applications located on servers resident within the firewall. VPNs are intended to replace existing dial-up connections such as remote access for employees and electronic data interchange (EDI) access for suppliers and customers. With a VPN, users simply place a local phone call to their Internet service provider and surf to the corporate web site to gain access to their applications. The company in turn avoids the expenses associated with acquiring, maintaining, and managing the banks of dial-up modems and the dedicated phone lines that comprise their private wide area network (Figure 9-9).

As might be expected, the VPN-enabling software architecture is fairly simple; it consists of client software on the remote computer and a VPN server that sits behind the firewall (Figure 9-10). The client software sets up each TCP/IP message with the IP address of a "real" server (i.e., the one on which the desired application resides) within the firewall, but before actually sending the message, the software encapsulates and encrypts the entire TCP/IP message, including the source and destination TCP/IP headers. The encapsulated message is then given the IP address and service number of the VPN server within the firewall and sent to that destination. Upon its arrival at the VPN server, the message is decrypted, validated, and sent on the actual IP address and service number embedded in the message. Any response from the application server then returns first to

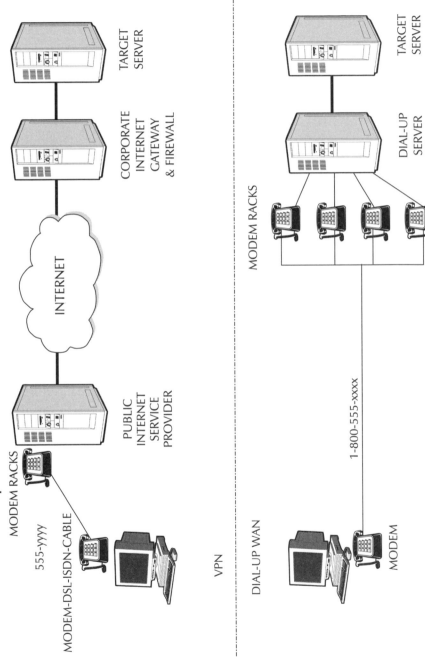

Figure 9-9. VPN versus dial-up WAN.

Figure 9-10. VPN architecture.

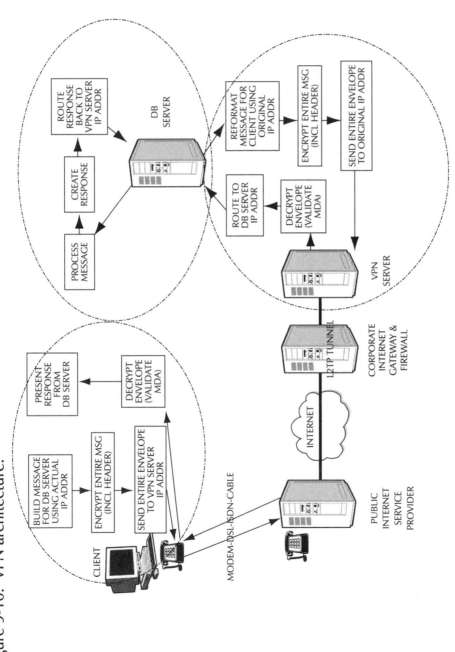

the VPN server to be encapsulated and encrypted before it is forwarded to the originating client.

In this way, VPN software provides not only the confidentiality and authentication for TCP/IP transport-level security, but it also extents this protection to IP addresses. An eavesdropper on normally encrypted communications can see the destination addresses of the TCP/IP messages and, over a long enough period of time, may be able to infer the functions of various servers. The eavesdropper can then use that information to mount an attack on one of those services. By encapsulating the actual IP addresses, as a VPN does, the only destination IP address visible to potential eavesdroppers is that of the VPN server. In this manner, the addresses and port numbers of all other services are kept confidential, reducing the chances of a successful attack.

Most VPN packages offer users a range of options regarding how encryption and authentication services are performed. A VPN package can use:

- Proprietary encryption and message integrity facilities
- Third-party PKI/CA and IPSec software
- SSL facilities and services
- Customized facilities provided by the individual installation

Minimally, a VPN must provide message security equal to that of SSL—that is, message encryption, user identification, and message integrity by means of message digests or hash counts. Communications to and through the firewall to the VPN server should follow the Level 2 Tunneling Protocol (L2TP) standard. The term *tunneling* refers to transmission of a TCP/IP message that has been completely encrypted, including TCP/IP headers.

VPN software is subject to many of the same performance issues that surround SSL, IPSec, and PKI authentication, plus the extra overhead of the additional network "hops" inherent in using a VPN server. These issues, however, must be balanced with the extremely large savings that accrue from eliminating existing dial-up and WAN facilities. Besides, without the level of security provided by the VPN software, many businesses might not be willing to surrender the privacy and confidentiality provided by private networks. In fact, VPN software can quite probably provide more secure communications than the existing dial-up and WAN facilities, simply because of the strength of its encryption and authentication services.

Browser Security Options

So far in this chapter, the discussion has focused on tools to secure Internet/intranet messages as they traverse the network. This section and the next focus on the two ends of the communication line: security considerations for the client and the host.

The discussion about client security can center on the browser once two assumptions are made:

- No rational users would initiate Internet/intranet communications without installing a reputable virus checker program on their computer and running it on a regular basis (at least once a day).

- Users have enabled a screensaver of some sort that locks the computer's display if no activity is detected for a period of time, preventing unauthorized use of the Internet/intranet connection during their absence.

Most browsers provide a screensaver facility, though it is not sufficient; there are other resources on the computer requiring protection besides the browser. Generally, an operating system timeout facility that is password protected is more efficient than just enabling the browser's pop-up.

The client's browser has a number of optional settings that have a significant impact on client security, and the vast majority of users are unaware of these settings. One of these options effects the browser's ability to download and run Netscape's plug-ins and Microsoft's ActiveX controls, objects that can provide new browser functions. They are modules containing machine instructions and function as part of the browser environment. They may be installed locally or downloaded from the Internet/intranet; locally loaded modules can generally be run without question. However, care must be exercised when downloading plug-ins and ActiveX controls from the Internet. The browser gives the user three options on whether to download one of these modules from the Web. The user can specify that the browser should:

- Download any of these modules requested.
- Download none of these modules.
- Prompt the user for permission to perform any such download.

More recent browser releases also allow the user the additional option of differentiating "signed" modules from unsigned ones and automatically accepting the signed modules with recognized certificates. Signed software is a normal executable file that has been digitally signed by the software provider. The public key used to decode the signature probably comes from a software publisher certificate issued by a CA, rather than an individual's certificate. The signature is used to ensure that the module the user downloads is the same one that the developer signed. Of course, it doesn't ensure that the original developer has not signed malicious code. It is a good idea to install the certificates of trusted software publishers, thus preventing the automatic download of signed modules from unscrupulous hackers. Digital signatures notwithstanding, downloading and blindly running a file containing executable instructions is not worth the risks involved. That's the stuff that viruses and Trojan horses are made of. As a general rule, browser options should always be set to prohibit automatic plug-in and ActiveX downloads.

Browser options concerning Java applets pose slightly different considerations. Java applets are not exactly the same as machine executable files. Rather, once downloaded, they run inside a Java Virtual Machine located within the browser. One of the features of this virtual machine is that the Java program runs inside a partitioned area called the sandbox and, except for being able to read and write to a specific disk directory, are isolated and cannot touch the rest of the computer's resources. As an additional security feature, the Java program is installed in the sandbox by a Java loader that performs some rudimentary security checking.

Browsers generally offer the following options regarding Java applets:

- Disable all Java applets.
- Grant any Java applet loaded locally access to all of the computer's resources.

- Restrict any Java applet downloaded from the Web from writing to the local disk.
- Prohibit any Java applet downloaded from the Web from initiating communication with any server other than the one from which it was downloaded.
- Allow any digitally signed Java applet full access to the local computer's resource as long as the signer has been preapproved by the user.

All of these restrictions can be modified to prompt the user for permission prior to performing any sensitive action.

A final set of browser options control the behavior of Secure Sockets Layer software. The major aspect of these settings deals with whether or not digital certificates must be exchanged and verified in order to establish secure communication with a remote server. The default settings permit secure communication without the exchange of certificates because the casual user probably does not have a personal certificate. If the user decides to acquire one, the browser settings should be changed to accommodate this addition. For truly secure communications, digital certificates are a must and individuals who plan to use their personal computer for banking or securities trading are well advised to request a personal certificate and modify their browser settings accordingly.

Host Security

Switching the emphasis from the client (where efforts concentrate on a single component, the browser) to the host means opening a Pandora's box—the web host server. Any discussion of host security must begin with a very basic security assumption: The web server software, be it HTTP with CGI or Java (or whatever new development comes next), must reside on a computer located behind a screening router in an isolated part of the IP network. All other hosts in an IP network should be isolated from direct access to the Internet. Also, just because they're behind a firewall and on their own subnets, these local resources are not exempt from normal, prudent security administration, as is appropriate for the various operating systems and applications. Web servers, though, are special cases and require additional administration and security. This special attention generally takes two forms:

- Limiting the various computing resources available to Internet traffic
- Minimizing the information available regarding the other resources and computers that exist behind the corporate firewall

Restricting the resources available to Internet traffic translates into configuring the host computer so that it has only the minimum necessary native services. Some prudent restrictions might include:

- Limiting the installed user ids to only those required to install and administer the operating system
- Defining only the TCP/IP, HTTP, or Java service, and any appropriate proxy services actually needed—even if it means that other services have to be manually removed from a preconfigured installation tape (or removed from the installed base delivered with the computer)
- Performing remote system administration only through services that require SSL (and assessing whether remote administration must be supported at all)
- Disabling any X Windows and Telnet facilities on UNIX systems
- Installing only proxy e-mail services that forward mail considered legitimate to actual mail servers sitting behind the firewall
- Never installing anonymous FTP (file transfer protocol) or RPC (remote procedure call)
- Never, under any circumstances, including a C compiler or any development facilities or libraries on the web server
- Monitoring access to CGI and Perl libraries very carefully

Physical security measures should not be overlooked, either. In most cases, the only way to update web programs and facilities should be through local floppy drives or CD-ROM readers. The web servers should also reside in a locked room where very few people have physical access. None of these security measures will be popular, especially with the programming staff, but they are necessary to protect corporate data resources.

Restricting access to information about the network resident behind the firewall requires a well-thought-out policy toward domain name server (DNS) services. DNS provides translation services between domain names and IP addresses. While the web server must have access to DNS services, it should not provide any information about computer names and IP addresses behind the firewall. To accomplish this, it is necessary to direct the web server's DNS needs to a special DNS server that acts as a cutout between the web server and the rest of the network. Similarly, the web server's native operating system's password files and directories should be secured with encryption, access lists, and other protections.

A number of different types of security verification tools have been developed to help identify host security weaknesses. These tools generally fall into one of three categories:

- *Tools That Identify Unauthorized Changes.* Tripwire and COPS, both available on the Web from Purdue University, produce and store message digests for every file on the server's disk(s). By running the program periodically, it will track the evolution of the server over a period of time, enabling the administrator to identify any unauthorized changes in the basic configuration of the server.

- *Tools That Identify Possible Exposures to Known Hacking Strategies.* The best known of these are SATAN and the Internet Security Scanner (ISS). Use of these tools is very controversial because they probe a target web site from the outside and therefore actually attack the web site. However, they only report exposures; they do not "crack" the site. The major point of contention revolves around the possible misuse of the information gained from these programs. The critics are missing an important point, however—the tools already exist, are in wide circulation, and no amount of criticism is going to make them go away. Prudent security administrators will make use of these tools so they know what the tools report about their sites. They can then take remedial action to prevent attacks.

- *Tools That Log Web Server Activity.* The single best way to monitor server activity is to gather as much information about server events as is practical. Most of the services that run on the web server can enable logging if that option is selected. Even if the volume of the events appears daunting, a number of analysis tools are available to reduce the raw logs to meaningful abstracts. Log data is invaluable when evaluating and recovering from security problems. It often provides the only way to reconstruct a series of events and determine exactly what went wrong.

One warning about system logs: Guard the access to the log files themselves. The same information that is so valuable to the security administrator is also of interest to potential vandals. Log tapes should be kept physically secure and might even be worth the bother to encrypt. They should never be analyzed on the web server itself, but on another machine. Some sites even go to the extreme of directly connecting (i.e., hardwiring) a personal computer to the web server. This machine's sole function is to receive and store the web server's log records in a place where they cannot be accessed from the Web. A completed collection of logs can then be analyzed and stored on disk or written out to a CD-ROM drive. While most would consider this excessive, it does point out that great care should be taken to protect the web server logs at all times.

The web server itself poses the greatest single threat to network security. Improperly configured, it offers a "welcome mat" to system hackers. The careless security administrator who overlooks web server configuration in effect posts a "hack me" sign on the corporate home page. The importance of subnets and restricting services available through the web server cannot be overemphasized for a secure Internet environment.

Final Thoughts

As is obvious, a multitude of security tools are available for use in an Internet/intranet environment. Communications can be encrypted, authenticated, and validated. Client computers and browsers provide a variety of security services. Host machines can be logged, validated, and stripped down to bare bones. All these technological services come with a wide variety of choices and customization options. However, the bottom line with all of these tools is that a distributed Internet/intranet system can still be hacked and cracked.

The best technological tools in the world are useless in the face of a situation where the organization has no security policy. All members of the organization, from the cleaning crew to the CEO, must be aware of their role in maintaining a secure environment. The policy begins with users knowing not to share personal passwords or write them on slips of paper and leave them on the desk, and extends to their knowing who should be notified if they suspect a security problem. The corporate security policy should encompass application architecture and procedures concerning system logs. Applications must be developed to embrace reasonable security, including user ids, if appropriate. New code should be tested thoroughly—"legitimate" bugs can unintentionally create security holes that are sought out by the experienced hacker. For example, if a process ends abnormally and leaves the user in the root directory, it is child's play for the hacker to move on to other, more rewarding locations in the corporate intranet. Administrators should also regularly monitor system logs, looking for traces of unusual activity and investigate the cause.

Above all, the organization's security policy must include contingency plans to deal with both successful and unsuccessful attacks on their web servers. On the World Wide Web, it is not a question of whether a site will be attacked, but rather a question of when it will happen. Even a company that has only an intranet is not foolproof against attack. These emergency plans should include fallback procedures to restore the environment to its "prehacked" condition and a blueprint to systematically investigate the circumstances leading up to the attack.

Maintaining an Internet presence can be a powerful asset to an organization, but Internet/intranet attacks cannot be entirely prevented. To do so would be far too costly in terms of both money and system resources. What is a company to do? Just because an attack may be successful is no reason to hibernate. The technological tools are available so that with prudence and some forethought, in the way of an enforceable security policy, the risk can be profitably managed and the bulk of corporate assets protected from even a successful attack.

10
WWW

Implementing a Distributed Data Warehouse

Ten years ago, many brokerage houses could have ascertained how many shares of stock they traded on behalf of their customers in an average month. Today, that same brokerage would likely be able to tell exactly how many shares of IBM were traded between 10 A.M. and 11 A.M. on the second Tuesday of the month, at what price, and if they were purchased on margin.

That is the advantage of a data warehouse. It gathers information from many different sources, organizes it, and makes it available to the appropriate people within an organization. The corporate data resources resemble a giant jigsaw puzzle, with each piece residing with a different department within the company, perhaps even scattered across several heterogeneous systems. All the pieces fit together seamlessly in the warehouse, allowing the entire picture, or any portion of it, to be viewed and analyzed. Decision makers can zoom in on a particular detail (e.g., IBM shares traded during a certain time span) or analyze the whole (e.g., total number of trades this month).

Most of the operational data processing systems within an organization are installed with a local view, their sole purpose being to solve a single isolated problem, such as trade clearance, client accounting, fee tracking, or accounts receivable. While not necessarily incorrect, this provincial approach presents problems when cross-directional views are required to understand the dynamics of a situation. Today's increasingly versatile and affordable technology makes it possible to access huge amounts of data from a variety of sources, analyze it, and distribute the results. The modern data warehouse is no longer bounded by a single computer; it can and does extend to encompass multiple systems, both within and outside the company.

Overview

Operational systems and data warehousing systems are fundamentally different in almost every aspect; they have a different life cycle, system configuration, and performance criteria. Instead of posting operationally focused transactions, the data warehouse is chartered to provide a tool to guide the business. Warehouses frequently use different computing resources than operational systems and almost always have deeper historical archives. Data warehouses are, of necessity, tuned differently to process applications not present in an operational environment. However, operational systems and data warehouses must share an important bond for both to operate correctly—they should use the same source data to be truly symbiotic. To do anything else endangers the success of the warehousing project.

Although the source is the same, the data used in the warehouse must frequently be transformed and consolidated to be useful. This is because the data stored in the decision-support system is processed in a different way; it is not even stored with the same schema as an online transaction processing (OLTP) system. To accommodate such variation, a number of architectural approaches are in use today to structure data warehouses.

Initially, data warehouse construction and implementation followed an all-inclusive approach. In this structure, enterprise data models were laboriously and meticulously constructed, with the data needs of the entire organization documented. Data was then extracted from many, if not all, transactional systems and fed into the warehouse. Until very recently, most major companies were working on, or planning to start, this type of warehouse. Constructing a centralized warehouse is such a gargantuan task that almost no one has actually completed one.

However, in the mid-1990s two technologies became commercially viable that fundamentally change the way data warehouses are constructed. These technologies are the World Wide Web, which makes information stored on computers linked to the Internet easily accessible, and distributed processing products, which make it possible for several different computing systems to work together as a whole.

The way information is obtained and analyzed is changing. Data published on the World Wide Web or the corporate intranet is easily accessible to nontechnical decision makers for query, reporting, and analysis tasks. For businesses, this network accessibility can offer an alternative, low-cost mechanism for making data available to individuals who need it. For the user, the end result is a much richer pool of easily accessible information from a wider variety of resources.

Distributed processing products can make things even easier for the users and extend their analysis capabilities even further. Properly used, they facilitate interoperability among a group of heterogeneous computing systems, making the data stored at any location available to anyone who has access to even a single system in the group (Figure 10-1). Using an appropriate decision-support tool, even inexperienced users can retrieve data from one or more remote systems without knowing the location of the information they want. Distributed processing opens the door to constructing an enterprise data warehouse from a series of data marts and operational systems, at significantly reduced cost to the business.

Data Marts

Organizations are beginning to realize that implementing the all-inclusive traditional data warehouse is an uphill battle with an extremely limited chance of success. More and more, they are constructing a series of limited, single-purpose systems instead that contain a carefully selected subset of information aimed at satisfying the data needs of a department. These data marts allow the organization to better control the data and are much quicker and cheaper to develop. Often, a data mart can be operational in three months and costs less than $200,000 in total.

There are four types of data marts that are commonly employed today:

- *Dependent Data Marts*. These data marts are constructed to satisfy the needs of a specific group, usually one or two departments within the company (Figure 10-2). They depend on the existence of a centralized data warehouse as the source for their carefully selected data. The dependent data mart is actually just a subset of the enterprise data warehouse, usually designed to improve performance for

Figure 10-1. Distributed processing products.

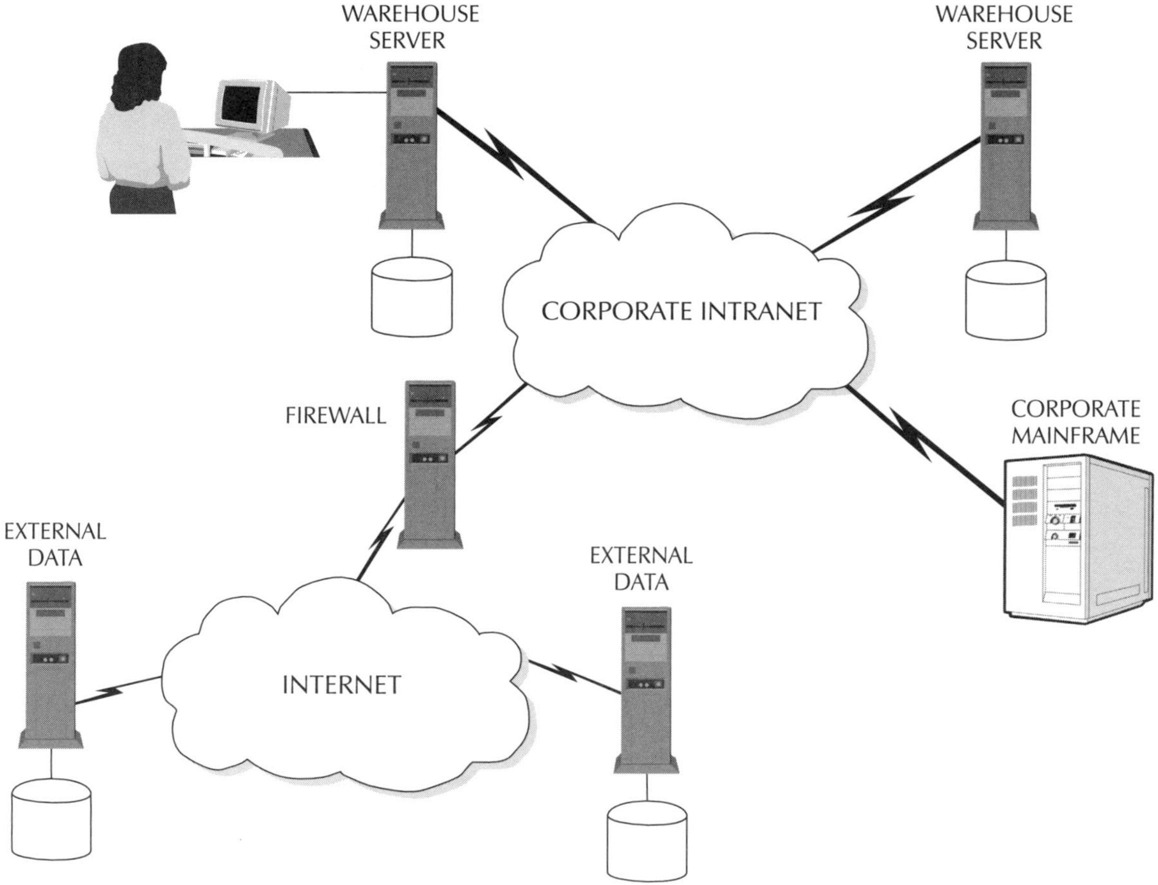

Figure 10-2. Dependent data mart.

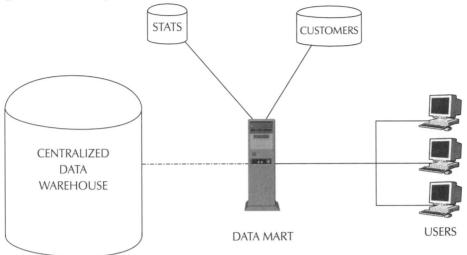

its user group. While the dependent data mart is fast and easy to build, its cost are enormous because of its reliance on the central data warehouse for information.

• *Independent Data Marts*. Here, individual applications are architected for specific departmental needs, with the required data obtained directly from operational systems (Figure 10-3) or other nonwarehouse sources. Care is taken to extract only what is absolutely necessary from the operational systems to limit the amount of time the downloads take them away from their primary transaction-oriented tasks. These data marts are easy to fund, fast to build, and generally enjoy good user support.

• *Integrated Data Marts*. These depend on there being a consistent data architecture behind the independent data marts (Figure 10-4). With a standard architecture, the independent data marts form an integrated group or "data mall." Like a shopping mall, the integrated data marts have a unifying theme and well-defined standards and rules for the participants. When using this approach, any new data mart that comes online has to comply with the rules of the mall. If it does not, it cannot participate in the traffic flow of customers (i.e., users) the mall attracts. A common example of a data mall is seen in electronic commerce. A group of merchants band together and agree to develop their web sites to a specific set of standards and link the

Figure 10-3. Independent data mart.

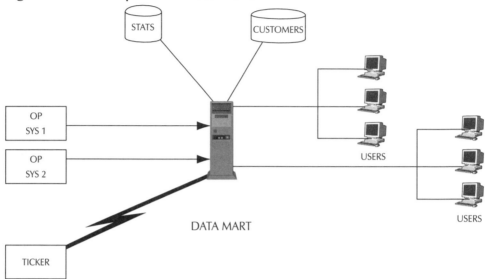

sites together. Customers are then presented with a common user interface (e.g., a shopping cart) with which they can peruse, shop, and order from any merchant in the group.

• *Point Solution Data Marts.* In this architectural construct, each mart is built to the specific needs of a particular group without adhering to any integrative architecture, standard, or other conformance with any other existing data mart (Figure 10-5). This is obviously the quickest data mart to build because no time is spent attempting to integrate the effort with any enterprisewide architecture. This is also the data mart most likely to need redesigning if it proves successful. Any possibility of cross-department analysis is difficult at best (if not impossible) because of the lack of standardization. The point solution data mart also puts the greatest stress on the existing infrastructure. If there is more than one data mart designed this way, all are extracting data from the same operational systems and a great deal of redundancy can result. The operational systems can be kept so busy supplying data to these marts that they have no time to perform their primary tasks.

To Be Considered

Obviously, there are several approaches available today for constructing a decision-support data warehouse system for a company. It

Figure 10-4. Integrated data marts.

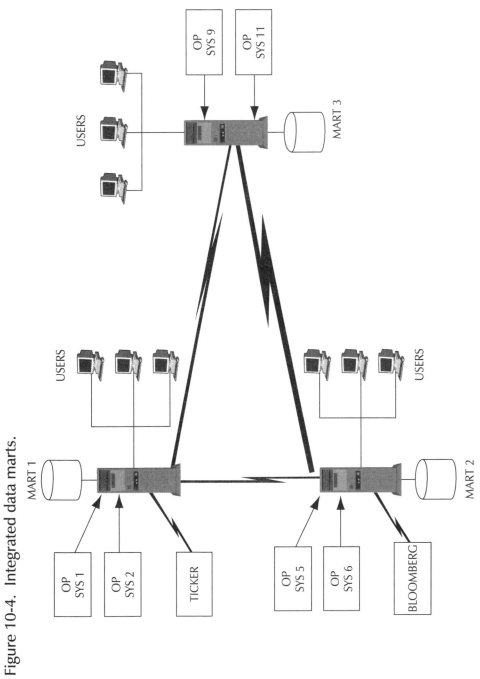

Figure 10-5. Point solution data mart.

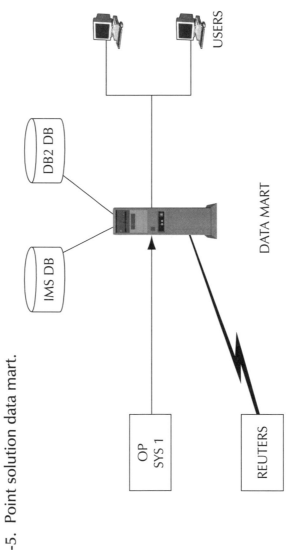

should be clear that regardless of the approach taken, certain underlying technology issues must be addressed first:

- *Performance* is one of the key factors in the success or failure of a data warehouse. The warehouse must not only deliver the right results to the correct people, it must do so in the right format, at the right time, and in a timely and responsive manner. Some symptoms of a failing system are queries that run for hours, frequent "system unavailable" notices, and obsolete data because of an infrequent load/refresh cycle in the data warehouse. If these conditions occur, the warehouse is in serious trouble. No user community will tolerate these obstructions for long.

- *Scalability* comes next after performance as a make-or-break warehousing factor. The warehouse, if it is successful, will be increasingly under stress as the amount of data grows, the number of users increases, and the level of sophistication of users and their tools develops. As users grow accustomed to the warehouse, they will try more complex joins, demand more variation in the models, and insist on greater functionality such as data mining. Implementations that cannot scale up to meet increased demands will soon become obsolete.

- *Availability* is another critical area because users will want the warehouse to be available when they need it, and sometimes their needs are not very predictable. When a competitor surprises the market with an innovative move or a change to the pricing structure, the warehouse must be in a position to respond with resources and analysis instantly, regardless of the time of day or day of the week. Increasingly, warehouses need to be 24×7—available twenty-four hours a day, seven days a week.

Organizations today are typically large and have a wealth of computing systems developed over the past thirty years. Often, these applications are owned by various departments, all of which use differing standards. These factors make coalescing the data into a warehouse a formidable undertaking. Certain characteristics of the data warehouse itself are critical to the performance and success of the system.

To assemble a complete picture about even a single aspect of an organization usually requires gathering data from many different systems. To build an enterprise data warehouse requires assembling and storing large quantities of data from all available sources internal to the organization and sometimes from external systems, too. For the type of analysis tasks most decision makers perform, raw operational data is needed as well as derived data such as summaries, averages, and deviations from the norm. This derived data soon adds up, consuming enormous amounts of storage, and it affects the warehouse in several different areas.

The first system impact is the time and computing power needed to scan such large databases in response to specific queries. The second area is the time and effort required to load, refresh, and maintain the warehouse in order to keep it tuned, current, and relevant to the organization. The larger the database, the more summaries, averages, and aggregations are needed, and the more time it will take to build them. Many businesses underestimate the database requirements of their systems. It is therefore very important to do the appropriate analysis up-front to ensure that the warehouse can expand to meet the demand when it comes.

A data warehouse is constructed to satisfy an unstructured query model, unlike the traditional reporting structures in operational systems, where the database queries are predefined before the system is even built. When E*Trade Securities, Inc., first announced its discount services, most other brokerage houses hurriedly began trying to figure out what impact E*Trade would have on their business and what response, if any, they should make. Countless models were built to determine the result of each proposed response, each based on different assumptions regarding customer behavior, advertising impact, and pricing structure.

Many brokerages have partial data warehouses in place to support just this type of decision making. It is clear that there would have been no way for the warehouse developers to have known ahead of time that this would be a subject for analysis and research. Each brokerage wanted to look at several potential scenarios and multiple responses for each. They needed to consider many iterations and permutations of queries into the demographics of customers, the effect of lowering trading fees, the revenue and profit impact of any pricing change, the force of an advertising campaign, and the trends in the marketplace. Given this example, it becomes clear that a data warehouse will be subject to significant stresses and will require considerable computing and input/output resources.

A crucial part of the demand on the warehouse will be for corporatewide information, which means that much of the analysis work performed will be cross-functional in nature. Users will need to combine information gleaned from several different views of the data. This requires the use of complex, multiway joins on the data tables. These joins consume considerable system resources, and when combined with a system where the tables themselves are very large, the problem is compounded. Any data warehousing veteran can tell apocryphal stories of queries that took hours or even days to complete.

Today's management philosophies have evolved considerably from where they were just a scant fifteen years ago when executive information systems (EIS) technology first surfaced. In fact, the very name suggested the exclusivity of these systems. At the time it was assumed that only executives in an organization were involved in the decision-making process, and only they would require the ad hoc analysis and summary information from a cross-functional perspective that would be provided by the warehouse.

Since that time, responsibilities and decision making have been pushed down the corporate ladder and into the hands of the professional staff. More and more people are demanding access to the information and cross-functional analysis required for sound decision making. As the importance of the data warehouse grows and its size expands, it is important that it be able to step up to the new challenges.

This expanded user base typically undergoes a learning curve in acclimating to the new technology. As they become more familiar with the data structures, query languages, and decision-support tools, they will build on their previous experience to develop more sophisticated models for analyzing their problems. This translates into more complex joins, more full table scans, more sophisticated mathematical computations, and in general, more demand on the warehouse. The hardware and software used must have the capacity and capability to ensure performance.

Pitfalls

It can be instructive to see where data warehousing systems have potential pitfalls. By identifying the areas where things can go wrong, the organization can better define countermeasures to avoid the problems. The primary technical issues are dependent upon the four elements common to all computer systems:

- Memory architecture
- I/O architecture
- Systems tools
- Application software (which utilizes the other three elements in order to deliver a solution to the end user)

The best place to begin almost any discussion of performance is the capability of the central processing unit (CPU) of the system. Decision-support systems, like warehouses, are only as good as their ability to satisfy the decision makers. The warehouse project is doomed to fail without a good, consistent architecture that can deliver performance and that will be stable and have the capacity to grow.

For a traditional, centralized warehouse, a good deal of attention needs to be paid to the ability of the selected computer to handle the demands placed by completely random searches into very large databases. While developers try hard to avoid full table scans and complex joins with careful modeling, the use of join indices, denormalization, and other techniques, the simple fact is that there is no way to avoid them completely. Therefore, there will be significant demands on the abilities of the CPU itself. The ability to load indices and other table portions directly into memory can significantly improve overall performance because memory access times are always much faster than disk access. Limitations on the size of memory could impede this process; indeed, this is becoming a significant problem for centralized warehousing installations today.

Recently, 64-bit architectures have emerged, allowing significant improvements in performance over their 32-bit predecessors. This architectural change directly affects many of the issues surrounding data warehouse implementations. A 64-bit CPU can address a memory space four billion times the size of the maximum memory space of a 32-bit machine. This allows the system to maintain frequently accessed portions of the database in memory. Since memory access times are orders of magnitude faster than they are for disk reads, the end user gains much faster response times, higher availability, and the capacity to do more work quickly. For example, a full table scan in a 64-bit system has been benchmarked as being eight times faster than in a 32-bit environment.

The way the system's memory is architected contributes to its ability to respond to the demands of a data warehouse. A significant aspect of this is the width of the memory. As the amount of data that can be transferred into and out of memory per clock cycle increases, the system's ability to deal with larger blocks of data in a timely fashion also increases.

In the distributed data warehouse, memory architecture is again key. In a multiprocessing environment, some amount of time must be devoted to synchronizing and coordinating the activities of the various processors. In the server-class shared memory machines (also known as symmetric multiprocessing) so frequently used, there may be times when the memory is busy servicing other processors, causing one or more processors to wait until the memory is free again. Minimizing latency, improving memory availability, and speeding up the access time to the memory will help keep more processors working at a higher utilization. In turn, this improves performance. Conversely, longer latency times, reduced availability, and slower access times will result in a poorer overall system performance.

Here again the 64-bit memory architecture can contribute to performance. In addition to being able to address vastly greater quantities of data, each access results in the transfer of 64-bits of data instead of 32-bits, which offers several benefits. First, doubling the number of bits transferred in a single clock cycle feeds the CPU with double the data, instructions, and addresses. This means that each transfer to memory is much more efficient. Second, it allows shared memories to service more processors, reducing latency and minimizing wait times. Finally, when combined with the increased clock speeds of today's CPU architecture, the effects combine geometrically to produce astounding performance increases.

Single processors can only address the finite amount of memory attached to them. By clustering memory and processors, each individual processor can have access to more memory. Where a single processor might have a 14 megabyte (MB) memory limit, when clustered with another similar processor it can have access to 28 MB. This increase in capacity can significantly affect performance of certain data warehouse functions.

When dealing with databases that are hundreds of gigabytes or even the terabyte range in size, it is reasonable to be concerned about the performance of the input/output (I/O) subsystems. A potential exists for operational problems related to the amount of time required to read and analyze large quantities of data, load large amounts of data, and maintain the database. Bottlenecks in the I/O process will cause longer load and refresh times and longer backup and recovery times. Each of these can cause reduced availability to the user community. The alternative, of course, is to make fewer backups or to refresh the data less often. In the former case, the action is imprudent; in the latter, the warehouse risks failing because it does not provide timely information to the users.

As expected, a 64-bit architecture also provides substantive improvements to the I/O subsystem if the architecture is carried throughout. Again, the combination of faster clock speeds with doubling of the bus provides a multiplicative effect for much greater throughput. In data warehousing, there is likely to be heavy I/O traffic, so it is vitally important that the architecture extend to the peripherals and I/O subsystems.

In a centralized warehouse, the data can be partitioned over multiple disks running in parallel. The amount of bandwidth provided by a 64-bit system makes it possible to think of supporting large user communities in a decision-support environment. For distributed warehouses, the improved clock speeds and bandwidth also make for extremely improved performance. Table joins across participating systems are much faster, and cross-system performance is improved overall. For both types of warehouses, load and refresh times are much improved, allowing more frequent refreshes of current data or even real-time updates where necessary.

Yet very large databases are not the only size-related problem facing warehouses today. If a warehouse is successful, chances are that there is a constant flood of users asking for access to the data for their own needs. The users are probably clamoring for admittance because they have heard from their peers how responsive and effective the warehouse is. The success stories circulated by their colleagues have intrigued them to the point of joining in.

The warehouse that cannot gracefully scale with these growing demands runs the risk of not only alienating the new users who have been enticed to join, but of disaffecting the loyal users who were spreading the good word to begin with. Clearly, data warehousing implementations must seriously consider the implications of scalability in their project plans—especially since the ultimate size of the warehouse system is often very difficult to predict.

The problems associated with scalability plague the centralized warehouse more often than they do the distributed system. With a distributed warehouse, it is easy to start small (e.g., a single-server data mart) and gradually add equipment as additional data marts come online or as demand increases. In contrast, the centralized warehouse begins, and all too often ends, life as a single monolithic system. While it is possible to increase memory, storage capacity, and user connections, all of these has a finite limit that is reached all too quickly, either leaving some users without access or providing poor performance to an inflated user base.

A final point of concern for the developers and managers of data warehouses is the integration and architectural consistency of the applications and support software with the overall warehouse architecture. Although vendors endlessly advertise the high-performance, state-of-the-art nature of their products, some application products do not have all the bells and whistles needed to take full advantage of today's technologies. It is important that the purchaser look under the covers of any proposed purchase to ensure that it has been written or updated to extract all the performance available from the warehouse system architecture. A good example of this is the many products now available that claim to be compatible with a distributed environment. While most will work in a minimalistic fashion, all too many are not yet designed to exploit the parallel processing capacity of the distributed system.

If warehouse developers intend to take advantage of a 64-bit system, they need also be aware that 64-bit computing is not limited to the CPU chip and its supporting systems. The database management system (DBMS) and applications must also be adapted to achieve the performance and scaling benefits. In fact, the operating system, compilers, and runtime libraries must be developed, coordinated, and tuned for the overall system to be a success.

As warehousing systems become more accepted, end users come to rely on them as a necessary tool to get their jobs done. Data warehousing applications are truly becoming mission-critical as their role in strategic and tactical decision making grows. With increased stature comes a corresponding need to avoid the pitfalls and provide reliable, consistent, and responsive performance to the user community.

Business Factors

The previous section focused primarily on technological concerns and how they can impact the success of the warehouse. The warehouse designer and manager must also address business and relationship issues to ensure a successful implementation. These issues center on other elements of the solution, such as selecting software that is capable of providing support services to enhance the value of the technology and customizing it to suit the business needs of the company. Integrating the correct set of components is key to a successful data warehouse implementation. Tools and processes that are compatible with the enterprise's business needs are required in each phase of warehouse development. All of these tools and processes must be compatible with each other and integrated into the overall architecture.

Initial Tools Selection

The operational life of the warehouse begins with the extraction of data and metadata from the operational systems (and any other data sources). There are many challenges inherent in this data extraction process, including issues of multiple data sources from incompatible and frequently antiquated systems that use outmoded data storage methods, such as flat files or custom-designed databases and tables. The task of assembling the metadata must start at the very beginning of the cycle if the programmers and users hope to have a reasonable chance of navigation through the tables in the warehouse and if they are going to be able to understand the nature and definition of the data. The tools selected for these tasks must be comprehensive and adaptable to the variety of data sources used by the organization.

To further complicate matters, most legacy systems were built without the benefit of any enterprise data standards. This often means that there is little or no data consistency across systems and even sometimes within a single system. For example, a brokerage has a decades-old database containing the names and addresses of all of its clients. No data standards were ever enforced concerning abbreviations, capitalization, name order, and customer Social Security number. To move this data to the warehouse, the information must be cleansed to check for accidental duplicates (e.g., J. D. Rockefeller and John D. Rockefeller, Sr.), transformed (e.g., Rockefeller, John D. versus John D. Rockefeller), and rebuilt into a consistent and well-defined system.

Of particular interest here is the fact that, in order for users to have access to correct data, the information must be extracted and cleansed/transformed without affecting business processes. In the case of large operational databases, the extraction/transformation cycle can be lengthy and laborious. The tools chosen must be flexible enough to adapt to operational cycles and perform their extracts in stages at convenient times.

The data base management system is the heart of the warehouse, critical to its function. The DBMS must be compatible with the rest of the architecture and robust enough to service the needs of the user community. There are several good vendor choices employing a number of technological strategies available in this class. For the centralized warehouse and the homogeneous distributed warehouse, this choice is made only once. In the case of the heterogeneous distributed system, several different DBMSs may be employed, but it is important that they share some level of interoperability and possess-compatible data storage methodologies (e.g., they are all relational, or a mix of object and object-wrapped relational) for the smooth functioning of the warehouse.

User access to the data once it is stored is of paramount importance. The need for good models to help users navigate the table structure and construct complex queries cannot be overestimated. There are a number of fine data access tools available that, in conjunction with the data model, simplify this process for the inexperienced user. Care must be exercised in choosing this application to ensure that it is relatively easy to install, customizable to suit the business' needs, easy to use with minimal training, and simple to maintain. Some of these products, while very flexible and simple to install, require extensive training to use effectively. The users must become expert in their operation in order to do their jobs. The warehouse should serve the users, not the other way around.

Customization

For any warehouse to deliver the best possible service to its users requires some additional work on the part of the developer. Warehousing is a technology that must be custom-fitted to the organization it serves. As a result, the business must take a methodical and structured approach to defining and building a warehouse in order to take full advantage of the system's potential.

This need for tailoring is so strong that vendors routinely offer customization services, either in partnership with management consultants or through their own staffs. Some vendors even employ the services of software groups to aid with the successful integration of their products into the overall architecture. Make certain that the technology implemented supports the business goals of the enterprise.

Prototyping

Prototyping techniques can be helpful in determining an information architecture, although prototyping poses a legitimate dilemma. On the one hand, it is desirable to have a complete information architecture and data standards before commencing any work on the data warehouse. This approach ensures that there can be consistent business rules for transforming data and for analyzing it. However, given the size, political diversity, and time constraints of business today, the likelihood of being able to produce a complete, agreed-to architecture is difficult at best and often virtually impossible.

By starting small and constructing prototypes upon which to gain consensus, some organizations are able to fashion enough of an architectural plan to build on in later iterations. With prototyping, the odds of having to redo the complete architecture are minimized while the prototype simultaneously improves the chances of a timely warehouse implementation.

Piloting the initial design also serves to gain consensus, prove the concepts, and increase the chances for success in any warehouse implementation, regardless of type. A successful pilot is likely to translate into a successful implementation—it increases user interest and awareness of the value of a warehouse and can point out areas of concern while the warehouse is still in the design phase, where any pitfalls are more manageable than in production. It is always more cost-effective to make mistakes on a small scale than a large one. Almost all pilots more than pay for themselves when the worker-hours and expenses they save the company are considered.

Implementation Plan

The overall objective of a data warehouse is to make all critical corporate data available for rapid inquiry, analysis, and reporting. To achieve this, it is necessary to locate, transform/cleanse, and in some cases, organize and move the data from the existing applications to the warehouse. Following a well-defined plan greatly simplifies these tasks.

The more the systems containing the source data adhere to some set of common data standards, the easier the warehouse implementation should be. For implementation, some of the major tasks are as follows:

• Identify the critical data subject areas (e.g., customer, vendor, inventory, accounts payable, general ledger). Often this step is accomplished using the enterprise data model. If there is no model, this is still a key first step. Specify the target performance for creating extract files. This is the rate at which conversion must proceed to be acceptable. If an operational system has an available window of fifty minutes once a day, then the extract must complete in that timeframe.

• Examine the source data, field by field, character by character, to establish actual content, mappings needed, and acceptable data standards for the organization. This is a laborious and thankless task and, as a result, is often skipped. Its importance to the success of the warehouse project cannot be overestimated—it must be done. There are a number of excellent tools available to assist in this type of analysis, and they do speed the process.

- Establish organizationwide standards for field size, type, and other characteristics for various common categories of field (e.g., names, addresses, phone numbers, postal codes).

- Establish content and format standards.

- Incorporate the developed standards into the conversion code to create standard versions of the source data.

- Develop and implement normalized tables within each subject area for the warehouse.

- Normalize source files and load into warehouse tables.

- Develop a common metadata dictionary of elements and tables to define the new standard elements, including data source information, to support future access by users.

- Evaluate results and implement additional changes as needed to complete cross-subject integration.

The result of completing this effort is that most application data, organizationwide, will be available in standard form. This careful planning is needed to allow access to historical data stored in the warehouse and to produce extract files that can be used to refresh the warehouse daily. Because of this daily transfer of data, the user is provided with consistent access to operational data and has the opportunity to replace existing applications reports with direct access to the warehouse data. In addition, the standards and content defined for the warehouse can be reverse engineered into a design for replacing the legacy systems, should that become desirable.

Of course, any implementation plan has possible areas of concern. In this effort, the constraints are as follows:

- *Inadequate Documentation of the Source Systems' Data Content.* This situation leads to the need for a character by character analysis of all data extracted from legacy systems to determine the exact content of the data, establish data relationships, and in some cases, discover if it is even the information desired.

- *Lengthy Processing Times to Extract, Cleanse, and Transform Data from the Source Systems and Load It into the Warehouse.* The more proprietary the source data structures and the more cleansing/transformation needed, the more likely a serious problem related to processing times will develop. In some cases the processing times are so long that it becomes necessary to change the legacy application code to bring the source more in line with the warehouse's needs. Another approach is to transfer most of the standardization effort to the warehouse after extracting the raw data from the source.

• *Inadequate Processing Speed for Data Mapping and Loading into the Warehouse.* For distributed warehouses, this can usually be resolved by using high-speed servers and parallel loads. In a centralized warehouse, parallel loads can again improve load times by as much as 75 percent.

All of the above-mentioned constraints deal, in one way or another, with the transfer of data from source to warehouse. These constraints are based on the premise that the needed data has to be extracted from the legacy system by some outside agent. There is another possible approach to data transfer that eliminates many of these issues. It is based on the publish/subscribe paradigm.

Moving Data into the Warehouse through Publish/Subscribe

At its most fundamental level, publish and subscribe is designed to provide three services:

- Coordinate processes
- Replicate data content
- Inform people

This is not a new concept, even in electronic terms. Such services have been available for years, providing daily news summaries based on subscriber's preferences. This service first became available by fax and cell phone, and later over the Internet and through e-mail. Although limited initially to a point-to-point feed of static text, now there are many services to choose from, with the Internet and e-mail versions offering live hyperlinks to other web resources and many including pictures and sound. Clients have only to specify at what interval they want an update and the messaging between client and server is automatic (Figure 10-6).

Figure 10-6. Publish and subscribe service.

DATA MART

REQUEST FOR CUSTOMER HOLDINGS
EVERY DAY AT 3 PM

SUBSCRIBE

PUBLISH

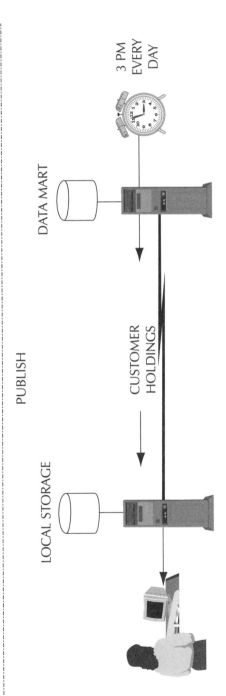

DATA MART

3 PM
EVERY
DAY

CUSTOMER
HOLDINGS

LOCAL STORAGE

The implications of this technology are enormous, especially for expanding the reach of all types of applications, and data warehouses in particular. Using the publish and subscribe paradigm, clients can tune in to broadcasts that provide not only content but also the logic required to view or even manipulate the data.

With a solid information infrastructure in place, the most efficient method of transferring data from one place to another is to publish and subscribe, which streamlines the information delivery process. It is being used in a limited fashion to deliver reports to users, and some organizations use publish/subscribe as a way to notify key users when certain events occur. The most effective use of publish/subscribe is to have legacy systems publish their information at intervals convenient to them, rather than having the warehouse extract, transform, and cleanse the data.

Using the publish/subscribe paradigm, a legacy system broadcasts, or "publishes," its new data in a predefined format at scheduled intervals to make it available to all interested parties. This can be accomplished with a few simple changes to the operational system's code, allowing it to accumulate and store the new information it acquires in the correct format, ready for publication. In the process of accumulating the data, the legacy system performs whatever cleansing and transformation processes are required to make the data suitable for the warehouse. Each time the data is broadcast, the storage file is cleared, and the accumulation process begins anew.

Once the information has been published and captured by a server, it is contained in a central location. This is especially useful in a distributed warehousing environment, where there are likely several copies of key data positioned throughout the network. Each data mart can subscribe to the data it needs when it is convenient, rather than having to adhere to a rigid extraction schedule. Publishing reduces the redundancy of extracting the same information several times, once for each data mart that uses it.

Publish and subscribe is a balance of subscriber control and administrator process management. Instead of "pulling" mass amounts of data from the legacy systems with extracts, it is published one time to the server. The subscribing data mart then determines when it wants the information and under what criteria. When the scheduled time or event arrives, the data is "pushed" to the data mart. Subscription is usually by time or event and does require the addition of scheduling and monitoring software.

Both the warehouse and the operational systems benefit from the use of publish/subscribe technology. For the warehouse, the data is available when it is needed, already cleansed and transformed. For the legacy systems, they need only accumulate their newly acquired data and broadcast it at convenient intervals, placing only a very minimal strain on their resources. This new method replaces the old extracts, which may have consumed so much of their time and resources to have been a serious impediment to their real function of transaction processing. Use of the publish/subscribe paradigm eliminates one of the major constraints of data warehousing.

Final Considerations

A data warehouse should be looked at as a means of organizing and improving data, not as merely a record-keeping device. Just supplying data on demand efficiently to the users is not enough. That data must be packaged within a context of frameworks, analyses, and rules. To be effective, the warehouse must challenge peoples' thinking, not reinforce it, and it should lead users to ask the right questions. Correctly deployed, a data warehouse can be a rising tide, improving the level of everything in the organization in the process.

No decision-support system delivers sustainable improvement unless it fundamentally alters the nature of work for the better. The greatest data surfing programs in the world will only have, at best, a temporary and localized effect if the analysis cannot be shared easily with others. Many data warehouses miss this component completely by focusing on data and reporting issues instead of the broader concepts of content and problem solving. The primary design goal of any warehouse should be flexibility—the ability to continuously evolve to meet changing user needs is even more critical than processing efficiency.

By its very nature, data warehousing is a technically demanding application because of its very large size and the need to integrate data from diverse areas. Businesses today have taken a broad range of approaches to solving this problem, from creating monolithic centralized warehouses to distributed data mart–based systems or isolated point solution data marts with no integration attempted. Regardless of the approach taken, the fundamental characteristics of the problems remain the same: Data warehouses that derive their information from many other systems will still require faster, larger, and better memory and enhanced I/O capacity to absorb data in a timely fashion.

The growing number of users who want access to the warehouse, combined with the increasingly complex analysis they will want to perform, will require a high level of computational performance. The increasing penetration of user queries into multiple areas of the business will require scalability. Increasingly sophisticated users will demand more complex tools (e.g., data mining and graphic visualizations), and as the warehouse gains acceptance in the user community, its need for availability and reliability increases.

Today's enabling technologies can play a big role in making data warehousing affordable and performant. The use of 64-bit technology will be invaluable, perhaps even mandatory, for addressing these issues in the months and years to come. The performance gains of 64-bit technology are well documented, and the move to this technology is as inevitable as was the move from the 16-bit to 32-bit architecture. The easiest way to accomplish this move is with a series of interconnected server-class 64-bit machines.

Organizations that make the move to 64-bit technology early will benefit in a number of areas. First and foremost, they will have a much easier time of addressing the needs of their constituency. Beyond that, the projected growth trajectory available through this technology ensures that their investment will be leveraged for some time to come.

The use of 64-bit technology will make the inevitable increase in demand from the user community addressable. Furthermore, when 64-bit technology is used in combination with a symmetric multiprocessing (SMP) architecture and processor clustering techniques, smoother upgrades to realize increases in performance will be available. Enterprises that make the move sooner rather than later will be better positioned for success.

Publish/subscribe technology is the least disruptive, most efficient way to move data into a distributed data warehouse. There is a caveat, however, with this technique. Multicasting is a type of broadcast that allows information to be pushed over the network from many sources to many recipients. This is the equivalent to employing the technology in a many-to-many connection pattern. It is the most practical methodology for a warehousing application, and anyone contemplating the use of publish/subscribe technology should strongly consider its use. This technique, however, can prove costly in terms of the quantity of network traffic it creates.

Above all, the business should adopt a mission-critical approach to warehouse construction, not a project-oriented one, to enable the warehouse to be nothing less than the driving force for corporatewide improvements.

11

Future Developments

Advances in computing almost always present a paradox—on one hand, new technology can make business more competitive, more efficient, and most of all, more profitable, while on the other hand, there is always the threat of implementation problems caused mainly by nonstandard components, proprietary conflicts, limited prototyping, and short development schedules. This paradox is more of a threat today than any other time in computing history.

A number of technologies have developed over the past ten years, and their emergence offers information technology (IT) departments everywhere unprecedented opportunities for building state-of-the-art applications of real value to their businesses. With the rise of the Internet and World Wide Web, distributed processing architectures, object-oriented technologies, and of course client/server, the time is ripe to take advantage of new methods of applications development. IT departments must be made to face the facts and realize that the whole paradigm of computing has shifted to smaller, cheaper, faster machines interconnected by high-speed networks.

However, it must also be remembered that literally thousands of terabytes of information are locked up in proprietary systems using older technologies such as IMS/VS, CICS/VS, and VSAM, where it can only be accessed by a programmer trained in the intricacies of the transaction monitors and messaging systems that manage the programs and information. Add to this mix the complexities of relational databases and distributed object computing, and it is no wonder that building modern, scalable, reusable applications that access enterprise data can be so challenging and potentially risky.

How is it possible to capitalize on the new developments without first redesigning the existing transaction processing and messaging systems? The trick is to leverage the immense value of the information in the legacy systems while still taking advantage of all the benefits the new paradigms of computing have to offer. One way is to construct a bridge application—a data warehouse—and make it accessible to a wide variety of users via the Web with an equally wide variety of applications and information. This is true for both older, centralized warehouses and new distributed data warehouses; both can benefit from an infusion of the new technological paradigm. By serving as the "bridge" between old and new, a data warehouse provides the highest possible return in exchange for the investment on its construction.

Evolution

In reviewing the development of data warehousing, the retrospective should begin with an examination of the origins of the data that normally populate a data warehouse. What was done with that data before the evolution of data warehousing, and how was the data managed historically?

Throughout the history of systems development, the emphasis had always been on operational systems and the data they process. It was not practical to keep data in an operational system for any extended period of time; it was only as an afterthought, and out of necessity, that any structure was developed for archiving and storing the data that the operational system had already processed. For example, many brokerage houses have operated mutual funds for the past three decades. It was only when the Securities and Exchange Commission (SEC) passed a new rule in the early 1980s requiring the fund managers to be able to re-create, on demand, their trading activity for any given day in the past two years that the brokerages began archiving their trading activities (the rule was passed to prevent a mutual fund from manipulating the stock market to its own advantage). Prior to that, trading records were kept for a week at most (legally, they had to be kept for three days) before they were purged from the system. The old data was viewed as unnecessary and keeping it in the system only slowed performance. With the advent of the new rule, there was a mad scramble to develop archiving schemes to make the re-creations possible.

These brokerage houses were typical of most businesses of the time. In the 1970s, virtually all business systems development was done on IBM mainframes (or IBM clones) using the standard toolset—IMS, CICS, DB2, and COBOL. The 1980s ushered in mini-computer platforms such as AS/400 and VAX/VMS, but not much really changed. The late 1980s and early 1990s made UNIX a popular server platform with the introduction of client/server technology, but real change had not yet arrived.

Despite all the innovations in platforms, architecture, tools, and technologies, a remarkably large number of business applications today remain on the mainframe environments of the 1970s. By most estimates, more than 70 percent of business data for large corporations still resides in the mainframe environment. The principal reasons are that:

- Over the years, these systems have grown to capture the business rules and knowledge that are incredibly difficult to migrate to a new platform/application, so replacing them would be a tremendously expensive and time-consuming task.

- Until very recently, mainframes had higher I/O throughput and faster processors than other platforms, making them the high-volume transaction processors of choice.

These systems, usually called legacy systems, continue to be the largest source of data in any corporation. But the fundamental requirements of an operational system and one designed for analysis are very different. The operational system needs performance, where the analysis system needs flexibility and a broad scope. The one purges data as soon as it is done processing it, while the other accumulates this discarded information, storing it and searching through it to glean some business insight. Since it is never acceptable to have business analysis interfere with and degrade the performance of the operational systems, it is obvious that two entirely different kinds of applications are needed to fulfill the business's needs, even though they both deal with the same data. When operational systems do try to fulfill an analysis role, the result is usually the generation of countless reports and extracts based on archived data, each designed to fit a specific need. In most instances, the IT department assumes responsibility for designing and developing the programs for these reports, and the time required to do so frequently exceeds what end users think they can afford.

During the past fifteen years, the sharp increase in the popularity of personal computers on business desktops has introduced many new and powerful opportunities for business analysis. The gap between the end user and programmer has begun to close as business analysts now have the tools required to do spreadsheet analysis for themselves and graphics packages to translate spreadsheet results into compelling pictorial representations.

Advanced users employ desktop database programs that permit them to store and work with information extracted from legacy systems. Many desktop reporting and analysis tools, targeted toward the end user, have gained popularity and expanded the end users' range of analytic abilities far beyond the simple spreadsheet. This model for business analysis has a serious drawback, however; it leaves the data highly fragmented and oriented toward very specific needs. Because they are not standardized, the extracts of the individual users are unable to address the requirements of multiple uses or users, and the time and cost of producing enough extracts for all users proves prohibitive. Truthfully, most users would rather not have to bother with data extracts at all, instead focusing their energies on the actual analysis and leaving the data extract issues for someone else to solve.

It was the attempt to organize the analytic needs of a business into a central facility that brought about the concept of a data warehouse in the first place. Not that it was called a "data warehouse" initially—the first primitive attempts were named "executive information systems" and generally provided a high level of consolidation and multidimensional views of the data aimed at giving the upper echelon of the company a chance to slice-and-dice the data any way they wanted. The next attempt, decision-support systems, were much closer to today's data warehouse and focused more on detail, targeting lower to mid-level management.

While these two similar and somewhat overlapping systems were the precursors to the modern data warehouse, the high price of their development and the coordination required for their production made them an elite product that never made it into the mainstream of information technology. Executive information and decision-support systems were characterized by the following:

- *The Use of Descriptive Standard Business Terms, Instead of Computer Field Names.* Data names and data structures in these systems were designed for use by nontechnical users who did not have many analytical or extraction tools at their disposal.

- *Data That Was Heavily Preprocessed with the Application of Standard Business Rules.* For example, data contained in these systems might be based on preallocating revenue by formula to products or business lines. In the early 1980s, the executive information system in a certain brokerage house calculated profitability thusly: The programmer assumed that if 23 percent of the company's revenues came from the sale of bonds, then 23 percent of their profits should be assumed to have come from the bond department. Because the senior partners using the system were unaware of the programmer's novel approach to calculating profits, this faulty "computer logic" led to some very curious, and nearly disastrous, business decisions.

- *Consolidated Views of the Data.* For example, data on products, customers, and markets were always prepackaged and readily available. Although the best of these systems featured drill-down capabilities, rarely was all the underlying detail available to the user.

Today's data warehouses come equipped with better analytical tools than their precursors, and their design is no longer dictated by the specific needs of a single group of analysts or executives. In fact, the modern data warehouse is the most successful when its design aligns with the overall business structure rather than the requirements of a few individuals.

Many factors have combined to bring about the rapid evolution of the data warehousing discipline. The most significant has been the enormous forward progress of hardware and software in the 1990s. The sharply decreasing prices and rapidly increasing speed and power of computer hardware, coupled with the development of software that is truly easy to use, has made possible data warehouses with storage capacities and processing speeds considered impossible just ten years ago.

The most remarkable of the hardware developments was the personal computer. Entering the marketplace as a novelty in the late 1970s, the personal computer has become a hotbed of innovation in the past decade. Initially used for word processing and a few other minor tasks, the personal computer, with the aid of powerful and easy-to-use productivity software, graphical interfaces, and responsive business applications, has become the focal point of computing today. Without the personal computer and powerful desktop software, client/server and the multitiered computing architecture could not have developed.

Today, all data warehouses, regardless of type, are accessed by personal computer. A wide array of software tools is available for this purpose, from the very simplest query products to incredibly robust graphical multidimensional tools. The extensive variety of access and analytic tools available to the users has in fact been a force propelling the data warehouse concept to develop so quickly.

Warehouses remained expensive to develop and maintain, however, so mainframe systems, with their reliability, capacity, and performance advantages, were a costly necessity. However, in the first half of the 1990s, server operating systems such as Windows NT and UNIX brought mission-critical stability and powerful features to the distributed computing environment. The operating system software has become feature-rich as the hardware and software costs have steadily dropped, making sophisticated operating systems concepts such as virtual memory, multitasking, and symmetric multiprocessing available on inexpensive platforms. These operating systems are constantly getting easier to set up and maintain, reducing the total costs of ownership of these powerful systems.

Just as revolutionary and critical to data warehousing development as the development of personal computers and server architecture has been the literal explosion of Internet and web-based applications. It is only now, a little after the fact, that businesses have finally jumped on the Internet bandwagon.

One of the most exciting and fastest-growing fields in computing today is the development of intranets and their accompanying applications. Intranets are, of course, private business networks that are based on Internet standards and designed to be used within the business environment. This Internet/intranet trend has two very important implications for data warehousing:

• *The use of the Internet/intranet can make the corporate data warehouse available worldwide on public and private networks.* This availability eliminates the need to replicate data across diverse geographic locations and can also save a multinational business thousands, if not hundreds of thousands, of dollars on communications lines.

- *The Internet architecture provides for a web server to function as a middle tier where all the heavy-duty processing takes place before it is presented to the web-browsing client to use.* This moves the organization from a fat-client to a thin-client paradigm, resulting in cost benefits by eliminating the need to support many different applications on all the company's personal computers.

Intelligent Distributed Systems

Where do all these developments lead? Where is data warehousing today and, more important, where will it be tomorrow? The rise of the Internet and World Wide Web, distributed processing architectures, object-oriented technologies, extended relational databases, client/server, and of course the personal computer have changed the face of applications development. Data warehouse applications are no exception.

While 95 percent of data warehouse efforts remain focused on centralized systems that have been under development for some time, there are a few pioneers willing to experiment with the newest technology and benefit thereby. Unlike their centralized predecessors that suffer from an 80 percent overall failure rate, the distributed warehouses built to date have been an unqualified success; to the best of the author's knowledge, not one has failed outright or been abandoned before completion.

Given the benefits of a distributed warehouse architecture, it is little wonder that distributed data warehouses are proving to be such a success. The distributed warehouse allows a company to start small, with as little as a single data mart, and expand the system at its own pace. As the need arises, new data marts can be brought online and networked together into a distributed system. The initial investment is small, and the overall costs remain modest, especially when compared to the expense of a centralized data warehouse. Because of the staged approach to development—one data mart at a time—the enterprise enjoys an almost immediate return on its investment and project management is reduced to controllable segments. It is almost a foregone conclusion that shortly all new warehouse development will take advantage of distributed technology, and many traditional warehouses, especially those plagued with performance problems, have already begun to migrate to the new paradigm.

Multidatabase distributed systems will grow in importance over the next few years as most large corporations begin to take distributed technology for granted. M. L. Brodie predicted as early as 1989 that the information systems of the future will be based not just on distributed systems (he assumed that as a given fact), but also on intelligent interoperability. Such systems will require not only the application of techniques from the field of distributed databases, such as are available today to support interoperation of systems, but also the incorporation of techniques from artificial intelligence, in particular knowledge-based systems and natural language processing, to provide the intelligence. In addition, richer information retrieval techniques capable of handling multimedia data will be required by future applications.

Merging Expert Systems and Databases

The rise of distributed systems has led to a major resurgence of interest in knowledge-based systems, yet their commercial success has not come anywhere near the amount of research and development effort that has gone into them. Expert systems (ESs) attempt to capture the expertise of human specialists in specific areas and transfer that knowledge to a computer application. Impressive results have been obtained in a number of limited domains.

One of the pioneering expert systems, MYCIN, was developed to recommend antibiotic therapy for bacterial infections of the blood (it has since been expanded to include other types of bacterial infections). MYCIN is just one of a host of expert systems developed in the medical field. The reason for the large number of medical ESs is the demand of doctors' themselves. Clinicians suffer from "data intoxication"—so much data on a patient's condition is generated by, for example, a blood analysis report that the doctor finds it difficult to sift through all of it and extract what is really important. By using an ES, the doctor can have assistance in separating the important from the less important.

Essentially, an expert system has a fairly simple structure (Figure 11-1). The flow of information is from the human expert (the

Figure 11-1. Structure of an expert system.

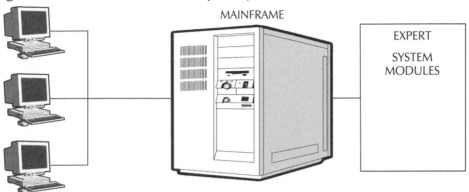

supplier) to the person seeking the advice (the user). The expertise is captured by means of a knowledge acquisition module. It is composed of logical rules or other materials forming the basis of reasoning, backed up by bare facts and evidence from sensors and tests. The inference engine manipulates the information in the knowledge base using some control strategy (e.g., forward chaining, which is the linking together of rules on the basis of results found so far) to select the rules to use in a particular circumstance. An explanation module is included so the user or supplier can ask the system to justify its conclusions to date.

There are two main reasons why expert systems are so seldom used today:

- Restricted domains
- Lack of integration

In the cases where expert systems have been applied, the domains are often too restricted and simplistic to be viewed as being of any practical use. Complex problems require more knowledge, of a deeper kind, than normally found in expert systems. Coupled with the fact that expert systems are normally developed as stand-alone applications that are not integrated into the general information processing environment, it is little wonder that they are underutilized. They are too stupid, restricted, and inconvenient to be of much value.

ESs and databases can, however, be coupled together in three main ways:

- Enhanced expert systems
- Intelligent databases
- Distributed systems

The result can be referred to as an expert database system.

Enhanced expert systems require larger knowledge bases. One way of tackling this problem is to use groups of smaller expert systems, such as those already in existence, in concert (Figure 11-2). Two predominate characteristics of enhanced expert systems are that they:

Figure 11-2. Enhanced expert system using several ESs in concert.

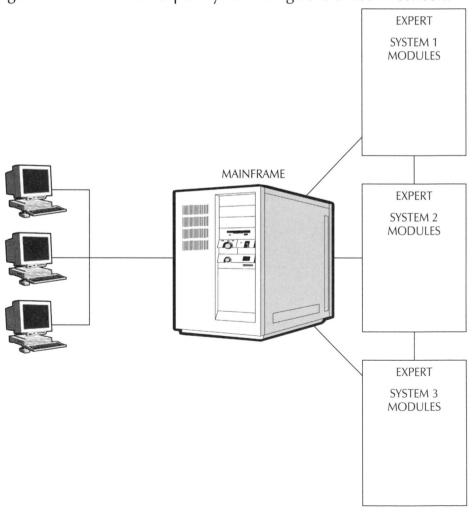

• Include deeper knowledge (i.e., reasoning from first principles) stored typically as rules in conventional expert systems.

• Link diverse expert systems that have been developed in isolation from one another, but which have overlapping domains.

With the intelligent database (IDB) approach, a deductive component is embedded in the database management system (DBMS), merging the expert system with the database (Figure 11-3). This type of expert system is often called a deductive database. A deductive database is one that is capable of deducing additional facts—that is, adding data to the data already present by applying inference rules to the information. Under the right circumstances, the facts can be

Figure 11-3. Enhanced expert system using intelligent databases.

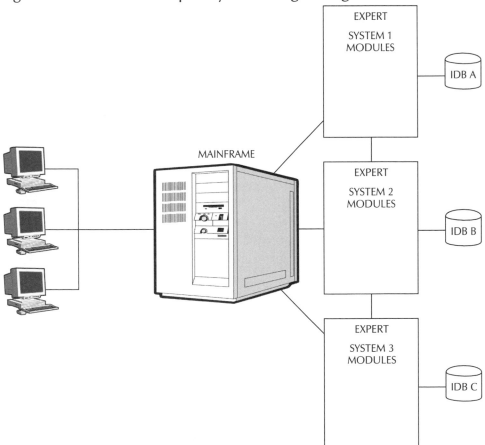

conveniently represented as relationships and stored in relational databases. An alternative is to use a standard DBMS and add intelligent modules to it. This approach can provide a very useful way of supporting certain DBMS functions, especially those that are amenable to a rules-based approach. Obvious candidates for this are optimizers, integrity constraints, and security functions, ensuring consistency and powerful and flexible constraint management.

In the third approach, using distributed systems, both expert systems and databases exist separately and communicate with each other via intersystem communications. Control may reside with either system or in an independent system (Figure 11-4). This approach is likely to be the most useful in developing systems based on interoperability.

The principle of intelligent interoperability is that several independent subsystems, each "expert" in a different area, cooperate together in problem solving. The subsystems in the information system based on intelligent interoperability might correspond to the data marts and ESs in the distributed warehouse of the future. One ES might be the expert in bond trading, another ES deals in stocks, while one data mart contains the bond information and another the securities trading information. Efficient management of the brokerage house depends on a cooperative effort among all of these subsystems.

As data warehouses grow and increase in size and complexity, the problems faced by users in understanding the data content and in trying to retrieve relevant data quickly become acute. Users often find themselves in the position of knowing that the data is "in there somewhere," but find it beyond their skill level to formulate a query to extract it. The field of man/machine interface has become enormously important, and nowhere more so than in data warehousing. If end users and organizations are going to be able to exploit their information resources to the fullest extent, then it is essential to provide easier and more user-friendly methods and languages. Today's web-enabled tools are good, but better, easier-to-use interface techniques are on the way.

Natural Language Processing

For the end user who is not a data processing professional and who wishes to pose an ad hoc query, an interface based on natural lan-

Figure 11-4. Enhanced expert system using distributed systems.

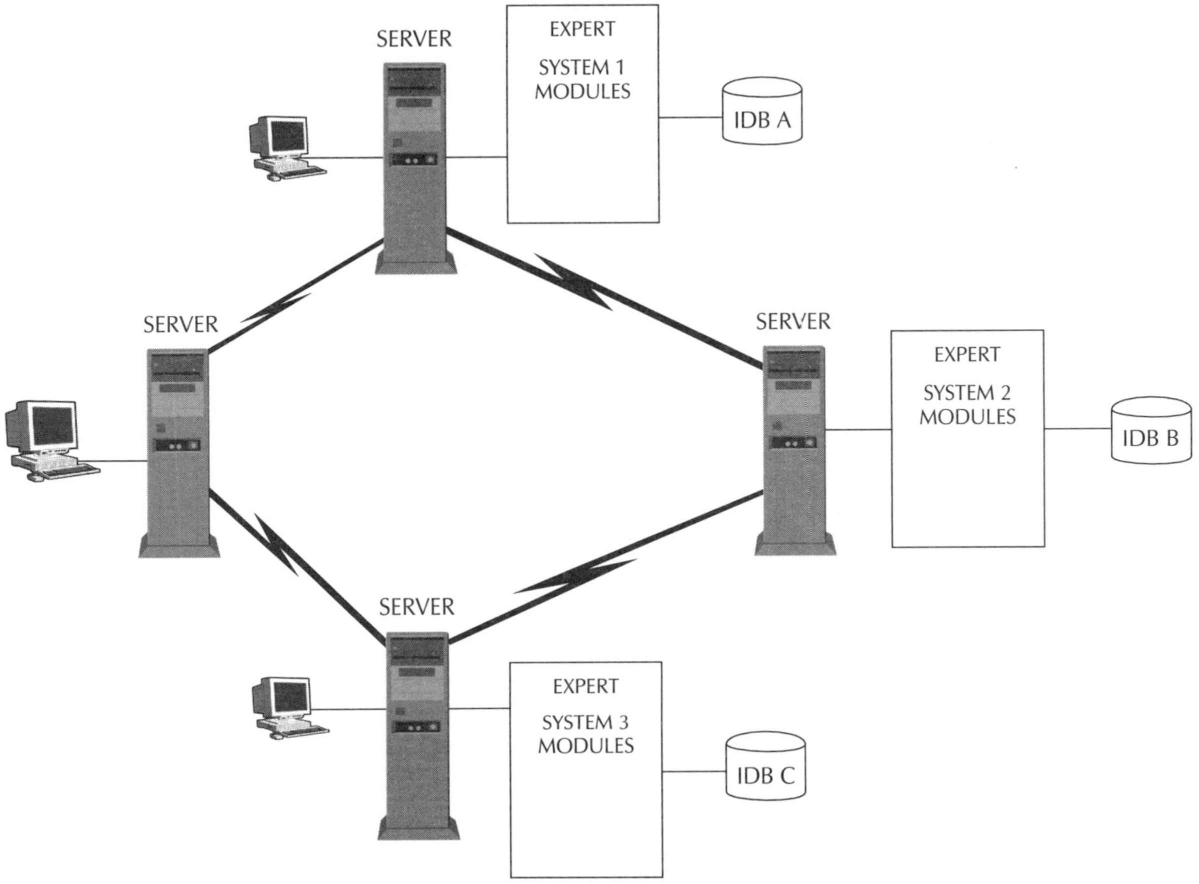

guage would offer tremendous advantages. Indeed, such interfaces were one of the first applications of natural language (NL) processing in the research laboratory. It soon became apparent that a general-purpose NL interface, which could cope with all of the semantic richness and complexity of spoken language, was not possible given the current state of the technology. It was necessary to limit severely the range of allowable NL queries, making the subset of queries so restricted and artificial that it offered no real advantage over conventional query languages and available ad hoc tools.

From the perspective of the distributed data warehouse, the benefits of a general-purpose, unconstrained NL query interface are considerable. For example, in a loosely coupled distributed data warehouse with a global schema, there would be no need for users to learn a new and complex query language to support interoperability. In fact, with full NL support, users could move freely from one data mart to another without any need for retraining or any special knowledge of data placement. This, however, is not yet available and by all indications will be at least another two years in development.

All this adds up to one simple conclusion—distributed systems are viable now and are the future of data processing. Current trends in research and development are almost universally geared toward making distributed systems more inclusive, efficient, and easier to use. Today's distributed data warehouse is cost-effective and user-friendly and gives responsive performance. Tomorrow's data warehouse may be smart enough to understand a question in plain English and do most of the analysis for us.

The Economic Reality of the Web

Throughout human history, crucial developments in "information technology" have helped accelerate the pace of human endeavor. The spoken word made it possible for people to exchange ideas in small groups, and tribal culture advanced from a loosely organized group to a tightly knit society. The written word allowed for communications over both distance and time, giving birth to recorded history, literature, poetry, and a host of other advances.

The invention of the printing press in the fifteenth century radically reduced the cost of distribution of written materials, providing an information broadcast capability for the first time in human history. What followed was an unprecedented advance in human knowledge, bringing about the Renaissance, the Scientific Revolution, the Protestant Reformation, and the rise of European Nationalism. Without Gutenberg's invention, which made possible the dissemination of the information critical to these movements, none of them would have occurred when they did.

The World Wide Web represents a paradigm shift of comparable magnitude to the invention of the printing press. Rather than broadcasting static information in the form of printed materials, the Web broadcasts entire software applications—the dynamic equivalent to the early books. The WWW decreases the cost of distributing a given piece of software by several orders of magnitude and makes it accessible to almost everyone.

For example, a group of stockbrokers, anticipating the increasing demand for individual investment in the stock market, created a program that allowed consumers to buy and sell stocks online through their brokerage house. They decided to deploy the program over the Web instead of mailing it to prospective clients. As everyone knows, this proved to be a huge success, and online trading was born.

What would have been the costs to implement the same system in what, at the time, was a more conventional manner? To allow for a pool of even 5,000 potential clients, the software developer would have had to mail 10,000 disks (assuming two disks per application), use 50,000 megabytes of hard disk space (provided the program utilized 10 megabytes of space on each user's personal computer), and print and ship two-and-a-half tons of manuals (if each manual weighed just one pound). Then, the brokerage house would have had to staff a help desk round the clock to answer user questions about installation and use. Imagine how much marketing would have been required to persuade all 5,000 potential clients to install and try the software package.

By the time the costs of materials, installation, maintenance, and support are totaled, the expense to distribute the application would have easily exceeded $1 million (that is a paltry $200 per package). The developers didn't even need to factor in marketing expenses to know that conventional distribution was a money-losing approach; at a basic charge of $8 per trade, of which less than $2.50 is actual revenue, it would take more than 4 million client trades to recoup distribution expenses. They choose the World Wide Web, not out of any desire to be a pioneer in a new media, but out of sheer economic necessity.

Comparing the web marketing to traditional marketing, it is easy to see that the Web offers massive economic advantages for those needing to distribute software broadly. The break-even point for web deployment is much lower, and the variable costs are also less, meaning that any application successfully deployed in this environment will be much more profitable.

In an instant, the Web has emerged as the low-cost distribution channel for software. In many cases, the cost is so low that it allows programmers to self-publish. The result has been a dramatic increase in the speed of information flow. Software expertise is distributed, tuned, modulated, and amplified at frightening speed over the Net. The collective knowledge of humanity, the fundamental engine of growth, expands and hopefully grows wiser.

The World Wide Web has provided the world with a revolutionary distribution channel. The data warehousing movement has resulted in a massive increase in the amount of data being captured for decision support, as well as an increase in the number of supporting applications available. The Internet/intranet can function as the transport system for this data, both in its "raw" form and its analyzed or "refined" phase. With the WWW as a distribution channel, it is becoming possible for some large corporations to turn their data warehouses into revenue-producing, rather than revenue-consuming, assets. Many insurers, phone companies, automakers, and others are now taking the first steps toward commercial data warehousing.

Explosive growth is imminent in this field because the value of a data warehouse is proportional to the number of people who query it, the frequency of their queries, and the sophistication of the analysis. As the number of users on the World Wide Web continues to grow, the number of customers for commercial databases will also increase. The result is more revenue to the data warehouse owners, encouraging them to invest in their decision-support offerings. As their decision-support facilities improve, they draw more customers, encourage more frequent usage, and in turn perpetuate the cycle.

Even smaller companies are cautiously beginning to use the World Wide Web in their everyday business. They often start by integrating their data warehouse into their intranet. Finding this to be a huge success, the business ventures into an extranet environment that allows it to provide dial-up access to its business partners, suppliers, and others. Other companies have gone straight from intranet to web-enabled applications, using a virtual private network (VPN) to grant the same level of access as dial-up to their critical business associates. Still others have gone to full web participation, encouraging their customers to visit their web site to learn more about the company and shop online, and allowing their employees to work from home over the VPN.

The level of information that companies have decided to offer via their intranets and web sites has followed a similar, cautious approach. Most businesses begin by putting up a set of static, canned reports. Almost all of the reporting packages available today will produce HTML pages that can be hosted by a web server, making this simple to accomplish. This static approach is fine if the users do not need to modify or query the reports, but this is normally not the case.

As the next logical step, most enterprises establish the capability for dynamic parameter entry, using a simple dialogue box that allows users to request a report and modify its behavior. More powerful and flexible tools are available, and in all cases, users demand more and better access. Soon, they are browsing the warehouse and generating multidimensional queries that will result in significant server load. Greater planning, administration, and system capacity are needed to support this increasing demand. Tomorrow's Internet/intranet-enabled data warehouse will need a flexible, high-performance web server and tight integration with the distributed database management system in order to provide quality service to all its users—both inside the company and external to it.

Of prime importance in this environment is security. A company needs a clearly defined security policy and must understand how to make both intranet and Internet access to the enterprise data warehouse consistent with that policy. An intranet, and especially the World Wide Web, can be used by unscrupulous people to their own advantage. The impact of a security breach on a mission-critical application, such as a data warehouse, can be devastating. Minimally, to survive in the future, a business will need a strong firewall, encryption, authorization, and authentication services.

The New Paradigm

Distributed processing systems, especially as used for data warehouses, are rapidly establishing themselves as the paradigm for the new millennium. Distributed systems did not suddenly arise out of thin air; they are an outgrowth of and the next logical step in client/server evolution. Given the fast-paced deployment of personal computers and advances in the speed and processing power of server-class machines, it was only a matter of time before distributed systems composed primarily of these smaller machines replaced their mainframe predecessors as the development platform of choice.

The impact of the Internet/intranet added to this volatile mix of technology should not be overlooked. Within two years, nearly all medium-size and large companies will have a corporate intranet in place and most will have ventured onto the World Wide Web, if only with a rather routine web site extolling the virtues of their company. True electronic commerce, in its infancy now, will take a while to develop, perhaps three to five years. But, it will happen, with numerous "false starts" and missteps along the way.

Right now, most e-commerce sites look pretty much alike. Smart corporations will want to find a way to differentiate themselves from their competition in both web interaction and in everyday transactions. In today's economy, everything is becoming a commodity. The leading providers of goods and services are finding their wares losing their luster mainly because consumers are overwhelmed with choices. They can obtain the same goods from a variety of stores (e.g., WalMart, K-Mart, Sears), the same services from many different institutions (e.g., banks, brokerages, insurance companies), and even a nearly identical laptop computer from a number of sources (e.g., Dell, IBM, Gateway, Toshiba, and many more). The retailers are barraged with new products all vying for the same limited shelf space. Capitalism has triumphed around the world, and it is threatening to cripple both itself and the consumer with the number of options it presents.

To distinguish itself from this cacophony of choices, a company needs to develop a new strategy aimed toward attracting consumers' attention and keeping their business. For the forward-looking company, this strategy will be built around inclusion of its enterprise data warehouse in its web mix to provide decision-support and analysis functions to its clients. A brokerage house can rise above its competition by providing decision-support software that analyzes stock movements individually and by category, displays price-earnings (P/E) ratios and trading patterns for each stock and within sectors, and tracks related stocks across sectors (i.e., an analysis of airline companies versus oil company stocks). A retailer can provide its customer with advance notice of a sale on the type of items the customer usually purchases, and information concerning the availability of selected items the customer will want (based on a customer-preference database). A computer vendor can provide responsive, easy-to-use online help tailored to the exact equipment the consumer just purchased. The result of these commercial decision-support systems should be happy customers who will tell their friends about the great service/company and make more frequent and larger purchases, leading to a greater market share.

One way to glimpse the changes the future may hold is to look back and track the impact of the first automated decision-support product, now thirty years old. The automatic teller machine (ATM), as it was first introduced in Columbus, Ohio, in the late 1960s, was a fairly simple device. It provided deposit and withdrawal transactions for City National Bank's customers. (City National, now known as BankOne, is one of the major "super-regional" banks and owes a good part of its success to its forward-looking policies.) Over time, ATMs have evolved into more complex devices, offering an array of services and decision-support functions, and they have replaced tellers as the primary method of interaction between most retail customers and their bank. They have become indispensable, a business necessity for any bank that hopes to attract retail business in today's marketplace.

A web-enabled commercial data warehouse system is a bit like an ATM network on steroids. It processes sophisticated transactions, provides rich analytical decision-support capabilities, can be upgraded at will (every week if necessary), and is available to tens of millions of potential customers at locations convenient to them near their homes and offices. The technology is applicable to nearly every business and is supported by thousands of industry vendors, suppliers, and integrators. For most people, the ATM is their only interface with their bank. In the future, their primary, and perhaps only, contact with many businesses will be their personal computer logged onto a web site offering data warehouse access and transaction services.

Conclusions

Historically, data warehouses have been a technical initiative designed to help control corporate costs and optimize operations. Almost all data warehouse initiatives, many thousands of them, are centrally focused, representing valid IT investments, and firms have benefited greatly from their use. Yet experience and statistics have shown that centralized data warehouses are very difficult to build—nearly 80 percent of these projects either fail outright or are redirected short of completion.

The convergence in the late 1990s of numerous technological developments—the Internet/intranet, the browser, and high-performance, high-speed servers—make possible a more cost-effective, easy-to-do approach to data warehousing. The practice of building a series of independent data marts and networking them into a distributed warehouse is rapidly gaining acceptance and promises to quickly become the paradigm for data warehouse construction. And why not? The distributed data warehouse can be started small (a single data mart), can be constructed quickly (three months per data mart), is easy to manage (short-term, achievable goals), provides quick return on investment (three months from initial investment to finished mart), is almost infinitely scalable (just add another server), and is usually less than one-third the cost of a centralized warehouse.

It is only in the last year that a very few corporations have broadened their warehousing horizons and found ways to deploy data warehouse access outside of their own employees. Through the World Wide Web they have reached out to their customers, business partners, suppliers, and investors and granted them access to their decision-support software and data warehouses. Distributed data warehouses are especially well suited for this type of extended business community because their architecture simplifies the security issues associated with web participation. Especially sensitive corporate data can be stored together on warehouse servers that do not participate in web activities, while still remaining available to authorized in-house users.

The World Wide Web is becoming more and more a part of life for people and corporations each day. Two of the hottest items on almost every corporate to-do list are finishing the data warehouse and building an Internet presence. The World Wide Web has officially arrived, with nearly 15 million web sites by a recent count. Statistics show that the number of Internet users doubles every year, and the number of web sites doubles every three months!

Most medium-size and large companies today either have or are building some type of data warehouse. They are taking their first tentative steps into the web environment, too. It is no surprise that these two popular technologies are beginning to join forces, enabling one another with the end product being easy access to large quantities of integrated information by a huge and geographically dispersed group of users. Some of the organizations currently developing distributed data warehouses are looking to the Web as the sole provider for the user interface.

The use of a web browser, coupled with web-enabled decision-support and analysis software, provides easy access to server-based distributed warehouses. This combination of hardware and software offers many advantages over traditional warehouse interface tools:

- It eliminates the need for many dispersed applications on user desktops that are nearly impossible to maintain and support.

- Unlike many custom-built interfaces, web browsers are cheap (they are already on most desktops bundled with the operating system) and easy to install.

- Web browsers are easy to use, and the training and ramp-up time are significantly reduced.

- The cost associated with expanding the corporate network to include all warehouse users is greatly reduced when using the Internet as the vehicle for access.

- The problems posed by multiple operating systems (or different versions of the same system) on the desktop are eliminated.

Many new tools are under development that will help leverage web/distributed warehouse technology. Already, some products allow SQL statements to be embedded in HTML text, which generates the results of the query directly to the Web in the form of text, images, or other data types. Other tools have a capacity that allows links to relevant information to be dynamically generated from the desktop. These are just the start of a flood of new products due on the shelves within eighteen months that will tie the Web and the warehouse more closely together.

Today, only a very few industry experts are predicting that a marriage between the Web and the distributed data warehouse will be the trend of the future. Granted, it is in its infancy now, but the combined technology of distributed warehousing and the Internet holds great potential for those forward-looking organizations that want to leverage information across the organization. With increasing investments in company intranets and servers, the next logical step is using that investment to harness the power of information—a distributed data warehouse. Regardless of whether the organization then uses the result simply to transfer knowledge within the company or as a revenue-generating storefront on the Web, the competitive advantage of a distributed data warehouse cannot be overestimated.

Centralized data warehouses are now a key component of the information architecture of many companies. As the warehousing paradigm shifts to distributed technology, it is not much of a stretch to predict that distributed warehouses will work their way into the fabric of the Web and become an integral, profitable part of the web-based revenue-generating strategy of many companies in the near future.

Glossary

Abort   A command issued by a program to a DBMS indicating an unsuccessful termination of processing.

Access control   A security principle that relates to the acceptance or rejection of a user requesting access to some service or data in a given system.

ActiveX controls   Objects that can provide new browser functions.

Agents   Represent the subtransactions at the various sites in the network.

Aggregation   A relationship between entities as represented by a higher-level object.

AH   *See* authentication header.

Analytic layer   Putting structured data on an intranet requires a server-resident layer whose job it is to generate SQL as needed, perform computations, and format reports based on user requests; the analytic layer provides these functions.

Anti-replay   In terms of system security, refers to a minimalist form of connection-oriented integrity where duplicate and/or very old data units are detected and rejected.

Applets   Fragments of Java code that run on the browser.

Application-coupled security   A network security scheme based on building security measures into the applications themselves.

Application layer   The seventh and final level of the ISO/OSI telecommunications architecture, where specific applications (e.g., e-mail, X.400, VTAM) reside.

Application software   Programs designed to a specific user-defined purpose.

Application-specific tags   Used to guide the web gateway in what buttons, dialogs, or objects to present to the user.

Architecture   The high-level description of the organization of functional responsibilities within a system.

ASCII   American Standard Code for Information Interchange, the common language for most personal computers.

Atomicity   The "all or nothing" property of a transaction; it is an indivisible unit.

Attack   In security terms, defines the details of how a threat can exploit a vulnerability.

Authentication   The ability of a system to recognize and verify users.

Authentication header (AH)   The part of IPSec that identifies the origin of a message and provides for data integrity through use of various message digest methodologies.

Availability   The ability of an application or system to respond with the resources and analysis instantly, regardless of the time of day or day of the week.

Balance tree (B-tree) index   An indexing technique that keeps track of the values for specific fields and points to the rows that contain them.

Batch window   A time period when relatively little system activity occurs, during which it is most convenient to perform loads and system maintenance.

Begin transaction   A command made explicitly or implicitly by the user/program to start execution of a transaction.

Bit-mapped index   An indexing technique where a single bit is used to indicate a specific value of data.

Breakpoint   In some forms of concurrency control, it represents a place where other transactions can safely be interleaved, allowing a greater degree of concurrency control.

Browser   A software program used to facilitate connection to the Internet.

B-tree index   Balance tree index.

Business objects   People, places, things, and events that are relevant to the business, all of which translate easily into an object-oriented schema.

Centralized data warehouse   A data warehouse implementation where all the data is gathered into a centralized location and managed by a single database management system, usually relational technology; a centralized warehouse is intended to serve the needs of the entire corporation.

Centralized deadlock detection A method for deadlock detection in a distributed environment where all the local wait-for graphs are merged into one, called the deadlock detection site, and examined for cyclic structures.

Certification Authority (CA) A third party that validates the information on a digital certificate.

CGI *See* Common Gateway Interface.

Challenge Handshake Authentication Protocol (CHAP) An extension of PAP where the user is asked to answer a question, usually something personal that only the user would know.

CHAP See Challenge Handshake Authentication Protocol.

Chunking In object-oriented technologies, it is the practice of building larger components from smaller ones.

Class A group of similar objects that are handled together; in object-oriented technologies, classes function like templates and are used to define the data and methods of similar types of objects.

Client/server technology A data processing architecture based on the use of personal computers on the desktop networked together with more powerful machines acting as application repositories.

Client side In client/server technology, it is the desktop machine employed by the user; in a client/server–based intranet environment, the client side is the browser.

COBOL *See* Common Business Oriented Language.

Commit A command issued by the program to the DBMS indicating a successful conclusion to the processing.

Common Business Oriented Language (COBOL) A mainframe computer programming language in wide use since the 1970s.

Common Gateway Interface (CGI) The interface between the web site's HTTP server and the other resources of the server's host computer; CGI is not a language or protocol in the strict sense of the word, it is just a commonly named set of variables and agreed-upon conventions for passing information back and forth from the client (the personal computer with a web browser) to the server (the computer that sends the web pages to the client).

Common Object Request Broker Architecture (CORBA) The

supporting architecture within which the object request broker (ORB) functions.

Concurrency control   The ability of a DBMS to control multiuser access to the data stored in the data structures.

Concurrent access   The ability of a DBMS to support multiuser access to the data (i.e., several users "simultaneously" reading and writing to the database).

Confidentiality   A security property that ensures both that data is disclosed only to those authorized to use it, and that it remains hidden from those not privy to it.

Connection-oriented integrity   In terms of system security, it ensures the order of transmitted data.

Connection-oriented protocol   Ensures that the receiving application sees messages in the same order and format as originally sent.

Conservative timestamping   A timestamp-based concurrency control methodology that substantially reduces the degree of concurrency but eliminates the need for restarts; transactions wait to process until the system knows it cannot receive a conflicting request from an older transaction.

Consistency   A property of a transaction; transactions change a database from one consistent state to another consistent state.

Constrained write rule   The assumption that a transaction reads data before it updates it.

Content standards   A consistent way of storing data, such as always storing only proper names in the "name" field and with the last name first.

CORBA   *See* Common Object Request Broker Architecture.

Countermeasures   In security terms, these are the actions taken to protect systems from attacks.

Counterstep   In some methods of concurrency control, it is necessary to undo transaction processing should the transaction fail; the measures used to reverse the effects of the transaction are called countersteps.

Critical data subject areas   The information that is most important to a data warehouse or data mart, such as customer, vendor, inventory, accounts payable, and general ledger.

DAPLEX A special-purpose system designed to be used as both a language and the common data model to which each local data model maps.

Data Individual pieces of information stored in a system; in object-oriented (OO) technologies, it is the private information portion of an object.

Database management system (DBMS) A software facility that stores and manages data. It handles all requests for database activity, for example, queries and updates, and permits centralized control of data security and integrity.

Database partition The division of a data structure into two or more parts along logical lines, each containing a portion of the original data; two types of partitioning schemes are in wide use today in relational systems, horizontal and vertical.

Database reorganization The practice of "unloading" all the data from a data structure, sorting it into a logical sequence, and reloading it to improve query response times.

Data definition language (DDL) A group of specialized commands within a relational database management system that allows the user to define data structures and other parameters to the system.

Data distribution The act of placing and maintaining duplicate copies of data at more than one data site in a mainframe computer environment or a telecommunications network. It can also apply to the placement of related data at different data sites in a distributed environment.

Data entity chart Describes how every item in a group relates to every other item, and what all of the many-to-many and many-to-one relationships between data elements are.

Data integration The process of ensuring that the quality and the structure of data conform to the selected standard.

Data integration tools Also called middleware; a group of software programs designed to extract, cleanse, and transform data from operational systems.

Data link layer The second layer in the ISO/OSI telecommunications architecture that ensures the integrity of the bit stream between any two points.

Data manipulation language (DML) A group of specialized

commands within a relational database management system that allows the user to manipulate data structures and other parameters within the system.

Data mart   A subset of the corporation's data, oriented to a specific purpose or subject area that has been stored and organized to support the decision-support process.

Data mart data model   A special-purpose data model designed to give the users a "road map" of the mart.

Data packets   Small, discrete pieces of a TCP/IP data transmission.

Data reservoirs   Another name for a data repository; it can include the logical, and sometimes physical, partitioning of data so that the data structures and the applications they support all reside in the same location.

Data transformation   The process of changing or transforming data within a common data architecture.

Data warehouse   An architecture for delivering information to knowledge workers.

DBMS   *See* database management system.

DCE   *See* distributed computing environment.

DCOM   *See* Distributed Component Object Model.

DDBMS   *See* distributed database management system.

DDL   *See* data definition language.

Deadlock   A situation that occurs when multiple transactions are queued-up waiting for a lock to be released and, for whatever reason, the lock continues in effect.

Deadlock detection protocol   A routine that is invoked periodically to check for deadlocks.

Deadlock prevention protocol   Concurrency control algorithms in which the possibility (not necessarily the reality) of deadlocks is detected and avoided.

Decryption   The process of applying a mathematical algorithm and an associated key to the ciphertext to re-create the original document.

Deductive database   Also called an intelligent database approach; a type of expert system that is capable of deducing additional facts and adding information to the data already present by applying inference rules to the information.

Deferred updates   A methodology for hiding partial updates where the updates of uncommitted transactions are not written to the database; instead, they are written to a buffer and only flushed out to the database when the transaction commits.

Departmental databases Databases that support the primary function of a workgroup or department, stored together at a single location.

Dependent data marts Data marts that rely on the existence of a centralized data warehouse as their source of data.

Desktop-centric Reliance on the applications resident in the desktop computer for the majority of the user's processing needs.

Desktop tools Software installed on the desktop computer, usually used for query and reporting and to facilitate decision support.

Destination IP address The IP address of the computer that is to receive the packet using TCP/IP communications.

Digital certificates A message that is encrypted and verified by a third party that ensures the recipient that the sender is who he claims to be; the certificate may include other information, such as the sender's public key or other keys to be used for message encryption.

Digital signature A field appended to a message that enables the recipient to verify both the signer's identity and the fact that the contents of the text have not been changed.

Dimensional modeling A technique for organizing data in databases in a simple and understandable fashion through the use of dimensions (i.e., time, product, sales).

Dirty read A situation that occurs when transactions are allowed to read partial results of an incomplete transaction that is simultaneously updating the database.

Distributed Component Object Model (DCOM) Extends COM to support communications between objects regardless of their physical location.

Distributed computing environment (DCE) A security architecture and specifications, developed by the Open Software Foundation, to provide tools and a framework for building secure distributed applications in a multivendor environment.

Distributed database management system (DDBMS) A type of database management system that allows the data residing in multiple locations joined by a network to work together.

Distributed data warehouse A logically integrated collection of shared data that is physically distributed across the nodes of a computer network; it focuses its approach on data marts that are built rapidly with the cost-effective, scalable distributed technology.

Distributed deadlock detection   A method of deadlock detection in a distributed system that employs an external agent in the wait-for graphs, allowing the sites in the network to exchange local wait-for graphs if there is a possibility of a deadlock.

Distributed object computing (DOC)   A computing paradigm that allows the objects to be distributed across a heterogeneous network, with each of the components interoperable to form a unified whole.

DNS   *See* Domain Name Server.

DOC   *See* distributed object computing.

Domain Name Server (DNS)   Provides translation services between domain names and IP addresses.

Durability   A property of a transaction; the effects of a successfully completed transaction are permanently recorded in the database and cannot be undone.

Dynamic invocation interface   One of the client-side services mandated by CORBA that allows for the specification of requests at runtime.

EBCDIC   Extended Binary Coded Decimal Interchange Code.

Electronic receipts   Messages exchanged between receiving and sending computers that verify the receipt of a previous message; used to ensure nonrepudiation.

Encapsulated security payload (ESP)   The part of IPSec that provides data confidentiality by encrypting the message's data.

Encapsulation   In OO technologies, the process of hiding internal information within objects.

Encryption   A technological tool frequently used to guarantee confidentiality by encoding a message so it is unintelligible to anyone without the encryption key; the process of applying a mathematical algorithm and some related key to a plaintext to create a ciphertext.

Enhanced expert systems   An outgrowth from expert systems, these systems require larger knowledge bases; one way to build an enhanced system is to use groups of smaller expert systems, like those already in existence, in concert in a distributed environment.

Enterprise data model   A data model that defines the data requirements for the enterprise as a whole.

Enterprise servers Servers that contain data and applications for use across the corporate environment.

Enterprise Systems Connection (ESCON) An IBM mainframe channel architecture and standard normally used to connect storage devices.

ES *See* expert system.

ESCON *See* Enterprise Systems Connection.

ESP *See* encapsulated security payload.

Exception programming It is the programming done to accommodate unusual circumstances in a mature OO-based system.

Expert system (ES) Data processing application that attempts to capture and imitate the expertise of human specialists in specific areas.

Fat client A personal computer loaded with application programs that is attached to a network and is reliant on those resident applications for the majority of its function.

File management layer Putting structured data on an intranet requires a server-resident layer whose job it is to allow users to continue work on the same copy of a report, or make their own copy for individual analysis; the file management layer provides these functions.

File Transfer Protocol (FTP) The oldest commonly used method of file transfer on the Internet.

Firewall Prevents undesirable messages from entering or leaving the secured network through a combination of special network configurations, special host configurations, screening routers, and proxy servers.

Flat files An antiquated data storage method where records are stored end-to-end in a continuous fashion.

Format Standards A consistent way of storing data, such as using a nine-number zip code instead of a five-number code.

FTP *See* File Transfer Protocol.

Function call A request to the system that activates one of the basic services provided by that system as a part of its infrastructure.

Generalization Occurs where a set of generic entities is considered to be a single entity.

Gigabyte (GB) One million bytes.

Global   Term often used when discussing a distributed system in order to distinguish aspects that refer to the system as a whole.

Global data model   A data model formed by integrating the various databases that compose the distributed warehouse into a DBMS-independent universal schema.

Granularity   Size of the data item that can be locked in a single operation.

Growing phase   The first portion of two-phase locking (2PL) when the transaction acquires locks.

Hash count   A method used to ensure message integrity that is generated by a special algorithm applied by the sending program to the entire message.

Heterogeneous distributed data warehouse   Resembles a centralized data warehouse except that the data is stored at more than one location within a network; it is characterized by the use of different DBMSs at the local sites.

Hierarchical data structures   A data storage methodology still used to support very high-volume systems; the primary data is stored in a record and related information is stored in a another, dependent (child) record.

Hierarchical deadlock detection   A method of deadlock detection in a distributed system where the sites in the network are organized into a hierarchy so that a blocked site sends its local wait-for graph to the site above it in the hierarchy.

Homogeneous distributed data warehouse   Resembles a centralized data warehouse, but instead of storing all the data at one site, the data is distributed across a number of sites in the network; the same type of database structure (database product) is used at each site, usually relational technology.

Horizontal partition   The practice of dividing a large physical table into several smaller sections, or partitions, using a key range to define partition members.

Hot spot   A situation that occurs when a processor is dedicated to a certain portion of a query and that portion requires much more processing than the others.

HTML   *See* HyperText Markup Language.

HTTP   *See* HyperText Transport Protocol.

Hyperlink   The software that enables users to navigate the World

Wide Web without knowing the exact location of each document and the network path that leads to the site where it is stored; users can click on highlighted text or an icon (with an attached hyperlink) to navigate to another set of information located literally anywhere.

HyperText Markup Language (HTML) Computer language used to create web pages.

HyperText Transport Protocol (HTTP) The transport language used with the HTML communications protocol.

IIOP *See* Internet Inter-Orb Protocol.

IKE *See* Internet Key Exchange Protocol.

Image copy An exact copy of a table or database made using an image copy utility or program, usually for purposes of disaster recovery.

Independence A property of a transaction; transactions execute independently of one another (i.e., the partial effects of incomplete transactions are not visible to other transactions).

Independent data marts Data marts that stand on their own, extracting the necessary data from operational and other nonwarehouse systems.

Information architecture Deals with data, describing the content, behavior, and interaction of the business objects.

Information technology (IT) Term usually used to encompass the entire data processing functions and systems of a company; often used to mean the division of a company that is responsible for the computer systems.

Inheritance In OO technologies, the process of creating a definition by the incremental modification of other definitions.

Integrated data marts Collection of independent data marts that all adhere to a consistent data architecture that governs the design of each.

Integrity In terms of system security, refers to the completeness and fidelity of the message as it travels through the network.

Intelligent database approach A type of expert system that is capable of deducing additional facts and adding data to the data already present by applying inference rules to the information.

Intelligent interoperability A futuristic data processing system based on the tenets of distributed processing and incorporating techniques from artificial intelligence and natural language processing.

Internet   The communications facilities used to interconnect the various sites on the World Wide Web.

Internet Inter-Orb Protocol (IIOP)   Sanctioned by the OMG, these specifications are used worldwide to develop and deploy applications for many different types of businesses.

Internet Key Exchange (IKE) Protocol   Formerly known as the ISAKMP-Oakley protocol, it is that part of IPSec that is used to identify the routers, firewalls, and hosts communicating and to set up the security policies for both authentication headers and encapsulated security payload protocols.

Internet Protocol Security (IPSec)   A series of open standards that address TCP/IP security issues at the system level.

Internet security scanner (ISS)   A program that probes a target web site from the outside to identify possible exposures to known hacking strategies.

Intranet   A telecommunications network within a company based on the design of the Internet; it almost always uses TCP/IP.

I/O architecture   The design of the input and output channels of a computer system.

IP addresses   In a TCP/IP network, the alphanumeric code that identifies a physical device to the network, usually written as four numbers that, in turn, indicate a network number and a host number.

IPSec   *See* Internet Protocol Security.

ISO   International Standards Organization.

ISS   *See* Internet security scanner.

IT   *See* information technology.

Java   Programming language commonly used on the Internet.

Java applets   Java permits software to be served to an intranet browser in code fragments called applets.

Java Virtual Machine   Located within the browser, it isolates the Java program so that it runs inside a partitioned area called the sandbox.

Kerberos authentication model   A network security method developed by MIT where both the client and the application server agree to trust a third computer, the security server, as to the identity and authorization of each other.

LAN *See* Local Area Network.

Legacy systems Existing, transaction-oriented systems that act as a data source for a data warehouse or data mart.

Level 2 Tunneling Protocol (L2TP) Ensures that even though a given communication is being transmitted over the Internet, it can travel via a private session limited to those members allowed to work within that channel by using data encryption.

Life cycle The phases through which an application passes, consisting of three main stages: introduction, deployment, and maturity.

Livelock A condition that occurs when a transaction is either repeatedly rolled back or left in a wait state indefinitely, unable to acquire locks, even though the system is not deadlocked.

Load balancing Relocating part of the data and attendant processing stored at an overworked site to another underutilized node.

Local Term often used when discussing a distributed system in order to distinguish aspects that refer to a single site.

Local Area Network (LAN) A group of computers, located at the same geographic location, linked together with a telecommunications network.

Locking The most frequently used method for concurrency control; there are several variations, but all share the fundamental premise that a transaction must claim a read (shared) or write (exclusive) lock on a data item prior to performing an operation.

Logic bomb A program that checks for certain conditions and, when those criteria are fulfilled, starts to damage the computer system in some fashion.

L2TP *See* Level 2 Tunneling Protocol.

Majority partition The primary copy of the data used to guarantee consistency across duplicate copies in a distributed system.

Man in the middle A form of electronic snooping where a transmission is intercepted in transit by the snooper and altered in real time; after passing on the changed message, the snooper waits for the response from the server, which, in due course, is captured, altered, and sent along to the client, leaving both sides of the message believing the intended legitimate transaction has occurred.

Massively parallel processing (MPP)   A computer architecture where the central processor function is replaced by a large number of smaller processors working in parallel, each with their own system resources.

Megabyte (MB)   One thousand bytes.

Memory architecture   The design of the CPU (central processing unit) of the system.

Message digest algorithm   A special type of encryption algorithm whose end result is a digital number of some known length.

Metadata   Data about data.

Metadata dictionary   A system dictionary containing all the relevant information about the data contained in that system.

Middleware   A special type of software used to extract and transform data from the source systems for loading into the data warehouse.

Missing writes   Using this strategy for updating replicated data in a distributed system, transactions operate in one of two modes; normal mode when all copies of the duplicated data are available and failure mode when one or more sites are unavailable.

MOLAP   *See* multidimensional online analytical processing.

Mosaic   The first user-friendly interface to the Internet that allows users to "surf" the Web without knowing the exact location of the web site they want to visit.

MPP   *See* massively parallel processing.

Multicasting   An implementation of the publish/subscribe paradigm that is a type of broadcast that allows information to be pushed over the network from many sources to many recipients.

Multidimensional database management system   A database management system that uses multidimensional databases for information storage.

Multidimensional data mart   Most often used for slicing and dicing numeric data in a free-form fashion.

Multidimensional online analytical processing (MOLAP)   Tools designed to work with multidimensional databases.

Multidimensional schema   A modeling approach in which data is preaggregated and stored in hypercubes.

Multitiered environment   A data processing architecture in which the HTTP server activity is separated from application-related processing that occurs on an intermediate server.

Network-centric   Centered on the network; a security approach in which the data security efforts concentrate on securing the network itself.

Network-coupled security   Concentrates security measures on the network infrastructure.

Network layer   The third level of the ISO/OSI telecommunications architecture that extends the concepts of the data link layer into multiple networks, which may or may not be compatible.

Nonrepudiation of delivery service   Provides the sender of an electronic message with proof that the computer message was successfully delivered to the intended recipient.

Nonrepudiation of submission service   Offers proof that a certain electronic message did in fact originate with a specific user at a noted time.

Non Uniform Memory Access (NUMA)   Allows MPP systems to share common memory.

Nonvolatile   Does not change rapidly, or at all.

Normalized tables   A method of design for relational databases that adheres to certain standards regulating table content designed to prevent storing the same data in multiple tables.

N-tiered environment   A data processing architecture in which the various system activities (e.g., HTTP server, applications server) are separated and occur on different servers.

NUMA   *See* Non Uniform Memory Access.

OA   *See* object adapters.

Object   The key element in OO technology, it contains both data and logic in a single package.

Object adapters (OA)   One of the client-side services mandated by CORBA that provide the means by which object implementations access most ORB services.

Object databases (ODB)   An emerging means of storage for hierarchical arrangements of data as objects.

Object-oriented (OO)   *See* object technology.

Object request broker (ORB)   The middleware of distributed object computing that enables objects to locate and activate other objects in a network, regardless of the processor or programming language used to develop either the client or server objects.

Object technology   A technological approach based on simulation and modeling, where models of the business are constructed and shared by all applications.

ODB   *See* object databases.

ODL skeleton interface   One of the client-side services mandated by CORBA that is called by ORB to invoke the methods requested from clients.

OLAP   *See* online analytical processing.

OLTP   *See* online transaction processing.

Online analytical processing (OLAP)   A group of software products that integrate query, analysis, and reporting into one product.

Online transaction processing (OLTP)   An application that handles transactions in "real time" as an event occurs; many online applications process extremely high volumes of transactions (10,000/per second or more).

OO technology   See object technology.

Open system   A data processing architecture where customers are free to mix-and-match multivendor (i.e., heterogeneous) components such as hardware, network protocols, operating systems, databases, access tools, and other elements.

Optimistic methods   A concurrency control method based on the idea that conflict is rare and the best approach is to allow transactions to proceed unimpeded without any waiting; only when a transaction wants to commit does the system check for conflicts and, if one is detected, force the transaction to restart.

ORB   *See* object request broker.

Organizationwide standards   A consistent format for field size, type, and other characteristics, such as names, addresses, phone numbers, and postal codes, that is adopted throughout the entire company.

OSF   Open Software Foundation.

OSI   Open System Interconnection.

Packet switching   The process of interleaved data packets from one message with all the other packets in the network.

PAP   *See* Password Authentication Protocol.

Parallel processing The ability to run two or more processes concurrently.

Password Used to identify and authenticate users, machines, and processes in a computer network.

Password Authentication Protocol (PAP) A system that maps users to their server account by verifying user names and passwords.

Performance The ability of an application system to deliver the right results to the correct people, in the right format, at the right time, and in a timely and responsive manner.

Physical layer The lowest layer in the ISO/OSI telecommunications architecture, which is responsible for the physical transmission of the data from the computer to the network.

PKI *See* public key infrastructure.

Plug-ins Objects that can provide new browser functions.

Point solution data mart A data mart built to satisfy the specific needs of a particular group with no thought given to integration with the corporate architecture.

Polymorphism In OO technologies, the concept that two or more objects can respond to the same request in different ways.

POP *See* Post Office Protocol.

Post Office Protocol (POP) Provides simple electronic mail services.

Presentation layer The sixth level of the ISO/OSI telecommunications architecture that determines what code set (e.g., ASCII, EBCDIC) will be used for the data exchange.

Prewrites A methodology for hiding partial updates where the updates of uncommitted transactions are not written to the database; instead, they are written to a buffer and only flushed out to the database when the transaction commits.

Private key The key used to decrypt a message as part of a two-key encryption scheme.

Private Methods In OO technologies, the private procedures portion of an object.

Protocol stack Another name for the seven-layer ISO/OSI telecommunications model.

Proxy server A special copy of an application program that has had supplemental enhancements made for web service.

Public key   The key used to encrypt a message as part of a two-key encryption scheme.

Public key algorithms   An encryption method that uses different keys on each end of the transmission, one to encrypt the plaintext and a different one to decrypt the ciphertext.

Public key certificate   A special type of digital certificate that identifies the entity, its public key, and various pieces of information about the entity such as e-mail address, physical location, and its distinguished name.

Public key cryptography   A popular form of encryption based on the use of two keys, one to encrypt the message (the public key) and a second, different key to decrypt the message (the private key).

Public key infrastructure (PKI)   An approach to authentication issues in which PKI provides management services to facilitate widespread use of public key encryption.

Publish and subscribe   A method of data distribution that involves the data being published by one system and stored at a convenient location from which other systems can subscribe the information when they need it.

Quasi-serializability   This method of concurrency control requires all global transactions to be submitted serially, while local transactions execute in the normal way (i.e., are serializable); local autonomy is maintained, but no global integrity constraints and no referential integrity between different agents of the same transaction are enforced.

Query   A method of obtaining data from a relational system, usually a question, written in SQL, requesting data.

Query transformation   In a heterogeneous distributed system, the process of restating a query originating in one system into a format understandable by another system.

RDBMS   *See* relational database management system.

Read lock   Shared lock on a data item, allowing more than one transaction to access the item at a time.

Read quorum   The process of acquiring a majority of read locks on replicated data in a distributed system to prevent a transaction reading out-of-date versions of a data item; if data integrity is to be assured, a majority of duplicate sites must be represented in the read quorum.

Read-write conflict The conflict between a read and a write operation.

Recovery manager The part of the DBMS that is responsible for ensuring that all transactions active at the time of failure are rolled back or undone.

Redundancy Repetition of information.

Relational database management system (RDBMS) A database management system that stores information in table structures and conducts searches based on indices and/or by using the data matching the search criteria in a column of one table to find corresponding data in another table. The number of rows of a table represents the record count, and the columns represent fields in each record.

Relational data model First proposed by E. F. Codd and C. J. Date in the early 1970s as a new paradigm for representing interrelationships among data, and was extended shortly thereafter to become the basis for a more efficient system of data storage/retrieval.

Relational online analytical processing (ROLAP) A group of software products designed to work with RDBMSs that integrate query, analysis, and reporting into one product.

Relatively consistent schedule A schedule that is nonserializable but that still guarantees consistency.

Replay A copy of a specific transmission is played back to the recipient, either in its original form or in an edited state, to serve the purposes of the snooper who illegally intercepted the original transmission.

Repudiation Either the sender or receiver of an electronic message denies their involvement in the communication.

Restrictions Can be placed on the generalized object or on a class of objects to obtain a subset of particular interest.

Reusability The practice of coding in modular components that can serve more than one purpose; for example, coding a basic sort in its own module that can be used in several different programs whenever a sort is needed.

ROLAP *See* relational online analytical processing.

ROLAP data marts General-purpose data marts that contain both numeric and textual data.

Rolled back   The process of undoing a transaction when a system fails; the effect of a rollback operation is to restore the database to the state it was in prior to the beginning of the transaction, back to consistency.

SA   *See* security association.

Sandbox   A partitioned area within the browser where downloaded Java programs execute.

SATAN   A well-known program that probes a target web site from the outside to identify possible exposures to known hacking strategies.

Scalability   The ability of an application or system to grow and expand if necessary as user demands increase.

Scheduler   The part of the DBMS that controls concurrently executing transactions so they do not get in each other's way.

Screening routers   Specialized routers that have the added functionality of being able to examine and discriminate among the network traffic based on certain criteria.

Secondary data   Information about the primary data; for example, the source, quantity, time imported, and location of external data acquired by a data mart.

Secure Sockets Layer (SSL)   The most common form of security used on the World Wide Web today, based on public key encryption; a separate layer of communications software that sits between the application layer and the transport layer.

Security association (SA)   The data structure established during the use of IPSec that keeps track of the communication.

Security layer   Putting structured data on an intranet requires a server-resident layer whose job it is to secure corporate data and protect it from any outside intrusions; the security layer provides these functions.

Security parameter index (SPI)   The structure established during the use of IPSec that accompanies each message in order to point to the appropriate SA record associated with the communication on both ends.

Serializability   The most common means of proving the correctness of the schedules produced by the scheduler.

Serializable   A schedule is said to be serializable if all the reads and writes can be reordered in such a way that they are grouped together as in a serial schedule, and the net effect of executing the reordered schedule is the same as that of the original schedule.

Serial schedule   One in which all reads and writes of each transaction are grouped together so the transactions run sequentially, one after another.

Server side   The web server in a client/server Internet.

Session layer   The fifth level of the ISO/OSI telecommunications architecture that manages the connecting and disconnecting of interactions between two computers.

Shortcut   A method for placing a web page link on the desktop; by double-clicking on this link the user signals the browser to automatically load the web page.

Shrinking phase   The second portion of two-phase locking when the transaction releases locks.

Simple Mail Transfer Protocol (SMTP)   Provides basic electronic mail services.

Single distributed database management system data warehouse   A single DDBMS manages all the warehouse's data, which is located at multiple sites within the network; this type of warehouse "looks" like a centralized data warehouse from the point of view of the user or developer.

SMP   *See* symmetric multiprocessing.

SMTP   *See* Simple Mail Transfer Protocol.

Snooping   The theft or compromise of data while in transit between endpoints of a network.

Source data   Data resident in source systems that will be extracted and used to populate a data warehouse or data mart.

Source files   Files containing data destined for loading into a data warehouse.

Source IP address   The IP address of the computer sending the packet using TCP/IP communications.

Source systems   Those data processing systems from which data is extracted for use in a data warehouse, usually transaction-oriented systems.

Special host configurations   Limit the resources available to intruders to a network should they get past the other barriers placed in their way.

Special network configurations   Special technique used to limit the number of computing and network resources directly exposed to Internet/intranet traffic.

SPI   *See* security parameter index.

SSL   *See* Secure Sockets Layer.

Star schema   A data modeling approach that produces a large "fact" table and many smaller "dimension" tables that extend the different aspects of the facts.

Static HTML documents   Can consist of almost any unstructured content such as text pages, images, and even audio files.

Static windows   The use of canned forms and reports at the workstation to access data.

Subject-oriented data   A collection of information selected for its relevance to a particular topic.

Subnets   Separately addressable segments of the network, uniquely and easily identifiable solely by the IP addresses of the components.

Subtransaction   In an environment controlled by a distributed database management system, a transaction may be required to access data stored at several sites and is broken into subtransactions, one for each site accessed.

Surfing   The navigation of users across documents or web sites.

Symmetric algorithms   A mathematical algorithm that use the same key to both encrypt the plaintext and decrypt the ciphertext.

Symmetric multiprocessing (SMP)   A computer architecture where instead of a central processor, there is a group of processors operating cooperatively using a common memory pool.

Syntactic transformations   Used to convert data to compatible formats when the record structure differs among the various local databases.

Systems tools   The utility programs that help to maintain the system environment, such as image copy utilities and reorg utilities.

Target performance   The estimated rate at which an application must function.

TCP/IP   *See* Transmission Control Protocol/Internet Protocol.

Technical architecture   Provides a blueprint for assembling hardware and software components, defining what and how tools and technologies will be used.

Telnet An application and set of protocols that allows a user's connected terminal to act as if it were directly attached to the host computer.

Terabyte (TB) One billion bytes.

Thin client The software on the users' desk is limited to those components that relate to presentation only; all other activity takes place on the back-end system as directed by the user, with only the result set shipped down line to the desktop PC.

Threat In security terms, an action or tool that can expose or exploit a vulnerability and compromise the integrity of a system.

Tiers Levels within a data processing architecture where various functions can be separated with each processing on its own dedicated server.

Timestamp The date/time at which a given activity occurred in a system.

Time-variant Data that refers to a specific point in time.

TLS *See* transport layer security.

Transaction The basic unit of work in a DBMS; it is a set of actions that must be carried out together.

Transaction manager The part of the DBMS that coordinates database operations on behalf of the applications.

Transmission Control Protocol/Internet Protocol (TCP/IP) The foundation of communications on the World Wide Web that is in wide use in corporations everywhere.

Transport language Works on top of the communications protocol and is used by the client and server to communicate.

Transport layer The fourth level of the ISO/OSI telecommunications architecture that works with the network layer to ensure that different transmissions, which are part of a sequence (message) but may have transversed the network by different routes, are appropriately resequenced at the receiver's site.

Transport layer security (TLS) Developed by the IETF, this security architecture is based on SSL 3.0.

Trojan horse A program that conceals harmful code.

Tunneling The transmission of a TCP/IP message that has been completely encrypted, including TCP/IP headers.

Two-phase locking (2PL) A common form of locking, thus named because transactions using it go through two distinct phases during execution; a growing phase, when it acquires locks, and a shrinking phase, while it releases those locks.

Unifying conceptual data model (UCDM)   Developed by starting with the relational data model and extending it incrementally by adding axiomatic extensions equivalent to various well-known data models.

Universal data servers   Database management systems, such as those from Oracle Corp. or Informix Corp., that manage a variety of data types extremely well.

Unrepeatable read   Occurs when transactions are allowed to read partial results of an incomplete transaction that is simultaneously updating the database.

User IDS   Used to identify and authenticate users, machines, and processes in a computer network.

Vertical partition   The practice of splitting an existing table vertically, moving a portion of the attributes to a new table. Both of the new tables thus created have the same primary key as the original and the same number of rows.

Virtual private network (VPN)   A combination of encryption software with Internet links to ensure message privacy for a group using the World Wide Web for communications; VPNs allow computers existing outside of an organization's firewall to securely connect via TCP/IP to applications located on servers resident inside the firewall.

Virus   Term widely used to cover a host of harmful attacks to computer systems; a bit of code, not an entire program, that plants versions of itself in any program it can modify.

Voting strategy   A method for updating duplicate copies of data where a transaction is permitted to update a data item only if it has access to and can lock a majority of the copies.

VPN   *See* virtual private network.

VRML   Virtual Reality Modeling Language.

Vulnerability   In security terms, a susceptibility to risk.

Wait-die   A timestamp-based transaction ordering methodology where the older transactions wait for the younger ones to either commit or roll back.

Wait-for graph A pictorial representation of the currently held locks in a system.

WAN *See* Wide Area Network.

Web The World Wide Web, a loose collection of interconnected computer sites, originally begun in the 1960s to service the government and universities.

Web-enabled Software specially designed to interface with and take advantage of the benefits of the World Wide Web.

Web gateway Acts as a translator between the HTML language used by web servers and the data warehouse application API/CGI.

Web server The server component of a client/server Internet environment; a web server acts much like a file server, responding to requests from its clients; it differs from the conventional file server in that it is responsible for passing requests on to other application servers when necessary.

Wide Area Network (WAN) A communications network used to link together computers at different geographic locations.

World Wide Web (WWW) Also called the Web or the Internet, it is a loose collection of computer sites networked together; originally founded in the 1960s to interconnect government and university sites.

Worm A self-contained program that replicates itself across the network, thereby multiplying its damage by infecting many different nodes.

Wound-wait A timestamp-based transaction ordering methodology where the younger transactions wait for the older ones to either commit or roll back.

Wrapper Functions as a bridge between existing relational databases and object-oriented technologies by encapsulating data that is stored in a relational database with code to make it compatible with an object-oriented system; the process of encapsulating data within code to ensure its integrity.

Write lock Exclusive lock held on a data item, permitting only one transaction to access it while the lock is in effect.

Write quorum The majority of locks on the duplicate copies required for a transaction to update replicated data in a distributed system using a "voting strategy" for updates.

Write-write conflict The conflict between two write operations.

WWW World Wide Web.

X.509 v3 certificates   A type of digital certificate that uniquely identifies an entity and its public key; different formats distinguish machines (server certificates), users (personal certificates), application programs (software publisher certificates), and the CA (Certification Authority) that issues certificates.

2PL   *See* two-phase locking.

Index